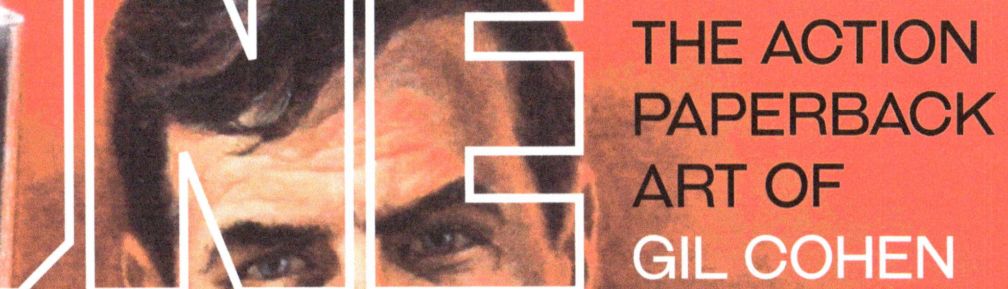

ONE MAN ARMY

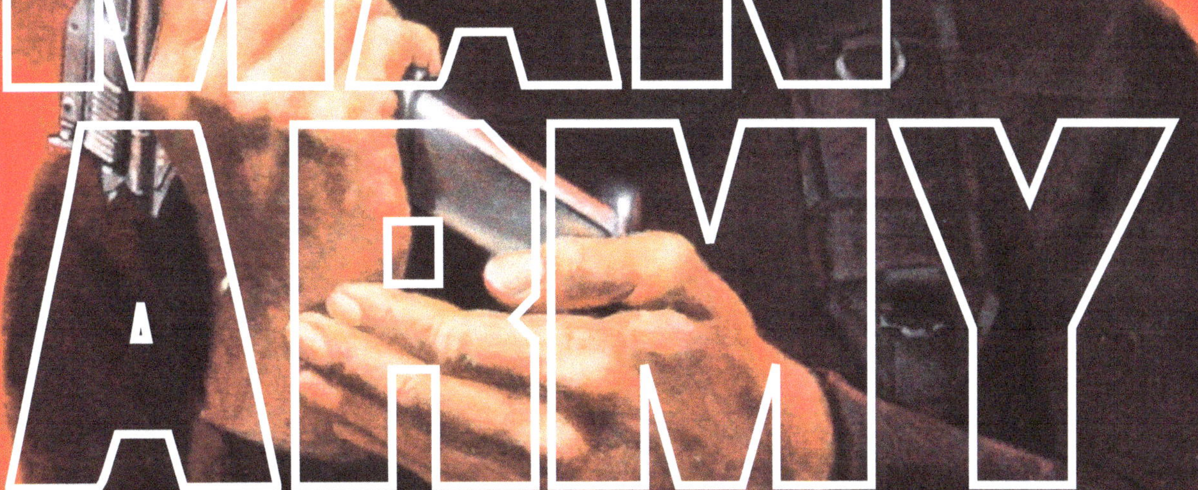

EDITED BY ROBERT DEIS & WYATT DOYLE

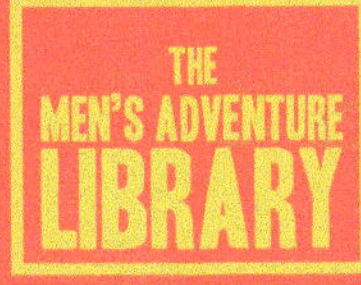

MensPulpMags.com

new texture

A New Texture book

Copyright © 2020 Subtropic Productions LLC

All artwork © 2020 Gil Cohen; reproduced by arrangement with the Artist.

All Rights Reserved.

Designed by Wyatt Doyle

The archival materials reproduced herein are included by arrangement with The Robert Deis Archive

Images in this book originate from a variety of sources; their reproduction here reflects this.

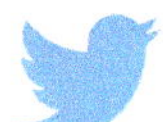 @NewTexture   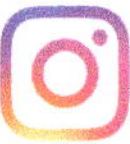 @ThisIsNewTexture   NewTexture.com

MensAdventureLibrary.com   MensPulpMags.com

To purchase original artwork by Gil Cohen, contact:

    Knightsbridge Press
    62 Creek Drive
    Doylestown, PA 18901

Booksellers: ***One Man Army*** and other New Texture books are available through Ingram Book Co.

ISBN 978-1-943444-57-1

Second printing

Also available as a deluxe hardcover with additional content.

Printed in the United States of America

10 9 8 7 6 5 4 3 2

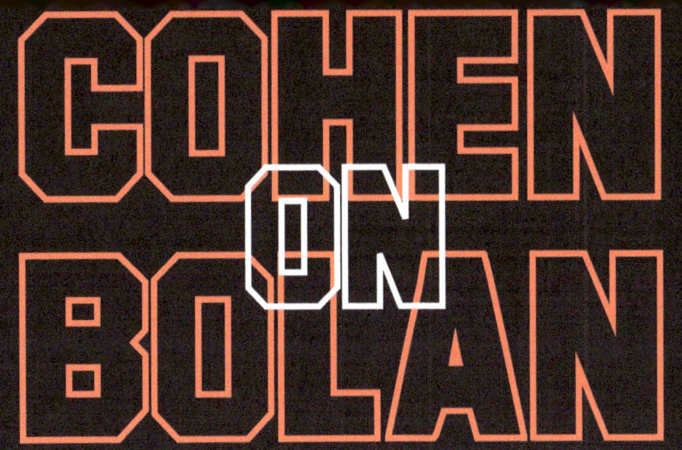

When I visualize Don Pendleton's Mack Bolan, I see Bolan as Gil Cohen portrayed him on the covers of Don's Executioner novels, and on numerous early Harlequin Executioners and spinoff series. Don loved Gil's cover art, and I still receive comments from Executioner fans who mention how much they like Gil Cohen cover illustrations. Seventeen years of wonderful Mack Bolan cover illustrations by a very talented artist! I'm sure the scenes on the covers helped to sell books.

Gil Cohen is very much a part of the Don Pendleton-Mack Bolan tradition of nearly half a century. The Executioner series would not be the same without Gil Cohen's illustrations.

—Linda Pendleton

THE FIRST Executioner book I did was No. 11: *California Hit* (1972). I actually got the assignment—the commission—in December of '71. I delivered it in January '72. Pinnacle asked me to take over doing the covers, and I redid a few of the first ten, including No. 1: *War Against the Mafia* (p. 16) and No. 2: *Death Squad* (p. 17). My head-and-shoulders portrait of Mack Bolan was used on newer editions of all the books.

I posed myself as Mack for *California Hit.* In fact, from No.13: *Washington I.O.U.* (1972) (p. 18) back, I largely used myself as the model for Mack Bolan and other male characters in the cover scenes. I posed for

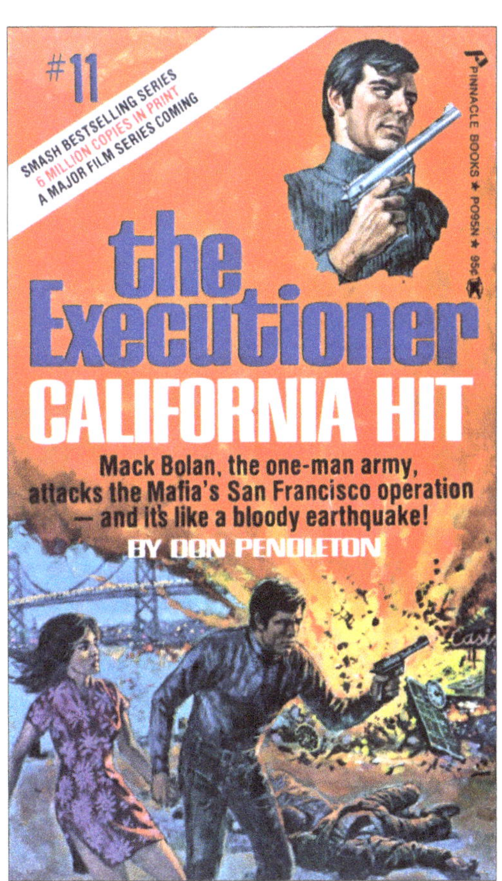

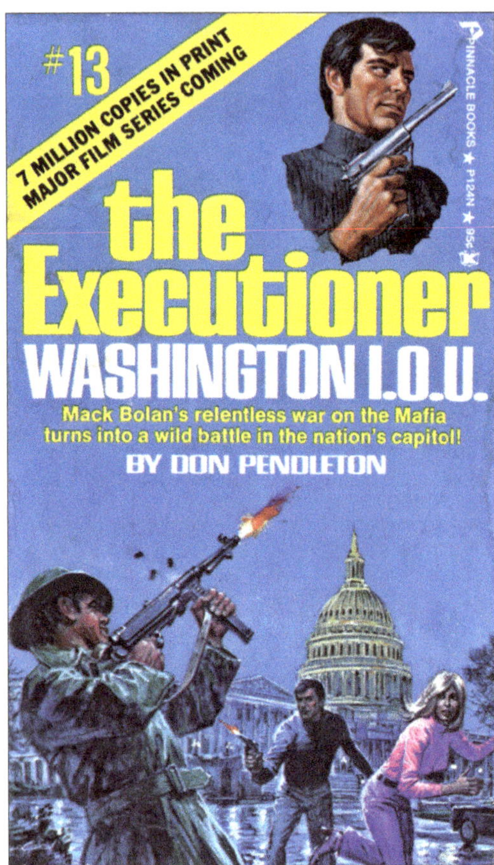

the reference photos, shot with a Polaroid camera. I could draw and transform myself into any kind of a character, and I did that frequently. Unlike a lot of other illustrators, I didn't use professional models for most of my illustration work.

At the same time, I was also asked to re-do the logo image of Bolan that appeared at the top of the covers. I more or less followed what the previous artist* had done, however I felt like that Mack persona was too thug-like. When I did the initial head-and-shoulders portrait of Bolan, I got a good-looking friend of mine to pose for

me. He didn't look much like the Mack I had in mind, but I had to meet a very tight deadline, and he was happy to help me out.

Now, he wasn't dark like Bolan. He was blond, as a matter of fact, and he didn't look a whole lot like Bolan. I did what I could to make him look like previous images of Bolan, but he's not the quintessential Bolan as far as I'm concerned.

Is there a quintessential Bolan by Gil Cohen?

The quintessential Bolan was done later, when I did the full figure of Bolan in black with all of his accoutrements, used for the first Stony Man novel published by Harlequin in 1982, *Stony Man Doctrine (pp. 84–85)*. If you want to know what Gil Cohen's idea of Mack Bolan really is, it is that guy. In fact, before I even did the *Stony Man* image, the Bolan I depicted in the cover scenes all along basically looked like that guy. Because even when I was working for Pinnacle, I was portraying somebody: Clint Eastwood. He most clearly personified Mack Bolan to me. I didn't just try to do portraits of Clint Eastwood, but I tried to get a *feeling* of a Clint Eastwood persona. So you'll see some physicality of Clint. But my Mack has dark hair, and reflects what I had in my imagination. That's *my* Mack Bolan. (I did sometimes change his eye color. He had brown eyes originally, but at times he's had blue.)

I did the Mack Bolan Executioner covers for Pinnacle, and then Mack Bolan for Harlequin's Gold Eagle line until 1987.

Did you work more frequently with professional models on the Gold Eagle covers?

In the Gold Eagle period, I did use some professional models for the female characters in the Mack Bolan cover scenes, but the models for my male characters remained

*Artist George Gross, who also did a lot of work for men's adventure magazines (MAMs) as well as earlier pulp mags, did the original cover paintings for most of the first ten Executioners. He also did the initial head-and-shoulders portrait of Mack Bolan holding his trusty .44 AutoMag pistol that was originally depicted at the top of the covers.

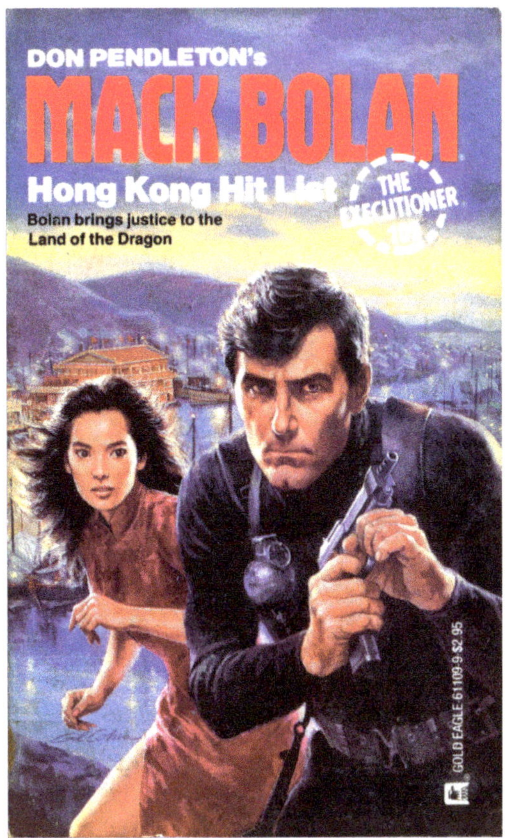

mostly non-professionals. I hardly used professional models until I did romance book covers for Harlequin. I would ask friends, "Would you mind posing for me?" Later, during the Gold Eagle era, I had to be a bit more fussy about the female models. So for a lot of the Gold Eagle covers, I used professional models for the women in the scenes. The painting I did for No. 60: *Sold For Slaughter* (1983) *(p. 46)*, is an example. (One of my favorites, by the way.) The girl who posed for that was a professional model. It's funny that I remember this, but her last name was Cohen.

But on that same cover, my brother-in-law Robbie Smith posed as Mack, as he did for many other covers.

(cont'd on p. 8)

I hope I don't disappoint any of the Mack Bolan fans, but when I got that assignment in 1969, I didn't know anything about Mack Bolan at all. To me, he was not a special character; he was one illustration assignment I had, of many hundreds that I had done. It was just another assignment. And so when I painted the character on a rooftop shooting a sniper's rifle down at (presumably) the Mob, I didn't think of the Mack Bolan character I painted later at all.

What would be the difference between him and Mack Bolan? Not a whole lot, really. It even looks like Bolan's hair, though Bolan's hair is black.

The weapons are right, I made sure of that. It's not only the two years that I had in the military, but my lifetime of interest in a lot of that stuff. Even in that first illustration, with his gun case opened up; I know the guns that are in there. I see a Mauser semi-automatic pistol, the first pistol of its type. It's from earlier in the 20th century, but people were still using them in the '50s. And I always thought it's a cool *looking* thing; it really is. Then you see a Luger, and you see all the accessories—silencers, scopes, magazine clips, things like that.

I never even became cognizant that this story was attached to Mack Bolan in any way until Bob Deis brought it to my attention not long ago. If I'd been reminded of it before then, I think I would have remembered, because The Executioner/ Mack Bolan has had a lot to do with my career!

I certainly remember the art, though I don't have it anymore. It was probably sold a very long time ago.

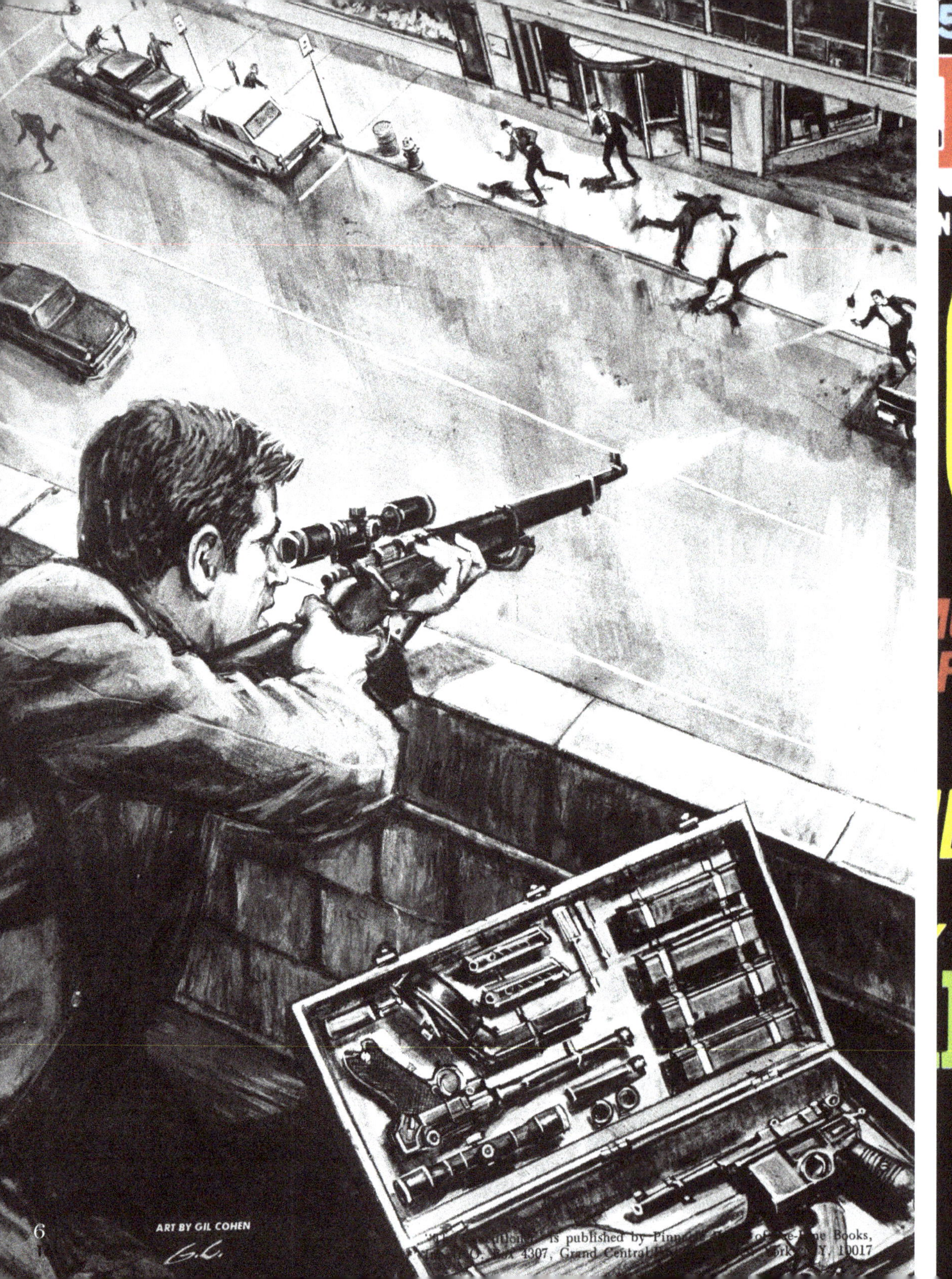

6

EXECUTIONE

THE MOB.....A TRUE-TO-LIFE STORY OF LUST FOR REVENGE WITHOUT LIMITS....YOU CAN'T PUT IT DOWN." —

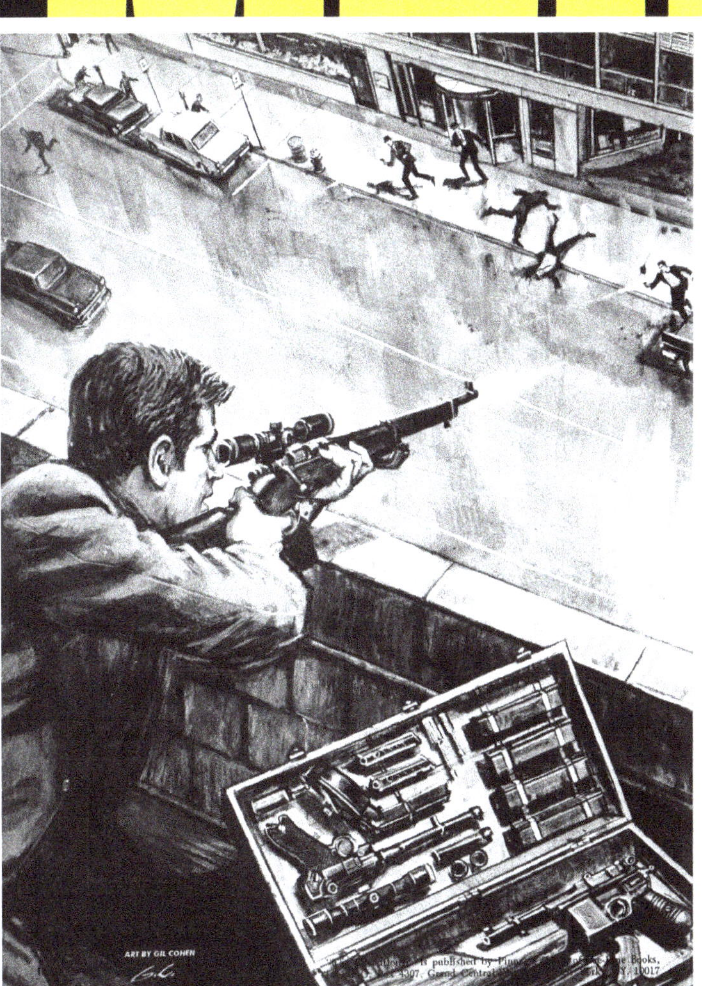

One Army-trained Killer against The Mob

THE EXECUTIONER

by DON PENDLETON

THERE WERE NO self-deceptions for Mack Bolan; he knew that he was the most marked man in underworld history. He had, overnight, become an American legend; a plum to be picked by every law enforcer in the nation; sudden riches to be

ACTION-PACKED BOOK THRILLER

cashed in by every two-bit punk with a gun in the country; a debt to be settled by each member of the far-flung family *(Continued on page 90)*

17

FOR MEN ONLY, October 1969; art by Gil Cohen

(cont'd from p. 5)

His day job was as a linesman for the Philadelphia Electric Company. He was movie-star handsome. I mean, he looked like a cross between Paul Newman and Burt Lancaster, he was that good looking. He made a great Mack Bolan. Maybe a little on the slim side; I tried to beef him out a little bit with the paintbrush. But he was a great Mack Bolan for a long, long time. So he became Mack Bolan in my cover paintings. Combined, of course with the Clint Eastwood aspect I had in mind at the beginning.

Funny story: In 1985, the Mack Bolan Convention was held in San Francisco. Bolan fans came from all over the country and lined up outside the hotel where it was held. The line went clear around several blocks; mostly men, sometimes women and kids. I was flabbergasted! For years sitting alone in my studio painting those covers, I had no idea how popular and far-reaching my audience was.

Harlequin had hired a man to strut around dressed in black, head-to-toe, wearing Mack's accoutrements; bandolier, grenades, cartridge belt, and holding an Uzi submachine gun. He approached my wife, Alice, and asked in a deep baritone, "Do you know who I am?"

Alice answered, "No."

He replied, "Why, I am Mack Bolan."

Alice then answered, "No you're not, my brother is!" "Mack" then backed up and sulked away.

But you sometimes shot reference photos outdoors?

Depending on the requirements of the scene, or if I wanted a more natural look, I sometimes did outdoor photo shoots. For No. 74: *Savannah Swingsaw* (1985) *(p. 56)*, I couldn't bring a jeep into the studio, so I rented one and did the shoot outdoors. There's one where Bolan and a red-headed girl are both shooting and they're in the woods—No. 57: *Flesh Wounds* (1983) *(p. 43)*; the photos for that one were shot outdoors.

For many of the scenes on the Bolan covers and for

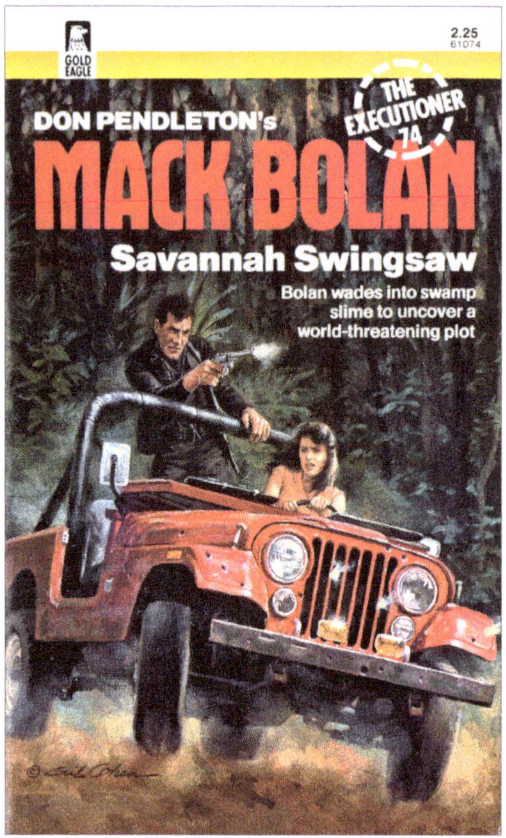

the romance covers I did for Harlequin books, the scenes had a certain theatricality. I wasn't after a completely naturalistic effect, therefore I preferred shooting indoors for those.

Were Bolan covers your primary work in those years?

I painted Bolan for Pinnacle for nine years. During those years, I was also doing a lot of work for many different projects. For example, I was doing a great deal of cover art for other Pinnacle paperbacks—a lot of work for Pinnacle! And I was still doing work for MAMs. And I was doing work for other clients—other books and magazines. But after Charles Kadin commissioned me to do the Executioner covers and spinoffs for Harlequin, Harlequin was without doubt my most important client for many years. They were giving me so much work, I hardly had the time to work for anybody else. I was doing one Mack Bolan every month. I was doing one Phoenix Force. And for several years, I was also doing one Able Team cover every month. That's a hell of a lot of artwork! So, overwhelmingly, Harlequin was my main client from about 1981 until the early '90s.

Did you expect to follow Mack to his new publisher?

I transitioned from Pinnacle to Harlequin via a rather odd encounter, and it would prove to be a pivotal event in my career. My last cover for Pinnacle was No. 38: *Satan's Sabbath* (1980); I wasn't sure then whether it would be my last Mack Bolan ever. I didn't know what was going on in the publishing world, but I got wind from the Pinnacle art director that they were no longer going to be doing Mack Bolans, that the series was sold to Harlequin. So I assumed it would be another artist doing it. And then I got a telephone call from the senior art director of Harlequin, a Canadian chap named Charles Kadin.

He called me and he said, "Would you be interested in continuing doing Mack Bolan? We changed the name. It's no longer called The Executioner series; we're going to call it the Mack Bolan series now. Would you be interested?"

I said, "Yeah, I might be."

So he said, "Look, I'm flying into the States and I'm going to fly into Philadelphia airport. But I'm not staying in Philly; I have to go somewhere else. But how about if I meet you at the airport in a pre-designated room?"

I said, "Yeah, fine."

We picked an office building at the airport and he said, "Okay, we'll meet."

Well, there was a huge thunderstorm. I mean it was an *enormous* thunderstorm. And I thought, "Geez, maybe his flight won't come in." This was not the kind of weather to go out in—flooding and thunder and

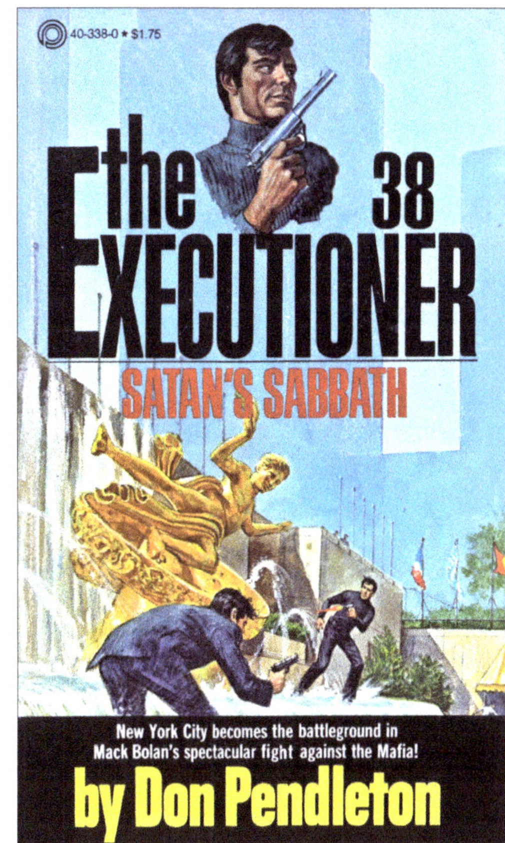

lightning. I had about an hour's drive plus down to the Philadelphia airport, but decided what the hell. I got in the car and I drove down there, figuring he's probably not even going to show. So, drenching wet, I went into the airport and into that conference room we had decided we would meet in. About a half hour later, the door opens and in comes Charles Kadin, also soaking wet. Tall, lean guy, about 6 feet, 3 inches tall, and very narrow and thin. We were each surprised that the other showed up in that weather.

He wanted to see the range of work I did, and I had my portfolio case. He looked at the work, was very pleased, and made suggestions about how we might work

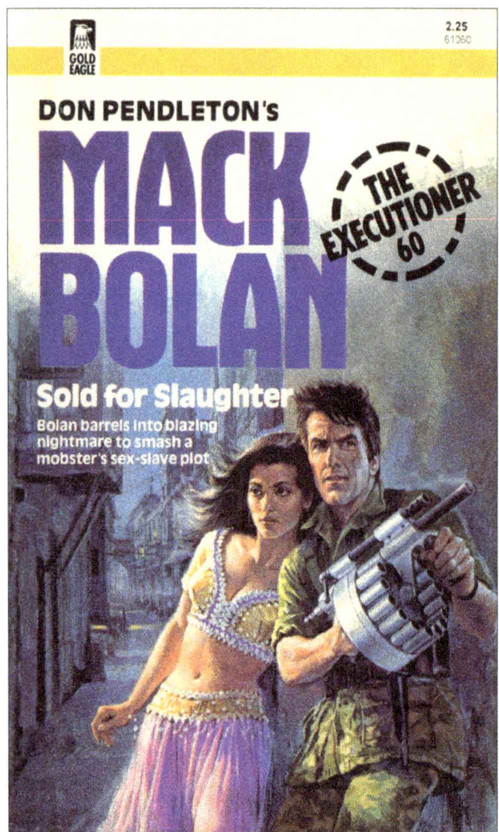

together going forward. Then it was goodbye. And the rest, as they say, is action/adventure history.

Rendering Mack's weaponry must have posed unique challenges.

Going back to No. 60: *Sold For Slaughter* (1983) *(p. 46)*, Mack is holding a kind of special machine gun that looks like something that I made up, but it existed: a Hawk MM-1 MGL Automatic Grenade Launcher. It had a huge barrel, where you had an array of different bullets and missiles and stuff that could come out of the different chambers. Now you can't just get that kind of weapon anywhere legally; even if you had a Class 3 license. I tried to get one for my reference photo and couldn't.

So, I figured, in order to get Mack—played by my brother-in-law Robbie—to hold it properly, I've got to kind of make a mockup of that gun. So I did. I got tubes, I got a pistol grip from a model of a .45 handgun…it took a lot of work. But I did it, and I was really proud of it. I posed Robbie holding it, and I thought it would impress the fans. Well, I brought those reference photos to the Mack Bolan Convention in San Francisco in 1985. Fans were looking at them, and one says, "What the hell is this? I expected you to have the real thing." They were disappointed! I was proud of the model I had done, but these guys were disappointed. They expected the real gun, and thought Robbie had been holding the real deal for the painting.

For the most part I only read a synopsis, which the art directors would send me, along with whatever guidance they gave me about what they wanted to see on a cover. And when it came to exotic weaponry, they would either send me some reference photos or I had to find some, so I knew what on Earth on they were talking about.

I would usually get a replica of the gun and have the person I was using for the photo hold it. I rarely had the actual guns, so I'd use a replica. I didn't just depend on photos of guns, because the hand hold is a very important thing. How the model was holding a gun was very important to me. I know how most small weapons need to be held.

I was in the service, and so you learn about those things. I was drafted in late 1953, less than 10 years after the Second World War ended. So a lot of the stuff we were trained with was from the Second World War—in fact, almost all of it. And so again, I know about that. I know what it's like to shoot an M1 rifle—or any rifle— and I know the kickback that it has.

When you pull that trigger, it kicks back against you. And if you didn't hold that rifle in the proper way, it would bang right into the hollow of your shoulder. (At the end of the day, you'd see guys black and blue in that area, and that was called *M1 shoulder*.) So things like that, I try to get right. I'm not saying I get it so right it's a manual, but I try to get them generally right.

That reminds me of the Mack Bolan convention again. The setting for the convention was the main hotel ballroom which was transposed into a wondrous tropical rainforest with palm foliage, tents and camouflage netting. While there, I finally met for the first time the very talented author of the Executioner/Bolan novels, Don Pendleton, and his gracious wife, Linda. I found Don to be a very intelligent and modest man.

I'm there, and I'm answering questions and all of that. There was a line, by the way, going around whole the block in San Francisco. People—mostly guys— wanting to get in. I was amazed. Absolutely amazed. I couldn't get over it. There were all kinds of people coming in.

One of the paintings that I brought was one of the Mack Bolan covers where I show Mack in a World War I aircraft; No. 78, Death Games (1985). Bolan is in the back seat of a biplane, shooting down a Russian MiG jet with a missile launcher; he'd just shot down a MiG-21. Now when Charles Kadin contacted me about that one he said, "Gil, this is what we want: He's in this old Austro-Hungarian patrol plane…" It's not even a fighter plane; it's an obscure biplane called a Lloyd C.II. It's a tandem thing—a pilot in the front seat, Bolan is sitting or standing up in the back of the plane. He's holding a surface-to-air missile launcher in his arms, and he's just shot down a modern MiG-21.

I said, "That just can't happen. Not possible. First of all, the heat seeking missiles of the MiG-21 would easily find that biplane and blast it out of the sky like swatting a fly. It would be nothing to knock that biplane down. And here you want him shooting down the MiG-21, and the MiG's going down in flames? That's ridiculous."

He said, "Gil, just go along with it. Do it."

So I said OK, and did it. And I figured, you know, *"Forget about it, Cohen! Just have fun. Do it, and have some fun doing it."* So I did. I looked up reference photos for the Lloyd C.II, and I did the painting.

I had that painting at the Mack Bolan Convention. And this nerdy young guy, maybe in his early 30s, walks

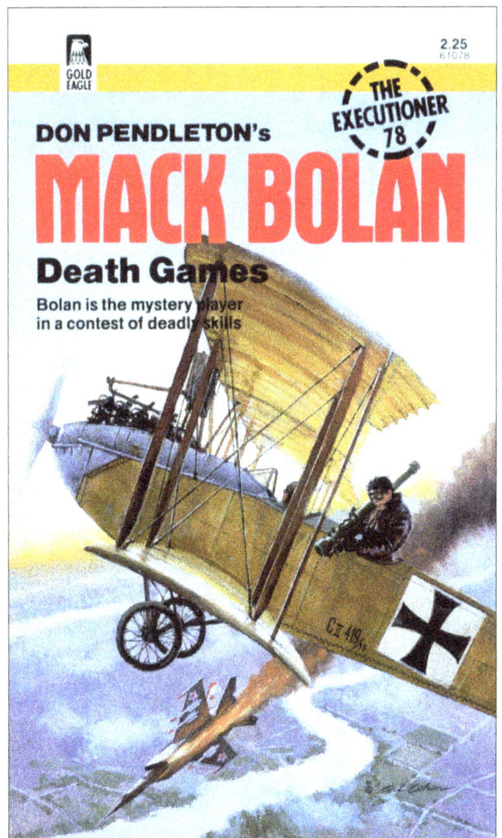

in with his tweed sport coat and his glasses and his neatly-combed hair, and he's staring at the painting. His nose is almost touching it. I'm looking at Alice, my wife, who is sitting next to me. I kind of nodded to her and whispered, "Here it comes."

So he's looking at the painting, and says, "Are you Gil Cohen?"

I said, "Yes."

He said, "Well, my name is ______, and I work in aerospace in nearby Silicon Valley." And I'm thinking, *"Oh God, he's going to tear this painting apart."*

And he said, "You know, that's very astute of you. This could really happen!"

I'm not saying anything, I'm just sitting there, letting him talk. He starts spouting technical aviation jargon—

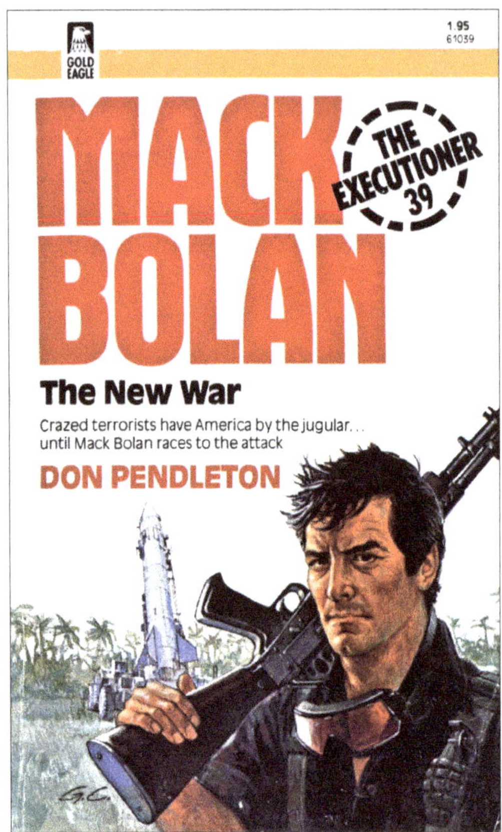

for the Phoenix Force and Able Team spinoffs. So I did them, too.

On Able Team, I did covers for a couple years, and then they gave it to another artist. They probably thought I had enough to do because I was also painting the Mack Bolan/Executioner covers and the Phoenix Force covers. I did one Bolan cover a month. Then, for quite a while I did one Phoenix Force and one Able Team a month, in addition to other illustration work I was doing. I could never do all that today, even if I tried. I mean, no way.

I continued to do Phoenix Force covers up until the early '90s, even after I was no longer doing The Executioner (though I painted covers for Phoenix Force that feature Bolan).

Again, you elected not to use professional models.

The models for the Phoenix Force and Able Team covers were not professionals. If I'm doing a romance book cover, yes, you bet I want to use professionals, because it's not easy to pose in the kind of romantic kinds of scenes with embraces. They are not easy. I mean if you ask the average guy, he'd say, *"Pose with some good-looking babe? I can do that, yeah."* But that's baloney; they can't. It takes a professional model—and not just a fashion model, either. It has to be somebody, whether it's a man or a woman, who is also an actor. They're the best models for things like that.

But when it came to the Mack Bolan, Phoenix Force, and Able Team characters, I put together my own tribe of people, and none of them were professional models.

There's one Phoenix guy, the older Israeli with one arm, Yakov "Katz" Katzenelenbogen. Well, an art school buddy of mine—a terrific artist in his own right—posed as that character. My model for David McCarter was the manager of a local video store. I asked him if he would pose, and he shrugged his shoulders and said, "Sure, why not?" Calvin James, I've forgotten the name of the guy who posed for him. But I remember he worked with his hands. I talked them and a few other regular guys into

vectors and this and that. Then he said, "…And the reason why this could happen is that the engine of the Lloyd aircraft is too tiny to generate enough heat for the heat-seeking missiles on the MiG-21 to pick up. Thus, it probably *wouldn't* be able to shoot down that biplane." So, the scene I painted was actually very valid, though I didn't know it! And he said, "That was very astute of you to think about that."

And I said with a straight face, "Well, you know, I kind of figured it out."

You also painted covers for two Bolan spinoff series.

I started doing the Mack Bolan books for Gold Eagle in 1981. About a year later, they asked me to do covers going to New York with me to pose for reference photos done by a professional photographer who specialized in reference photos for illustrators.

Your work appears on more Phoenix Force covers than Able Team covers.

You can tell most Able Team paintings were not done by me. As I said, I might have done maybe a couple years of them and that was it. Phoenix Force, I did for a much longer time. Now my Phoenix Force characters, as I mentioned, were not professional models—no more than Mack was. There were 58 Phoenix Force covers, from 1982 to 1992. I would have done all of those. I continued doing them even at the same time as doing romance book covers for Harlequin. So if my memory is correct, the covers during those years are all mine.

Phoenix Force as made up of five guys. And the books had wraparound covers, with front and back comprising the same scene. (I don't think any of the Pinnacle Executioners were wraparounds.) A panoramic cover of that type simply took more time to paint. They would have to, because there's more detail involved.

When did you and Mack Bolan part ways?

Around 1987, Gold Eagle had another artist start doing the Mack Bolan covers, because the editors noticed that I was aging Bolan. He was getting more creases on his face, more wrinkles. (So was I!) They were after a younger audience, and they didn't think the way I depicted Bolan was good for that audience, because young guys might not be attracted to reading about this old guy. But I was quite literal about Bolan's aging.

They got another artist or artists—I'm not sure how many—to do them, and their Mack Bolan is very different from mine. He looked like a model—which he probably really was. My Macks were never professional models. Maybe my style was copied a little bit, and maybe the look of Mack Bolan was copied a little bit, but this new guy was a pretty boy compared to my Mack. If you look at the Mack Bolan covers that came after

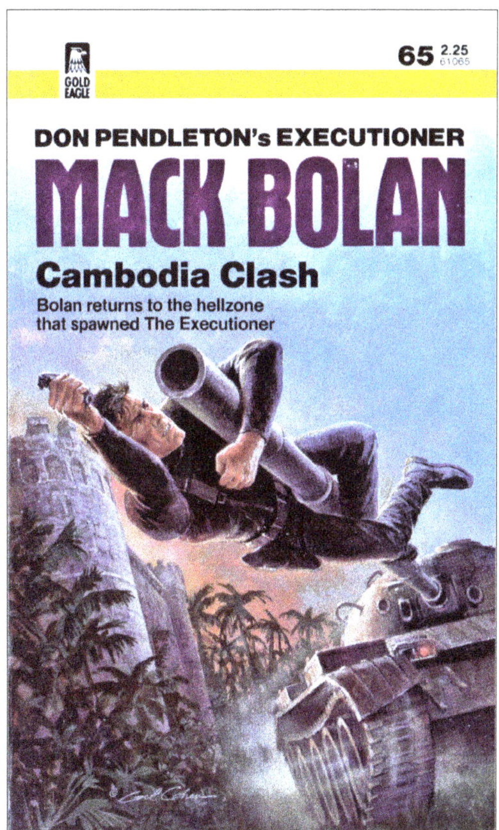

mine, he is definitely younger, smooth-faced, obviously handsome with a hot-combed look and all of that. My Mack was different. And I made sure he was holding his weapons right.

But, you know, there you go. They wanted a younger Mack Bolan, and the series is obviously still successful after all these years.

How has your technique evolved?

Over the years I have used different painting media and techniques to produce paintings for book covers and MAMs. When I first started doing the MAM artwork in the 1950s, they were either opaque watercolor (gouache) or pencil or charcoal line, with thin acrylic washes

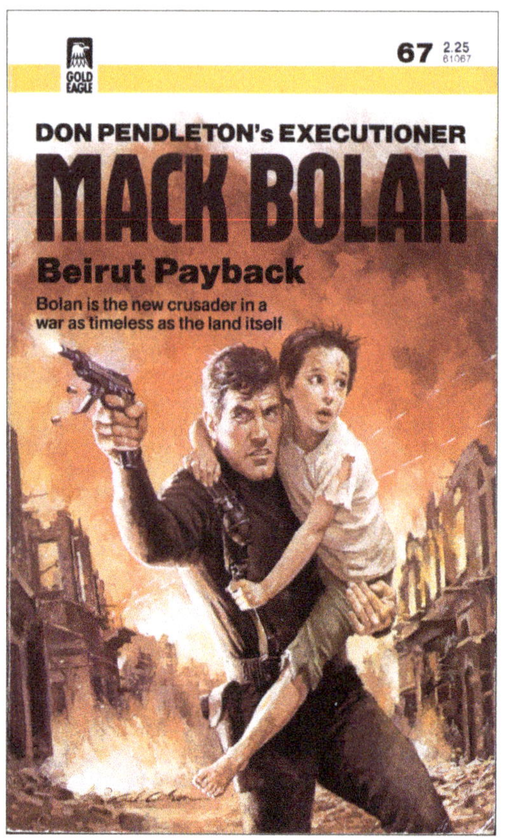

glazed over them. During the Harlequin/Gold Eagle period, I painted with acrylics.

Painting the covers in oil began in 1984 with No. 67: *Beirut Payback* (1984), where Bolan has a child with him and there is a great fire in the background. That was the first cover when I started using oil on linen-covered Masonite board. I had hardly used oil paints since my art student days, but starting with *Beirut Payback*, oils became my medium. I felt as though I had really found my favorite means of expression. After that, the majority of my paintings have been executed in oil.

Regardless of the genre, I am told that I have an easily recognized style in my work. Not only in my painting technique, but also in how I compose my paintings. You can tell a Gil Cohen perspective, or point-of-view. And I think I still do it that way today, even in the aviation art I paint now. I try to keep my technique as painterly as possible, while still revealing enough detail to tell the story. I have studied art history and have a certain partiality to the impressionists, as well as 19th century American Realism.

Your Bolan covers alone are an enviable legacy.

I've produced over 15 years of Executioner/Mack Bolan covers, something over 200 among Mack Bolan novels, the Phoenix Force series, and Able Team. I haven't done an exact count of all of them. It would be well over 100 Mack Bolans alone, and many Phoenix Forces. They were quite an undertaking for me, and as I look back I realize just how much I relished doing them. Mack has taken me to adventures around the world, and I enjoyed the ride. It certainly was a very significant part of my lifelong career as an illustrator.

But whatever I did from the time I became a professional artist (which really goes back to 1953), right up to today, I am a lucky person. And in more recent years, in the age of the internet, I have found out that some of my work has affected people and their lives in some way. And I think, *"Wow, that's OK."* It really is. Few have ever got terribly rich as an illustration artist, but I enjoyed most of what I did. So I'm lucky.

I also have a teaching career. I taught at what was then called the Philadelphia College of Art (now the University of the Arts) for 21 years. All during the time I was working as a freelance illustrator! In fact, I was invited by the American Society of Aviation Artists to give a talk and a class in figure drawing within a composition. I'm going to Dayton, Ohio for that on Wednesday.

I'm still a pretty active guy. I might be 88 going on 89, but I'm still pitching.

In conversation with the Editors

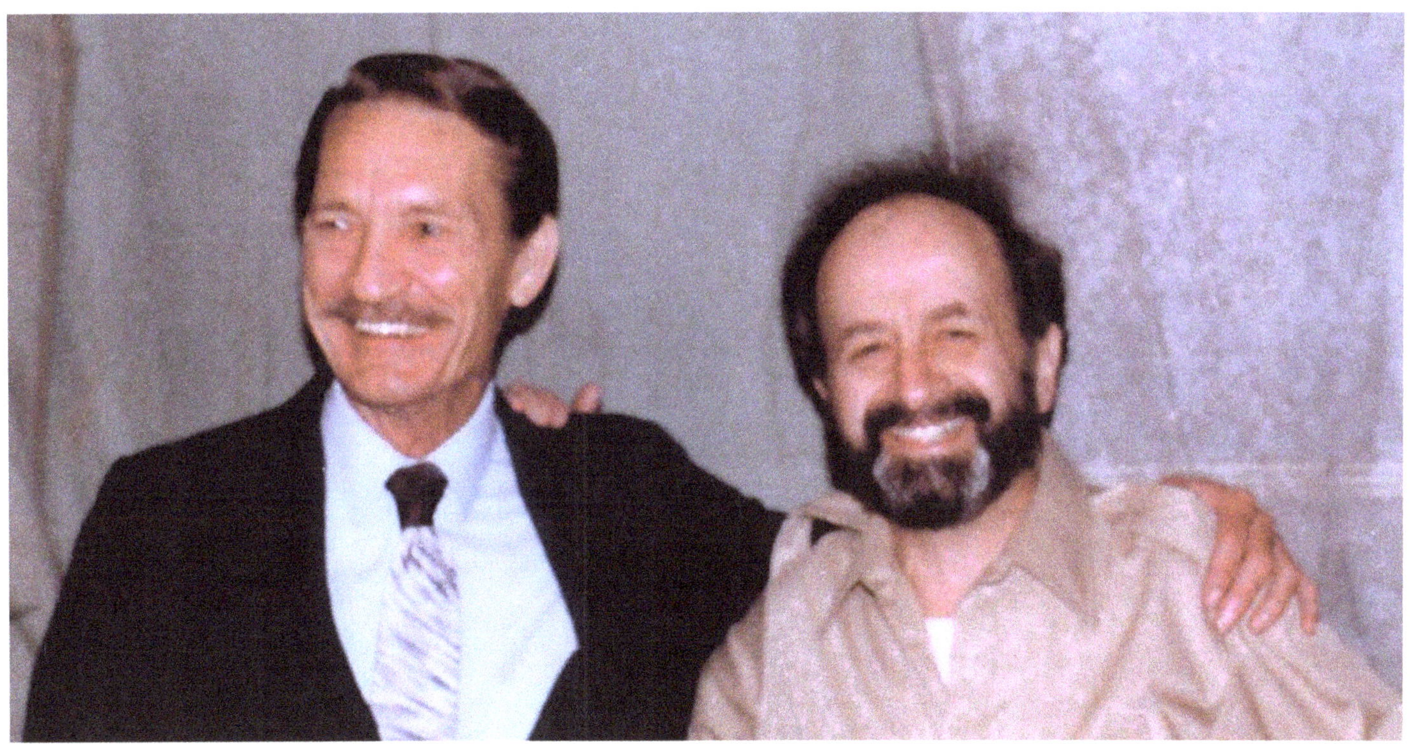

California Hit: *Executioner creator Don Pendleton* (left) *and Gil meet at last for the first (and so far only) official Mack Bolan Convention, San Francisco, May 1985. Pendleton passed away in 1995.*

ABOUT GIL COHEN

To many of his fans, Gil Cohen is the top cover artist for the hugely popular series of action/adventure novels featuring Mack Bolan, "The Executioner," created by author Don Pendleton.

To collectors of vintage men's magazines, he's one of the best artists who created cover paintings and interior illustrations for men's adventure magazines published in the 1950s, '60s and '70s.

To aviation enthusiasts, he's one of the top military aviation artists, his work shown in galleries and sold as high-end prints.

Gil Cohen is all of those things. He has also created movie posters, illustrations for books and magazines in a variety of genres, and other types of artwork.

Much of his illustration work from the mid-'50s to the mid-'70s was done for MAMs published by Martin Goodman's Magazine Management Company, such as Male, Men, For Men Only, Stag and Man's World.

His more recent military aviation paintings are featured in the book Gil Cohen: Aviation Artist.

Don Pendleton popularized the saying "Live large" in his Mack Bolan novels. Gil Cohen has done that as an artist. Along the way, he created an iconic, larger-than-life visual image of Bolan that's beloved by fans.

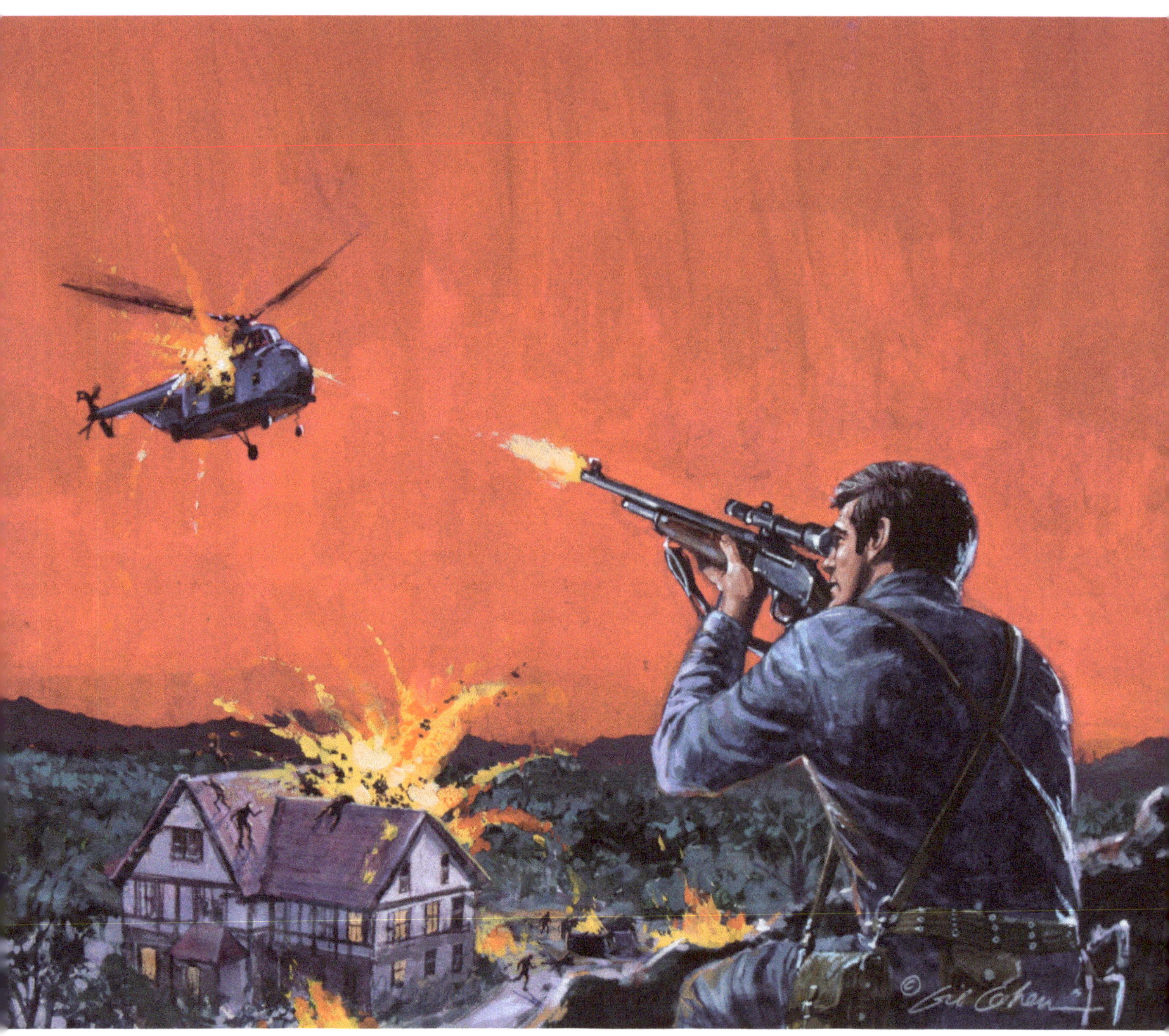

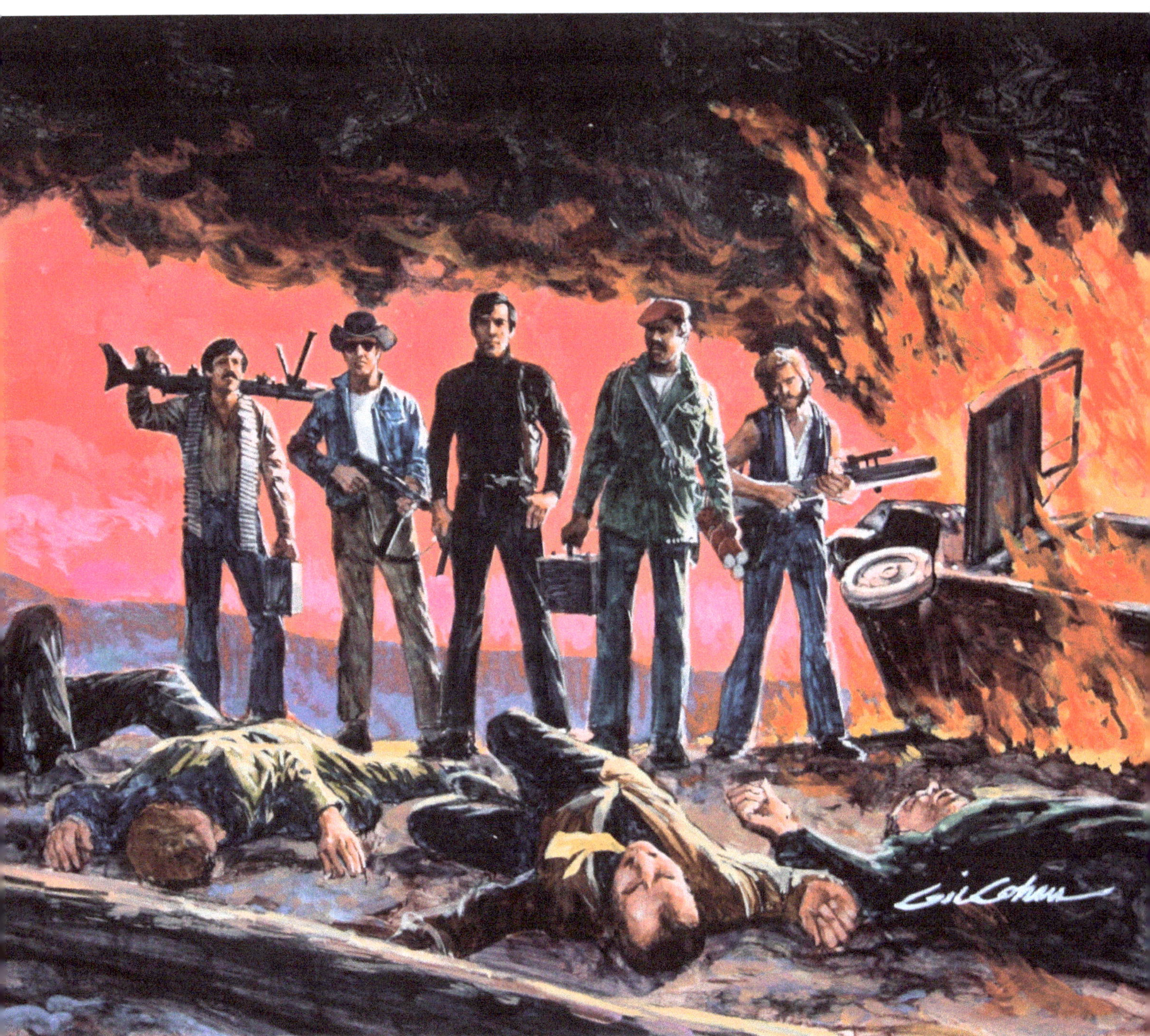

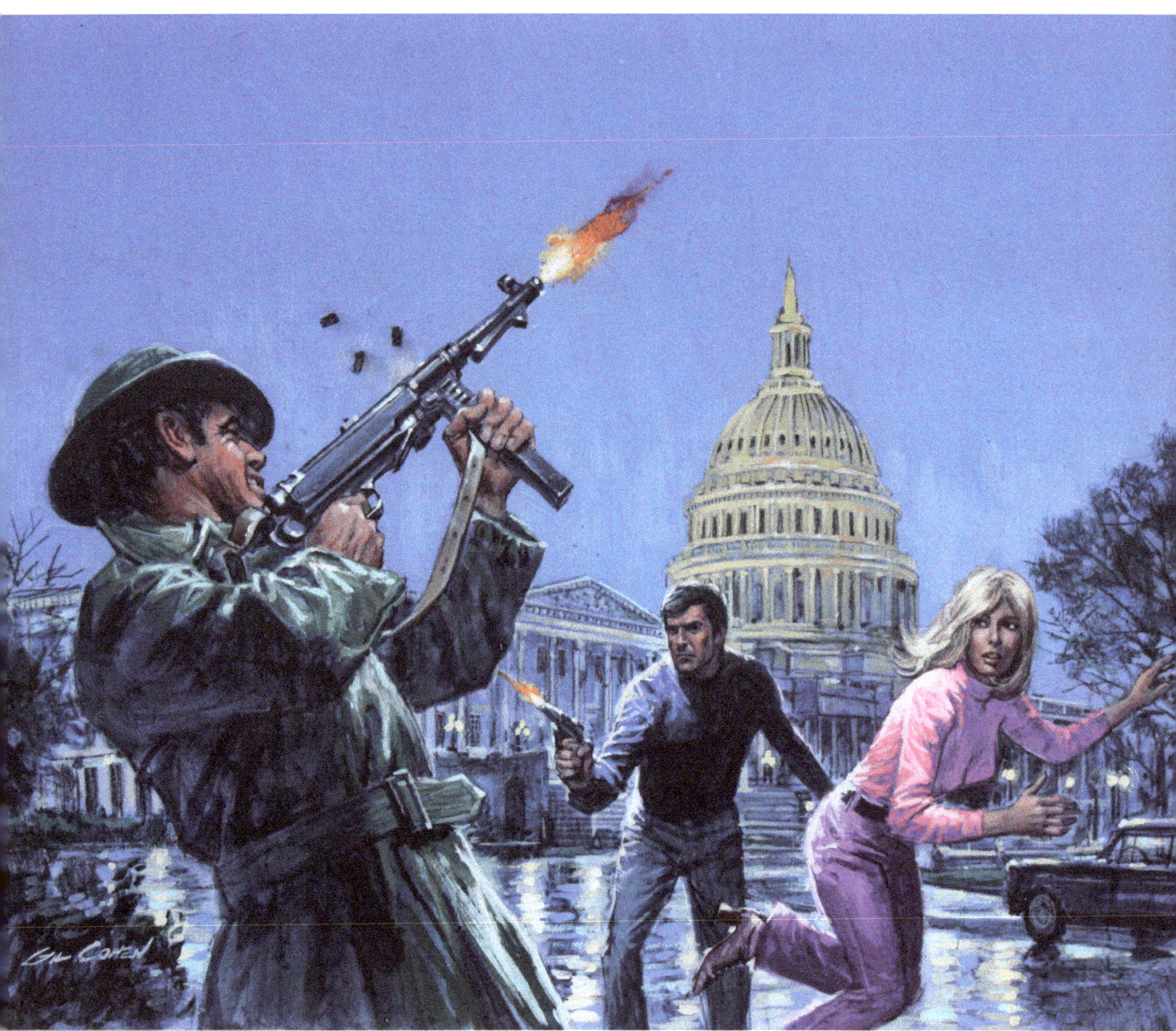

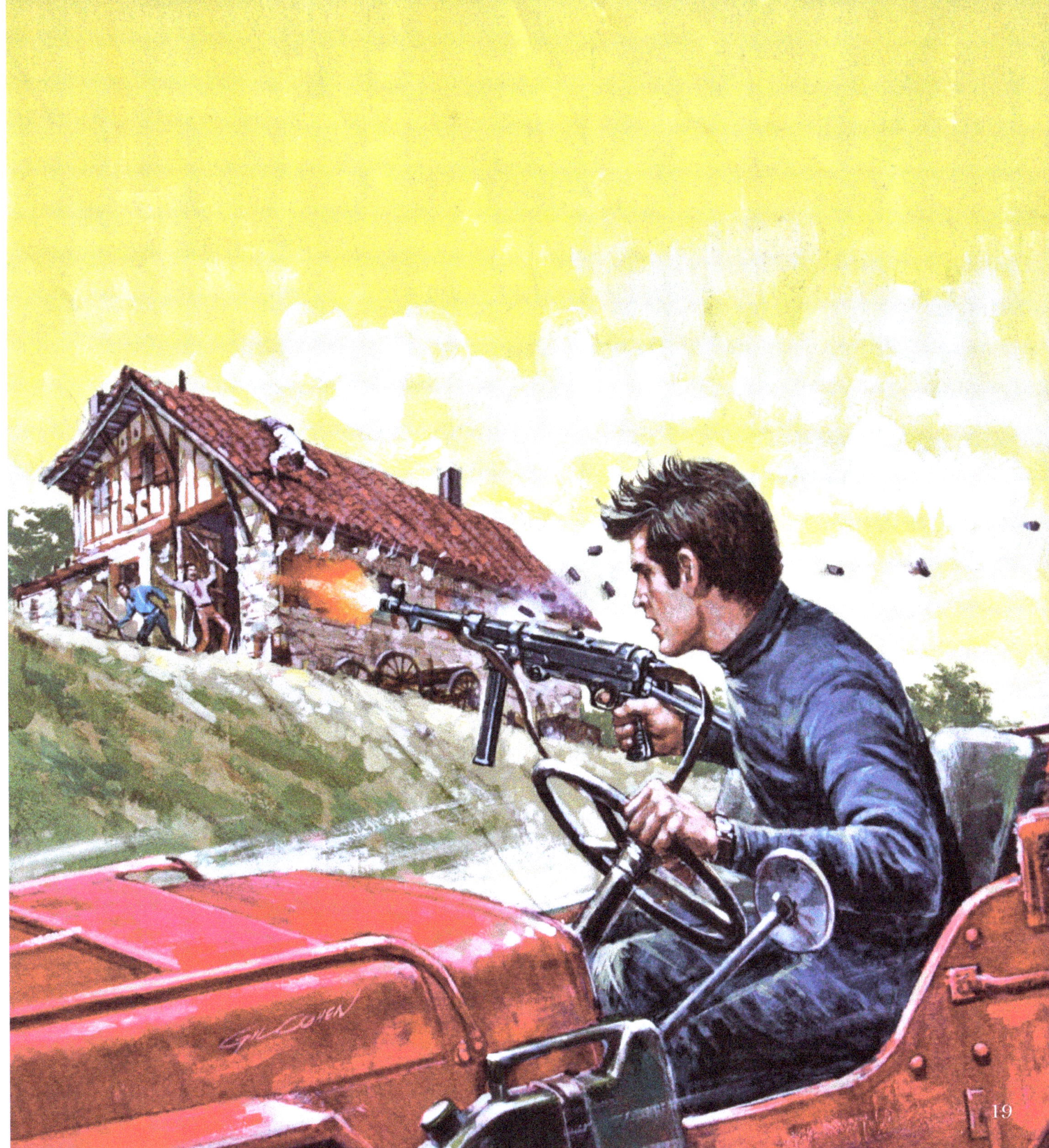

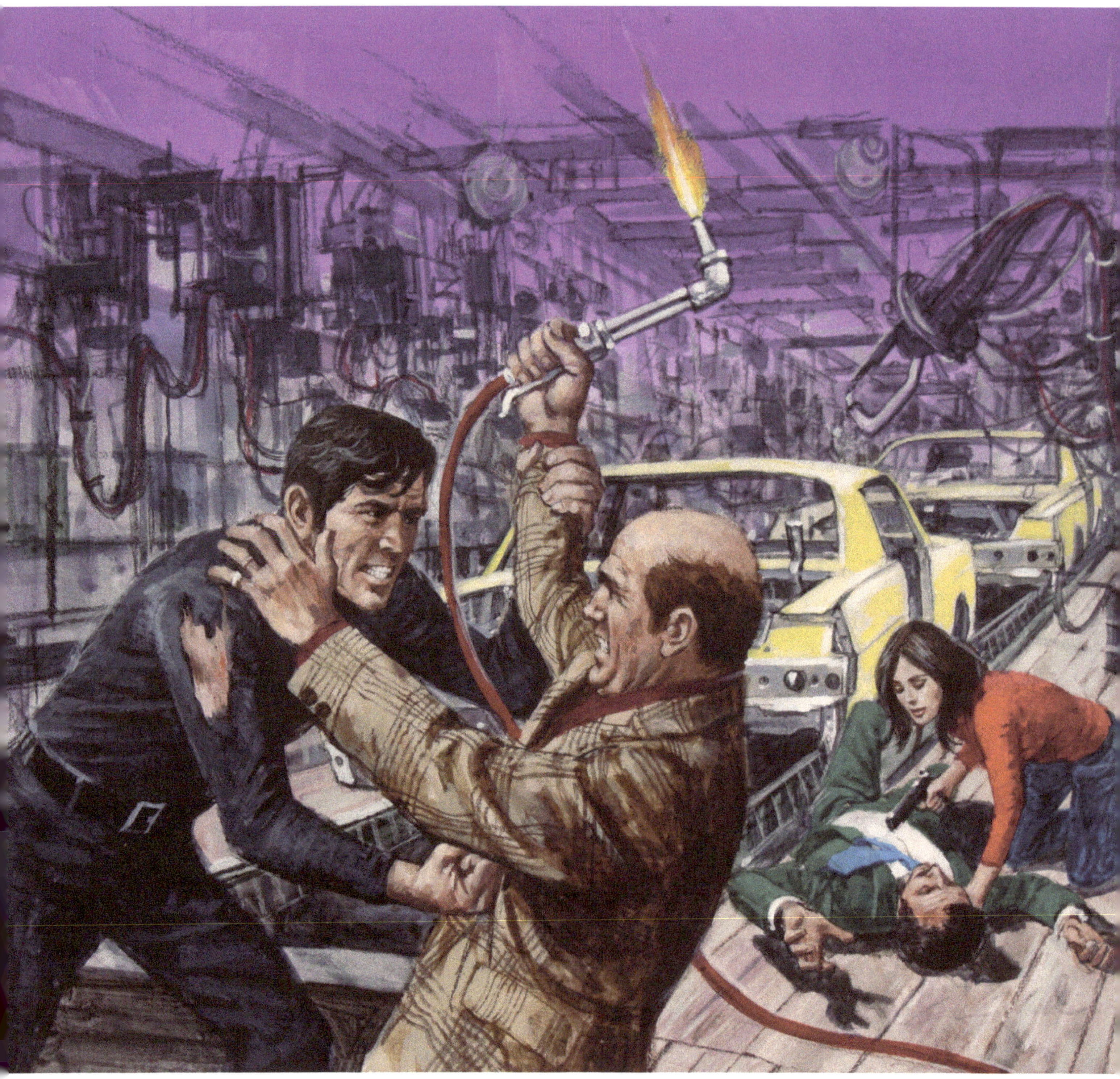

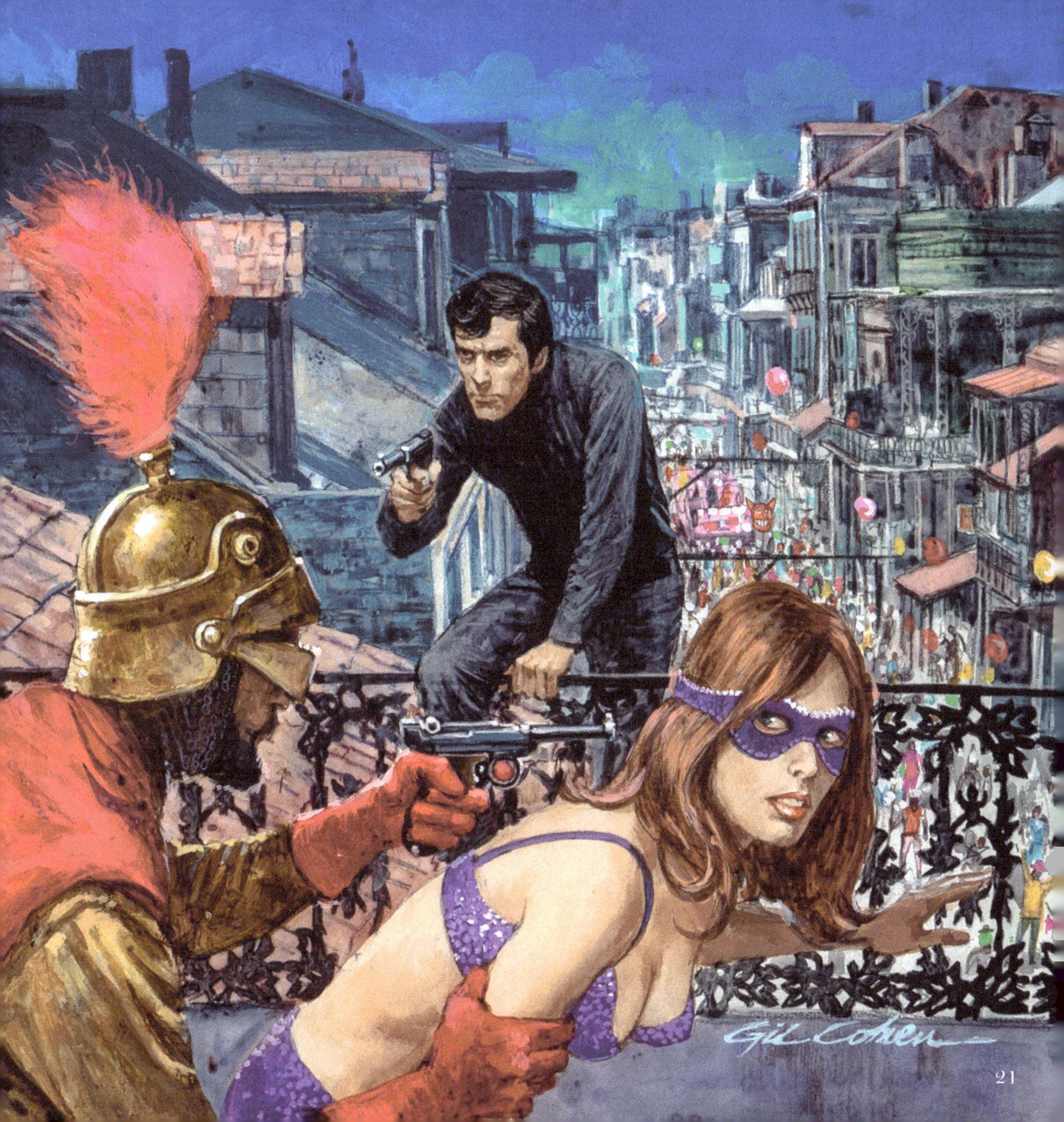
Gil Cohen

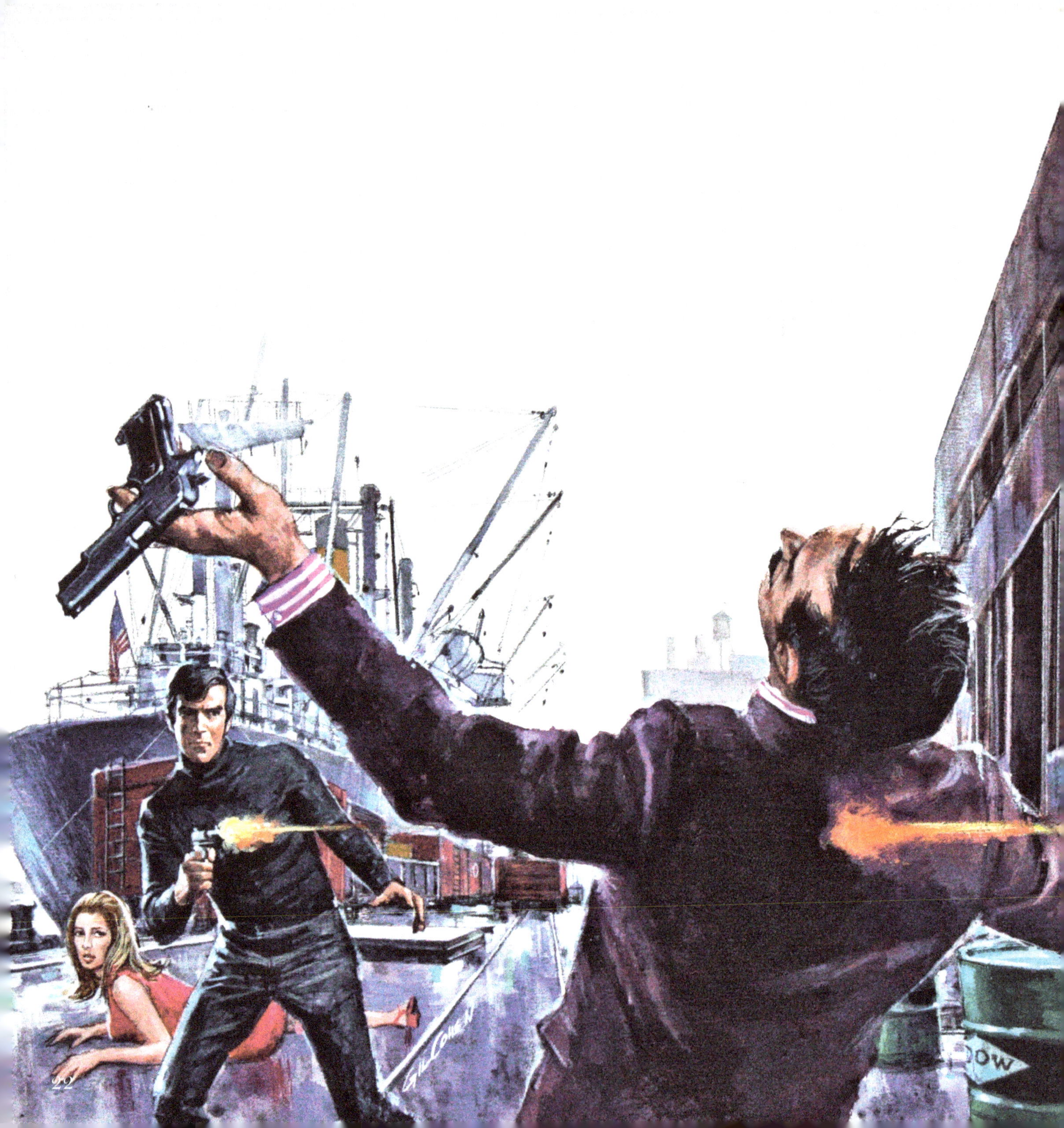

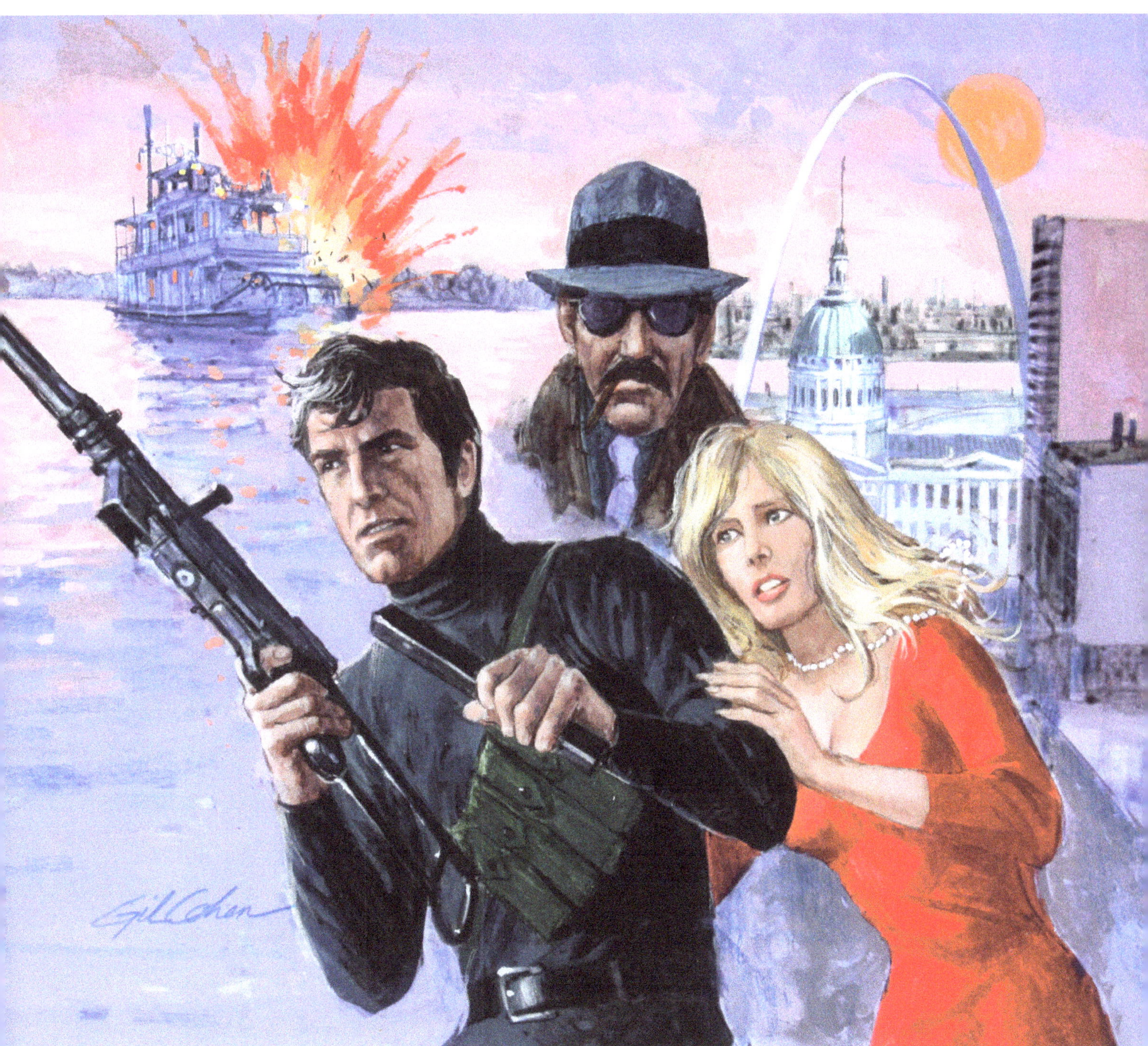

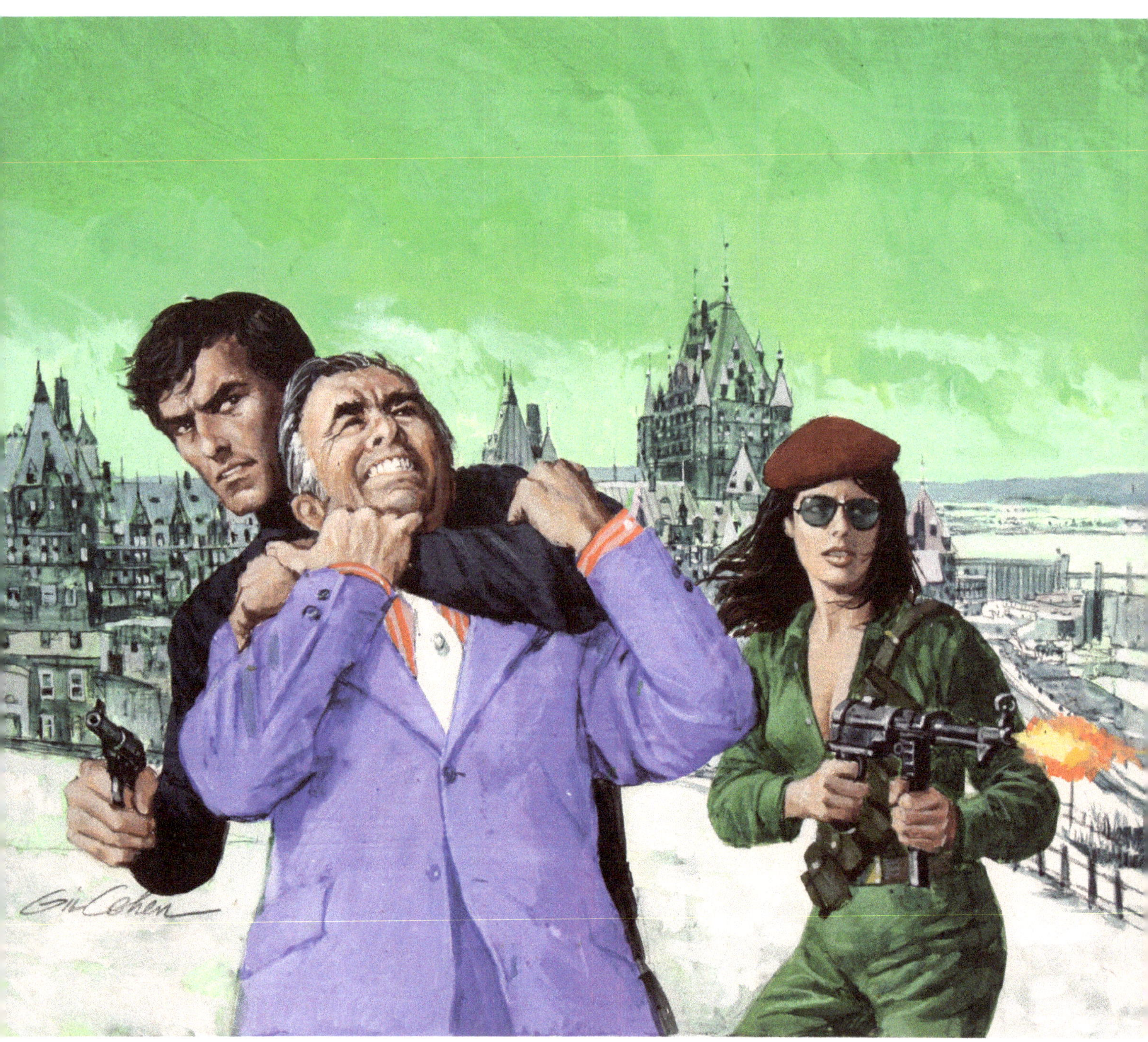

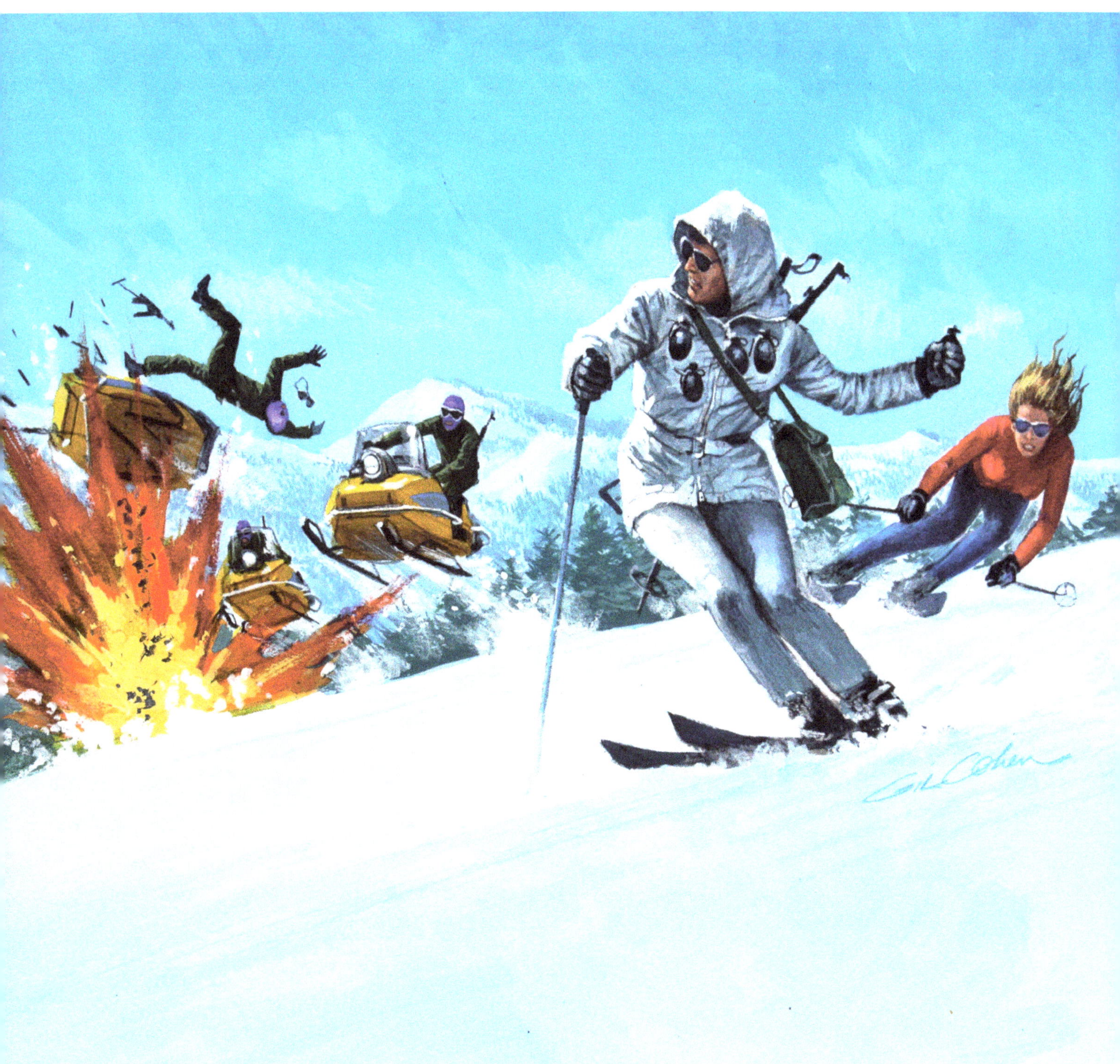

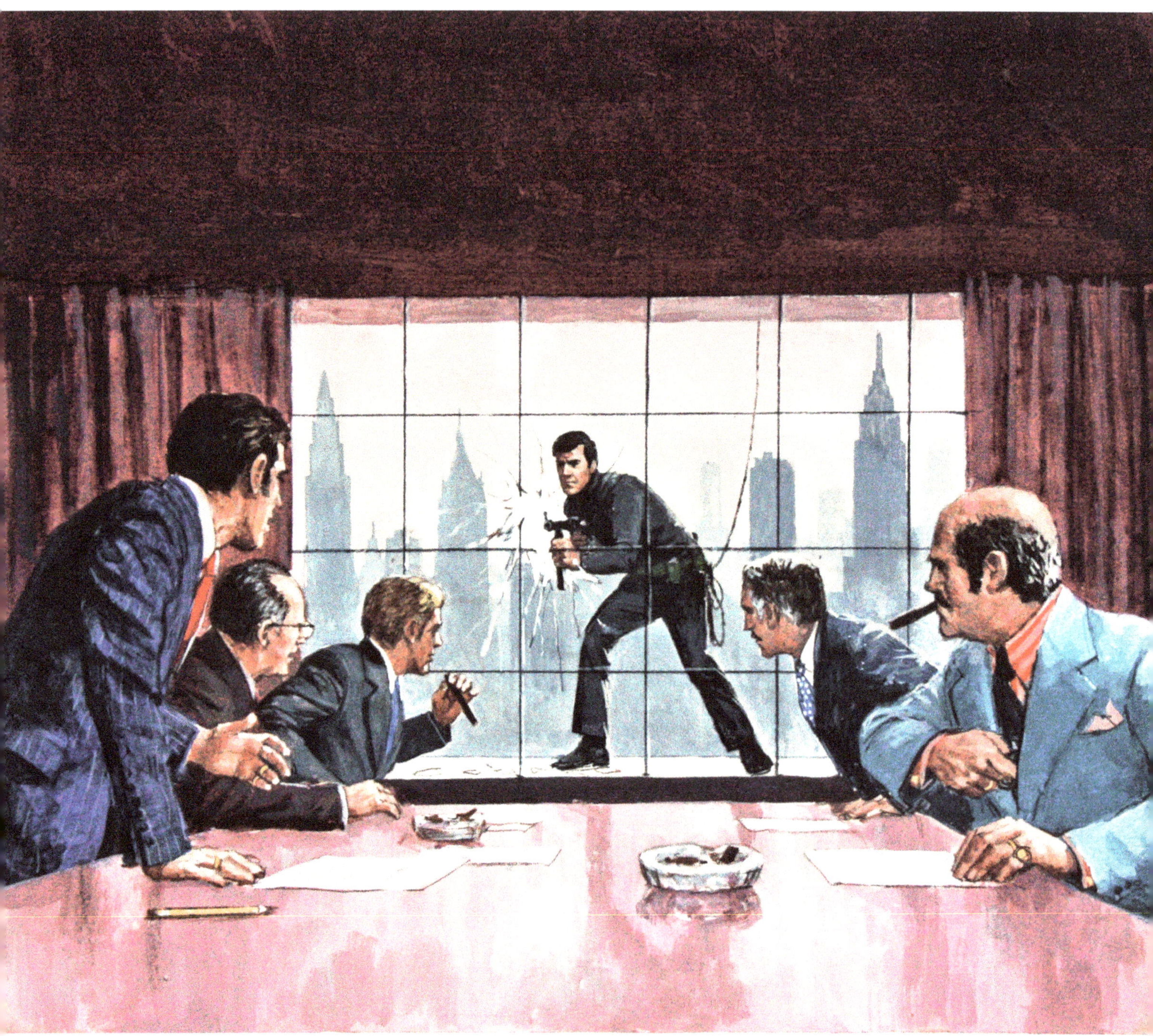

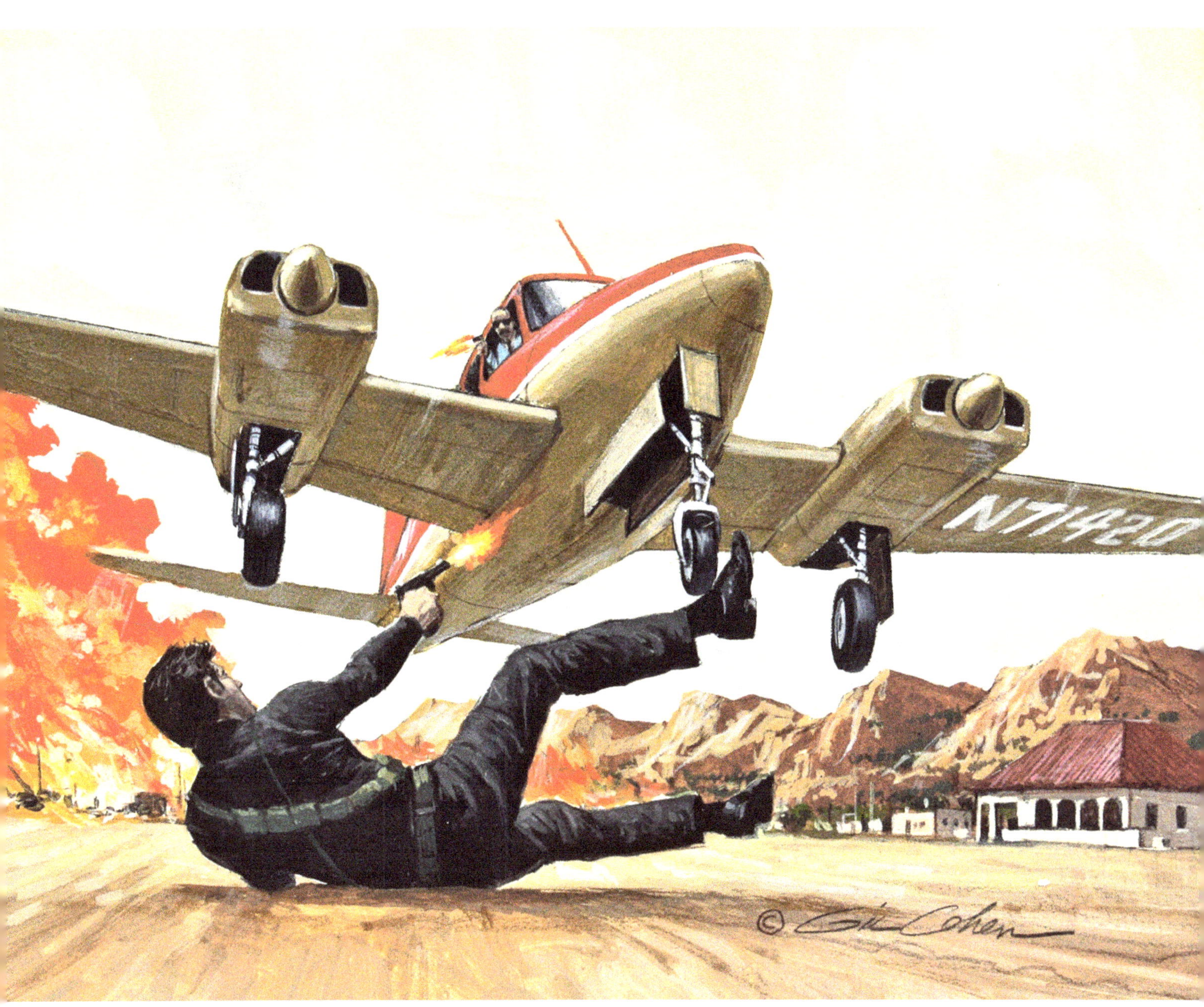

N71420

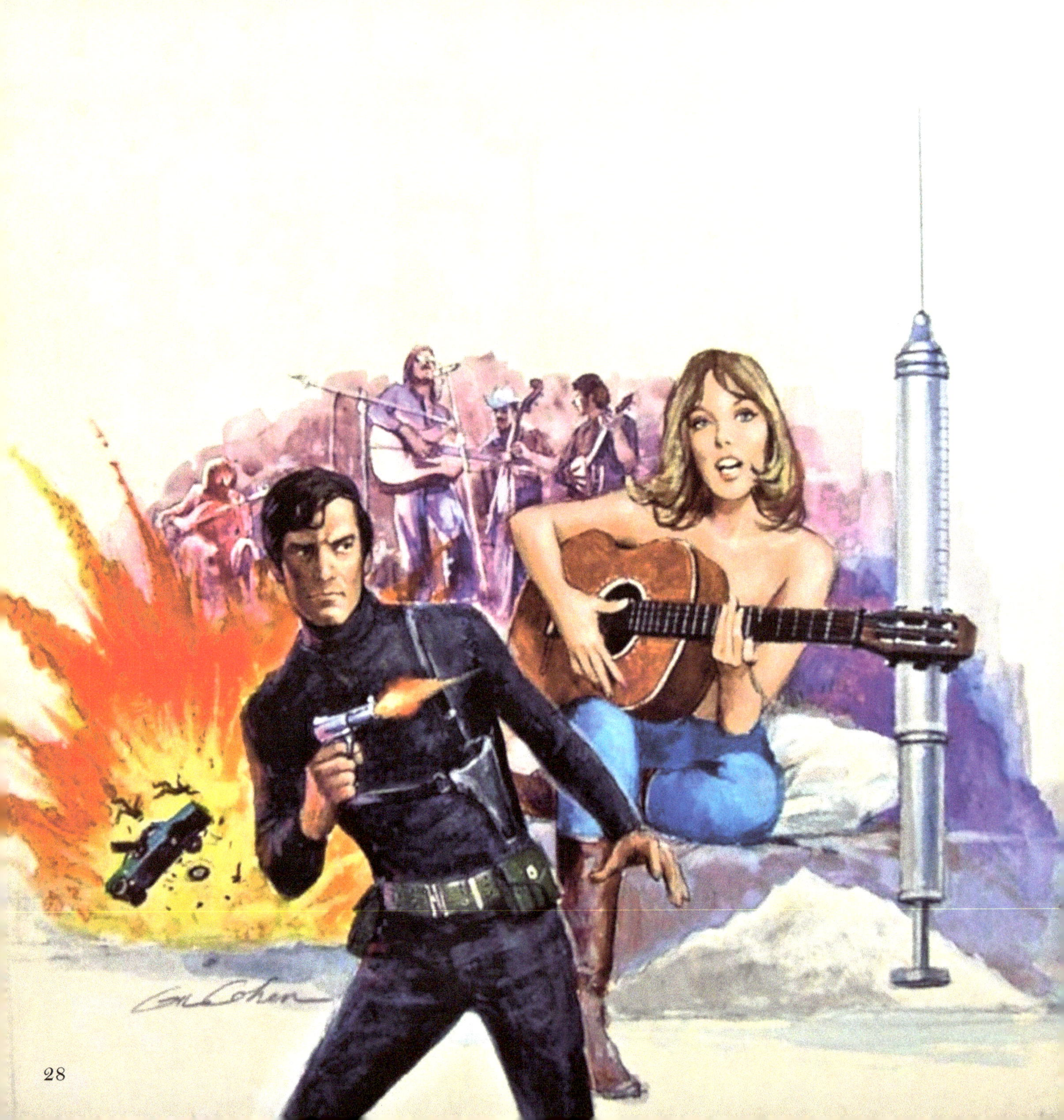

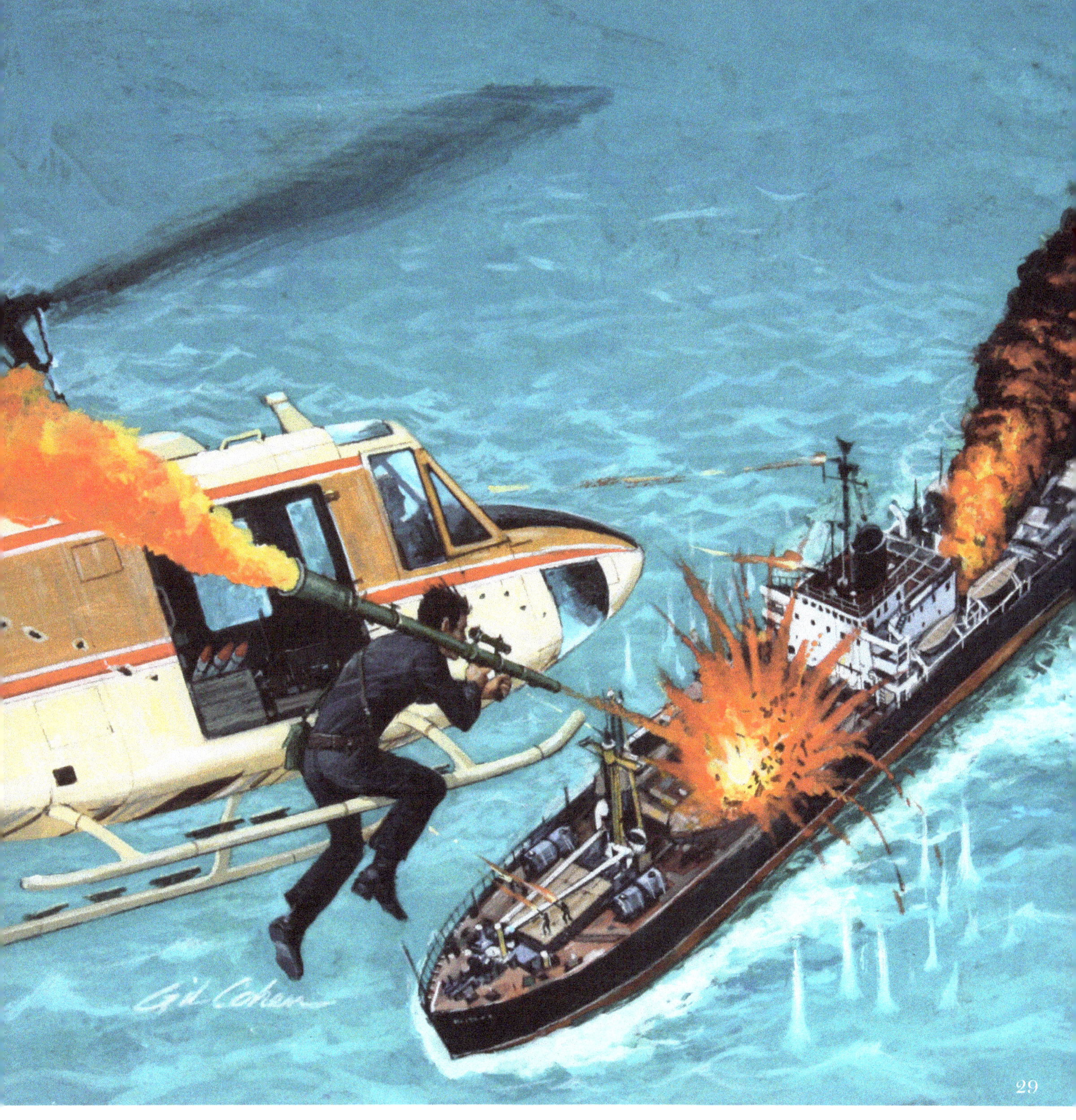

Gil Cohen

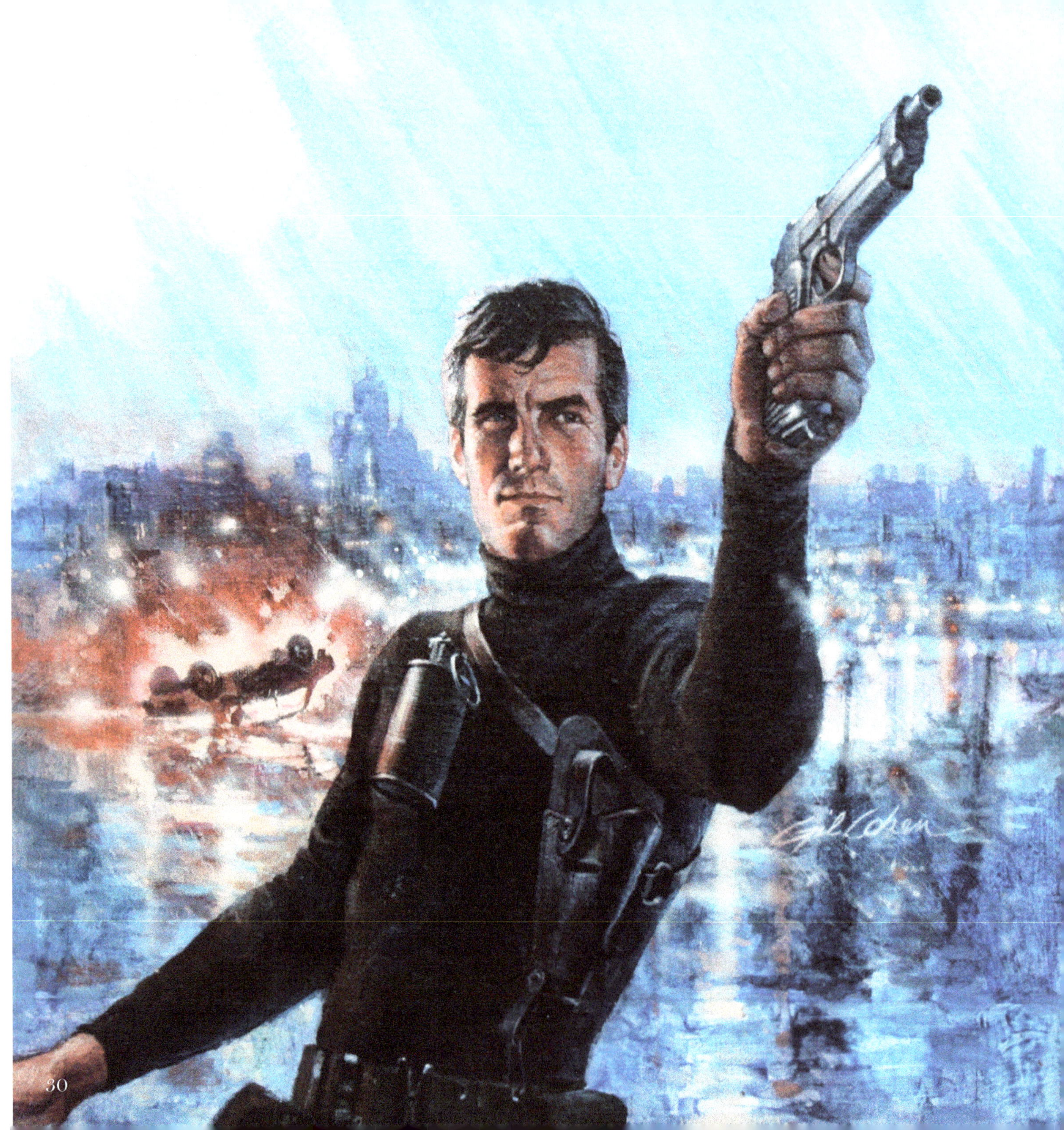

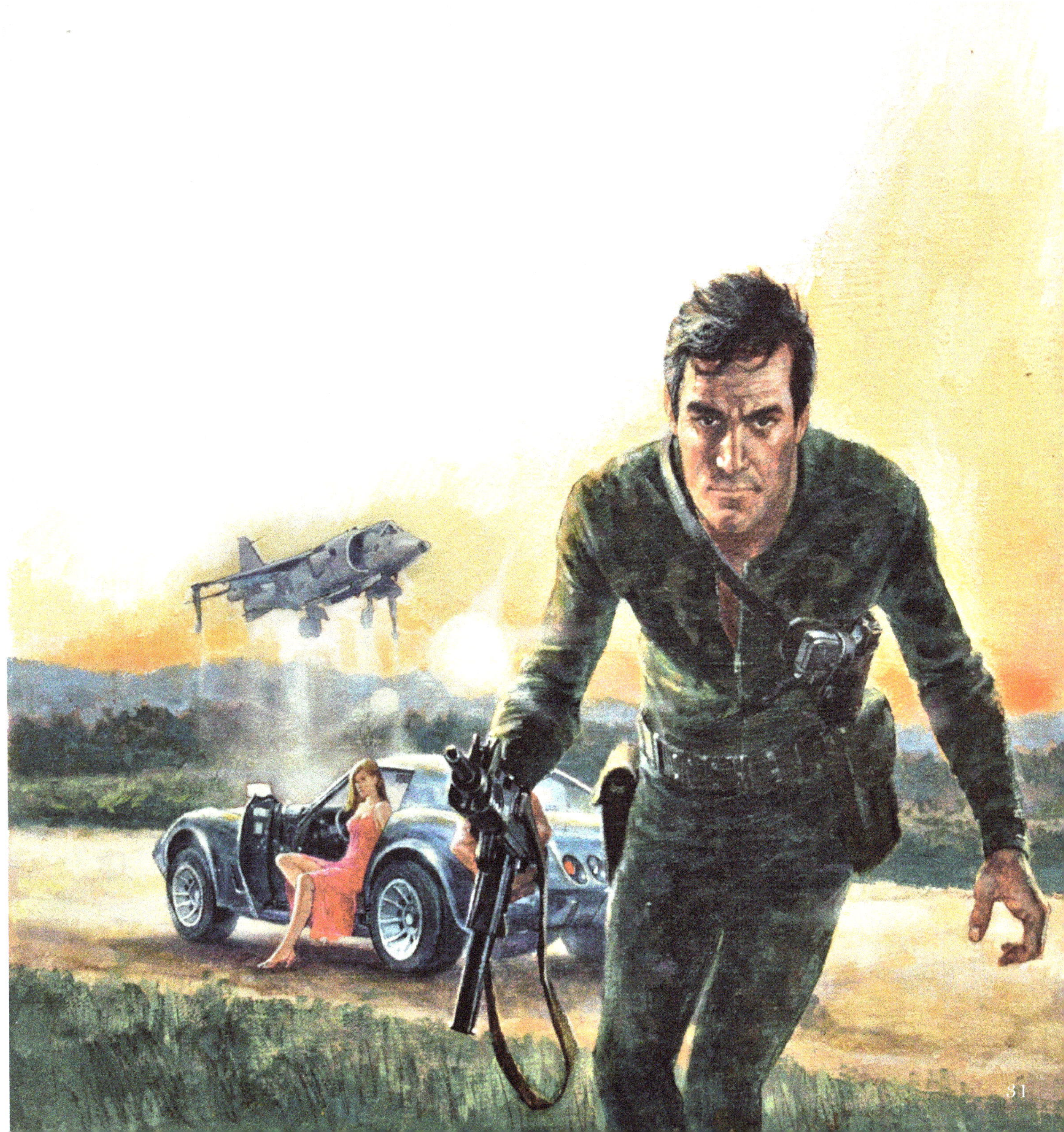

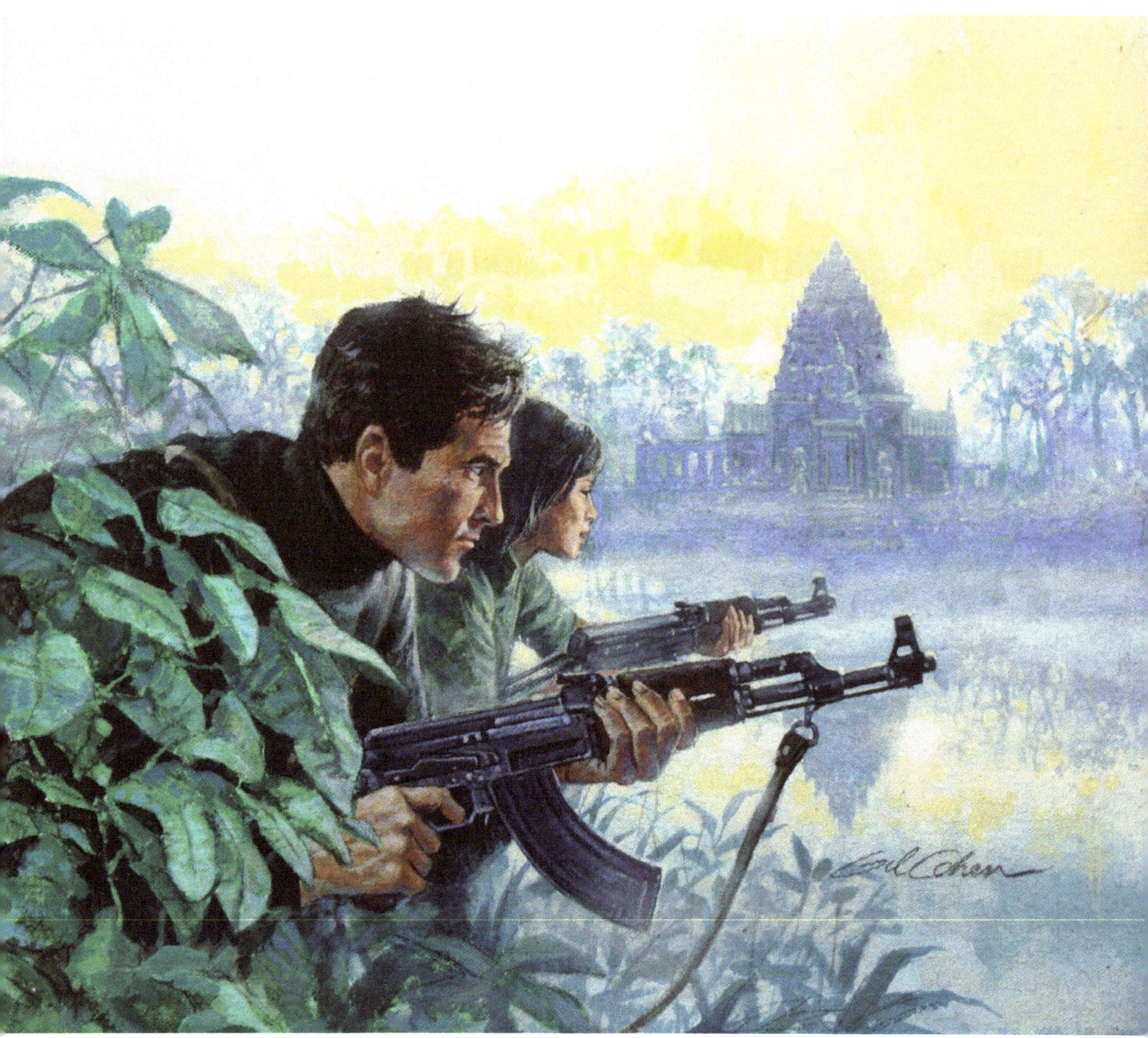

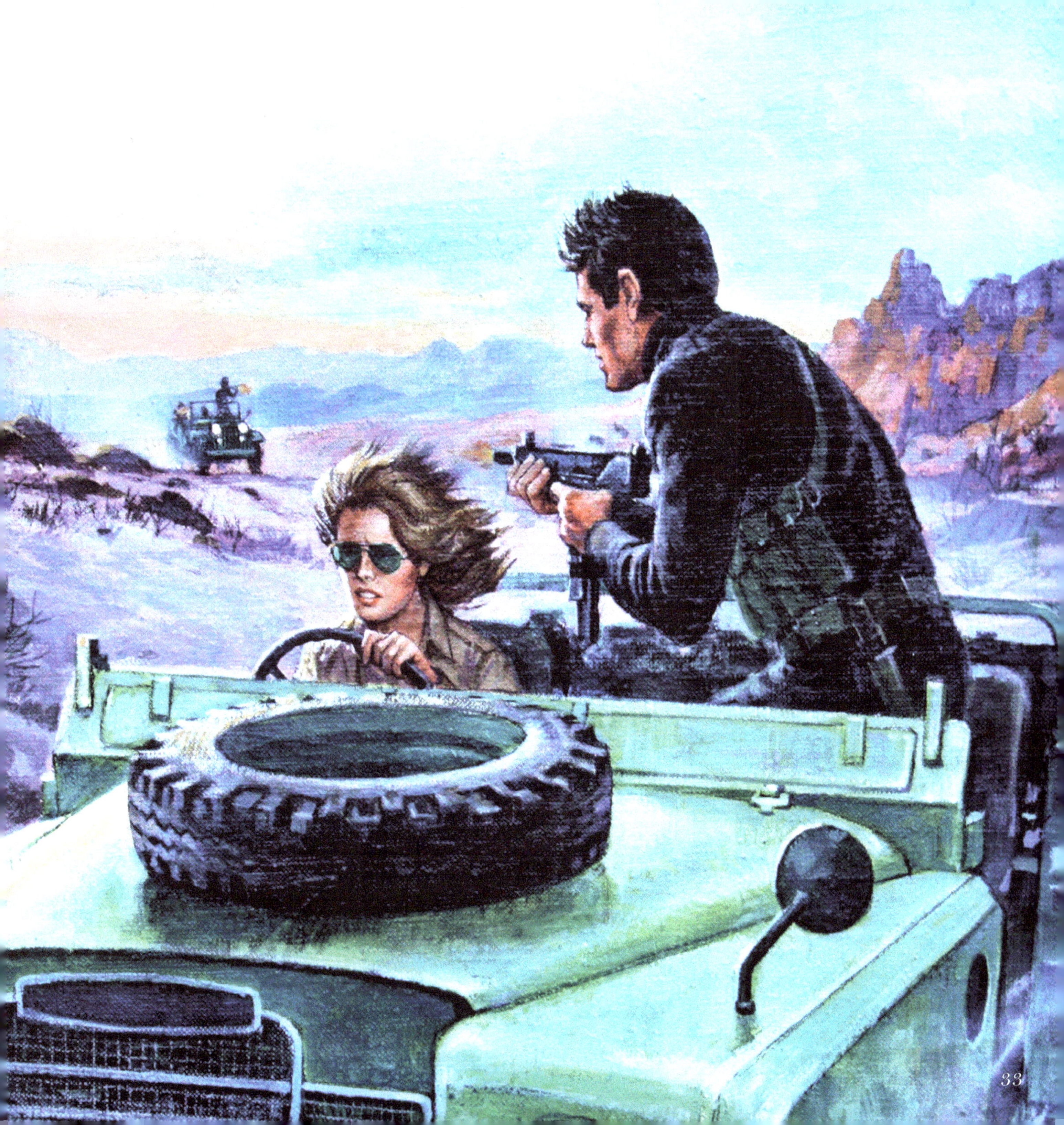

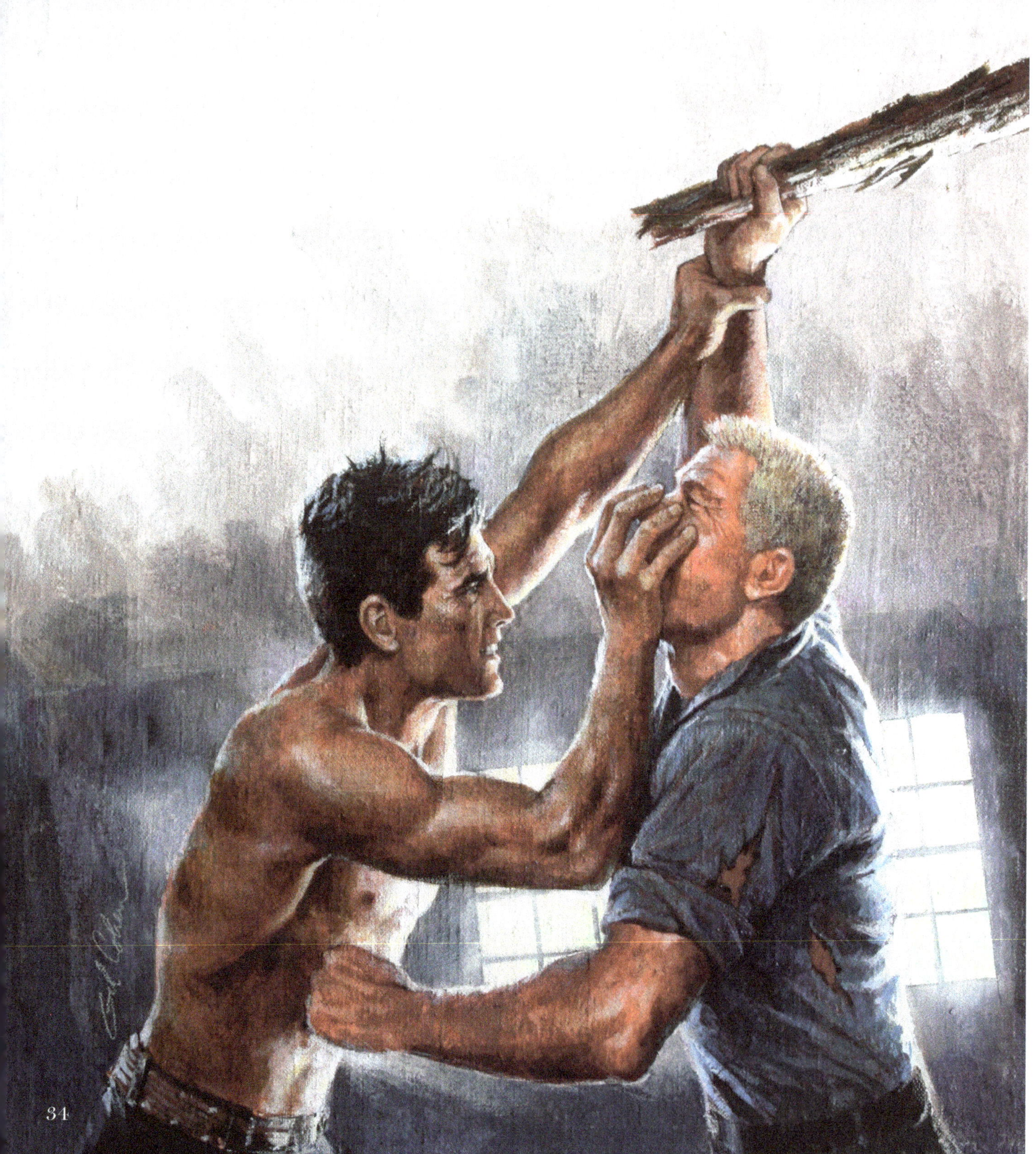

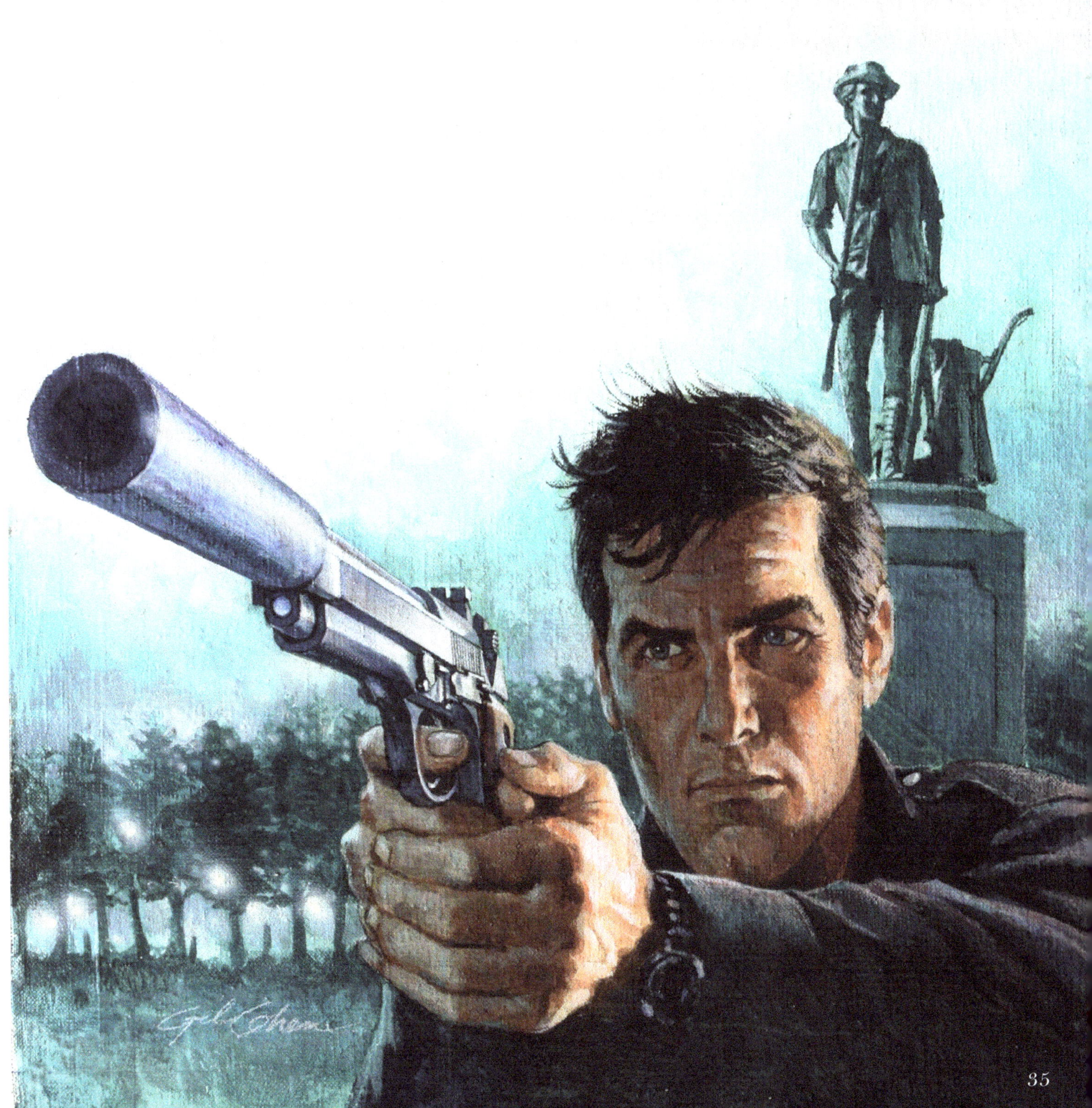

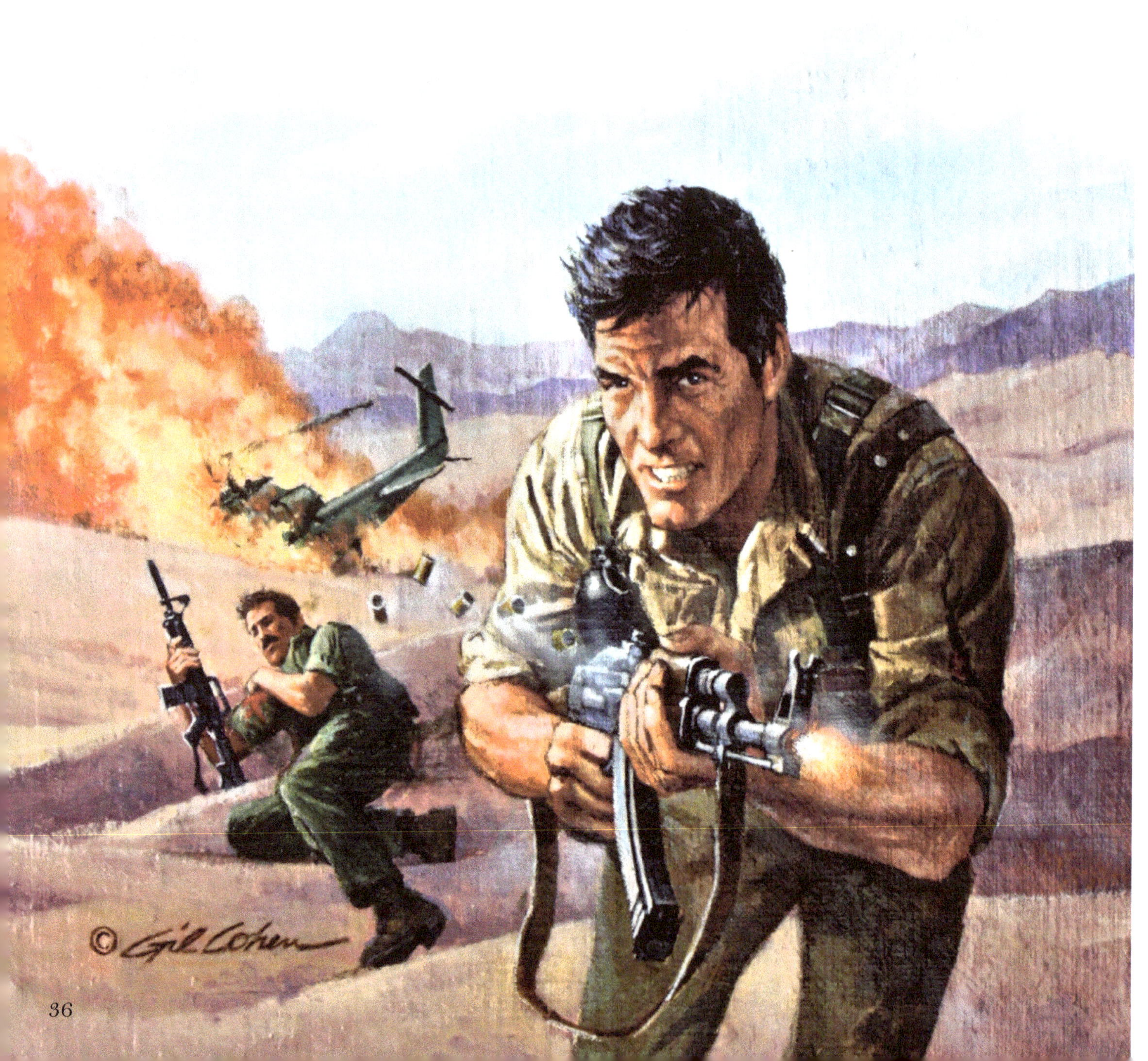
© Gil Cohen

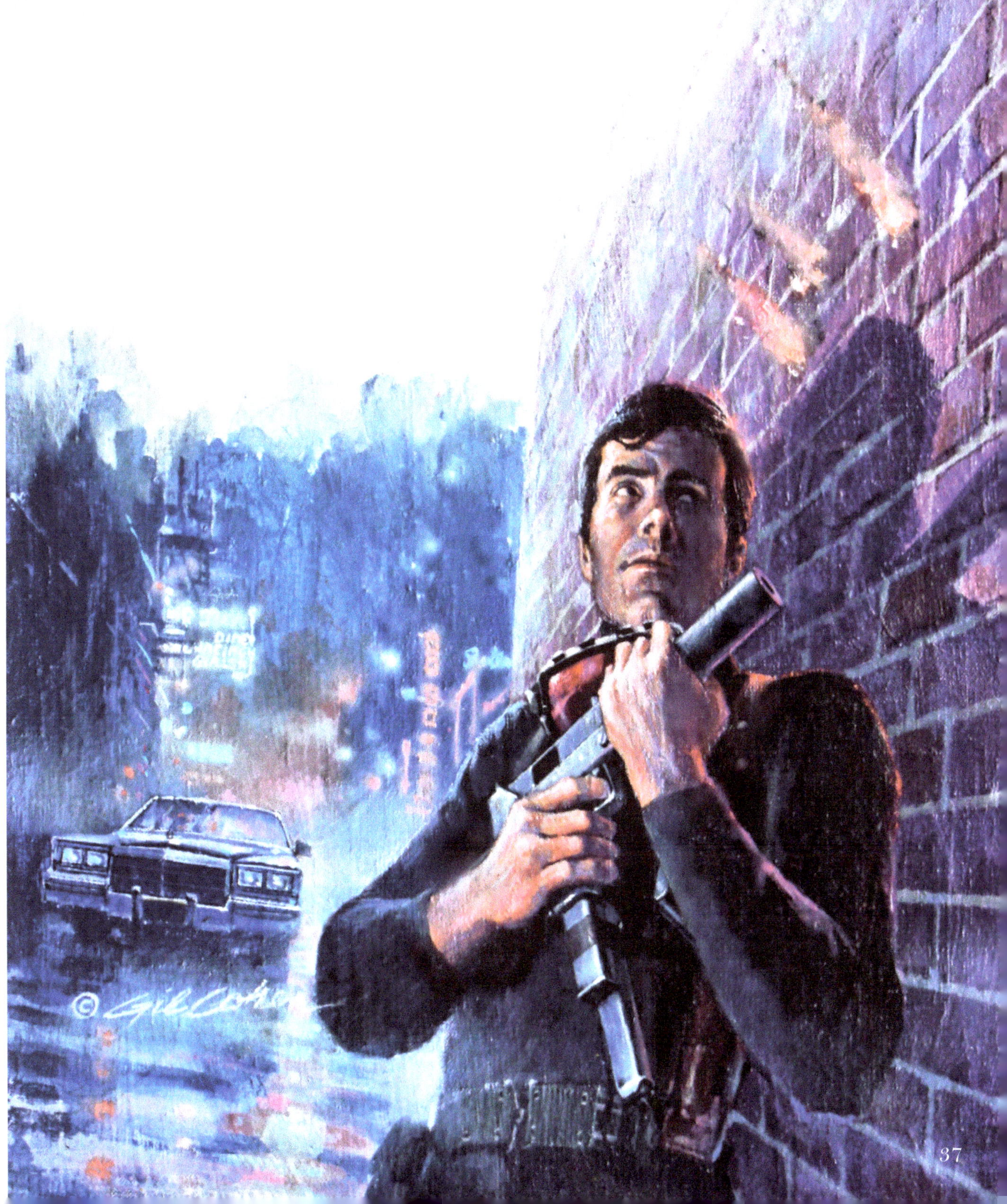

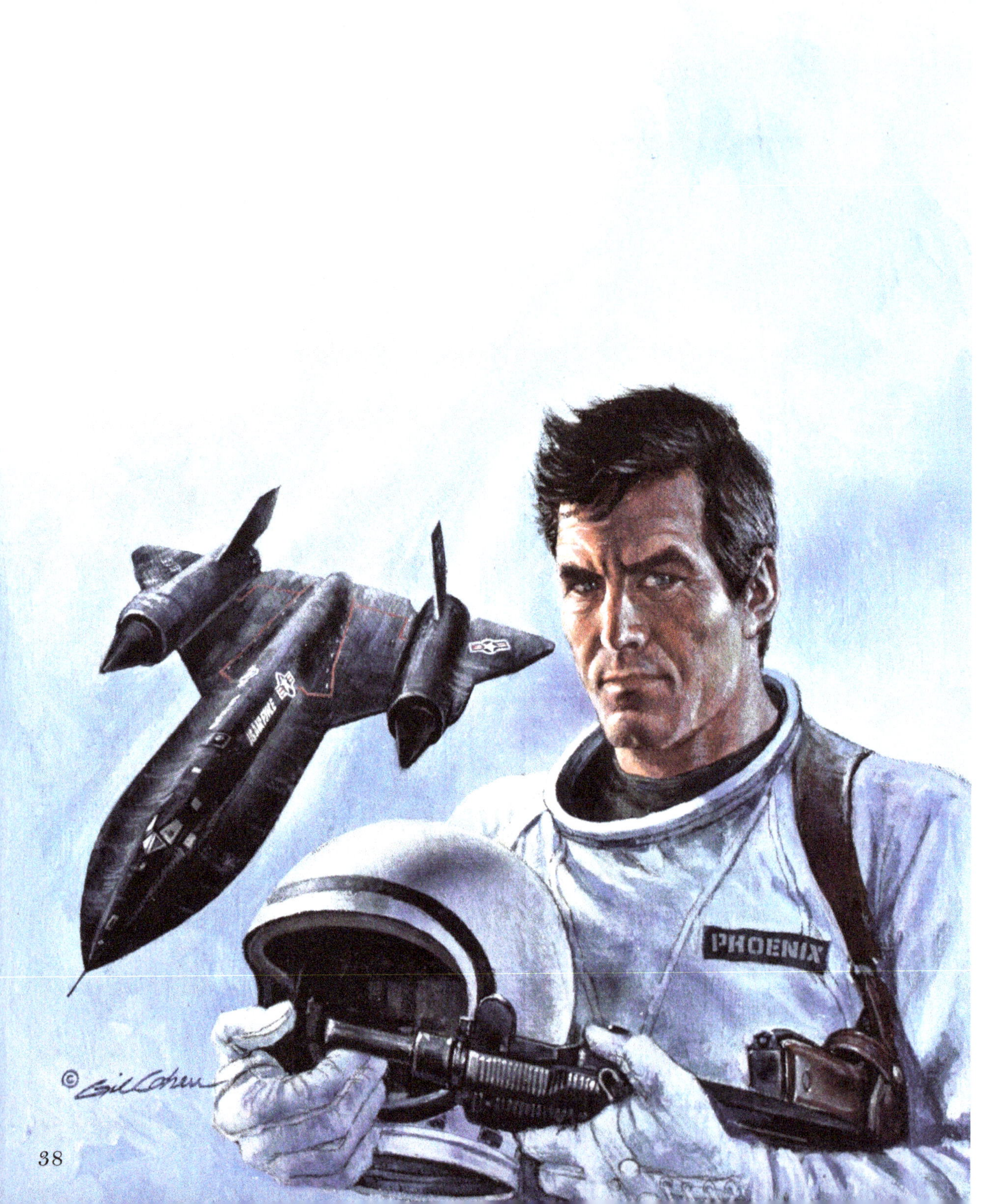
PHOENIX

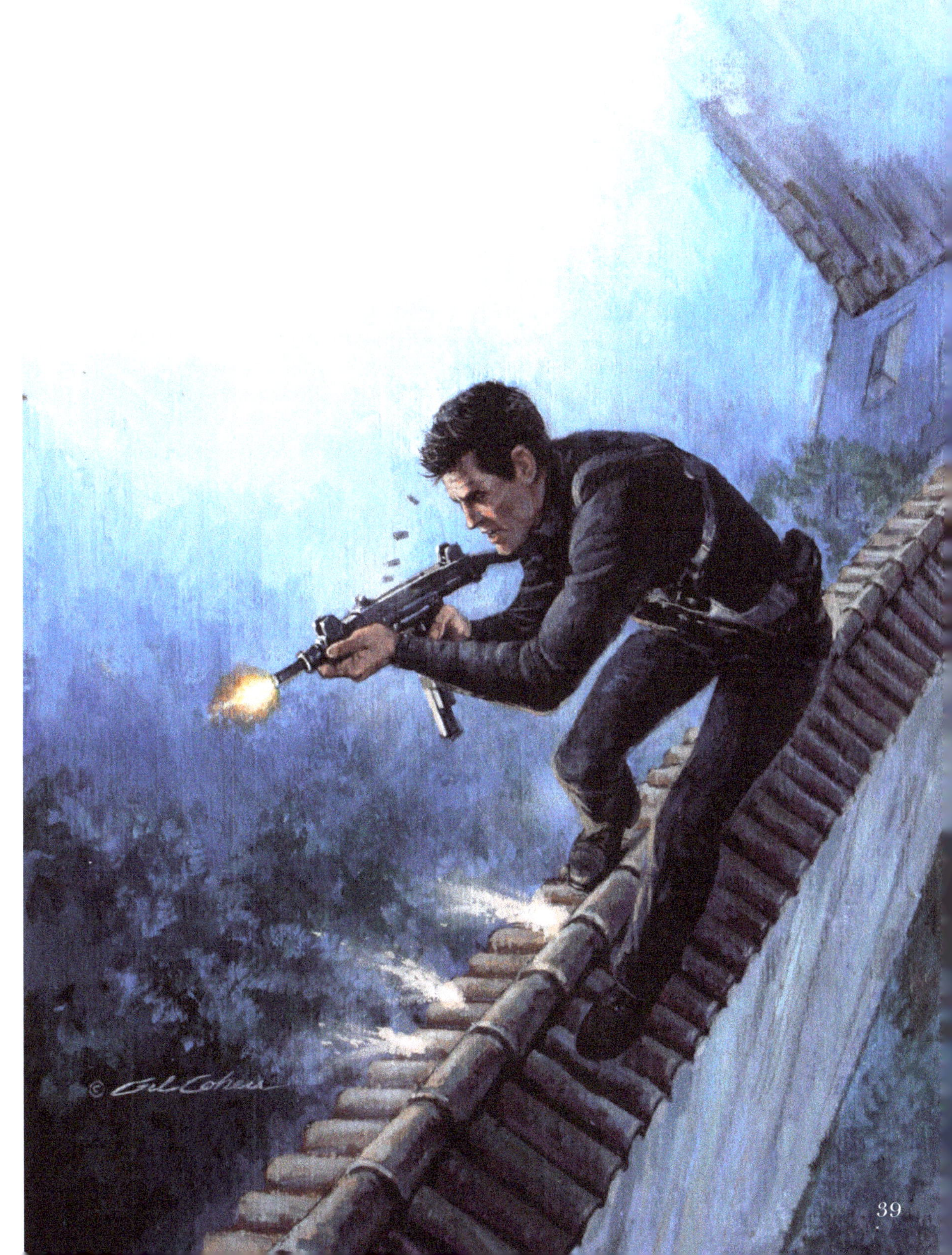

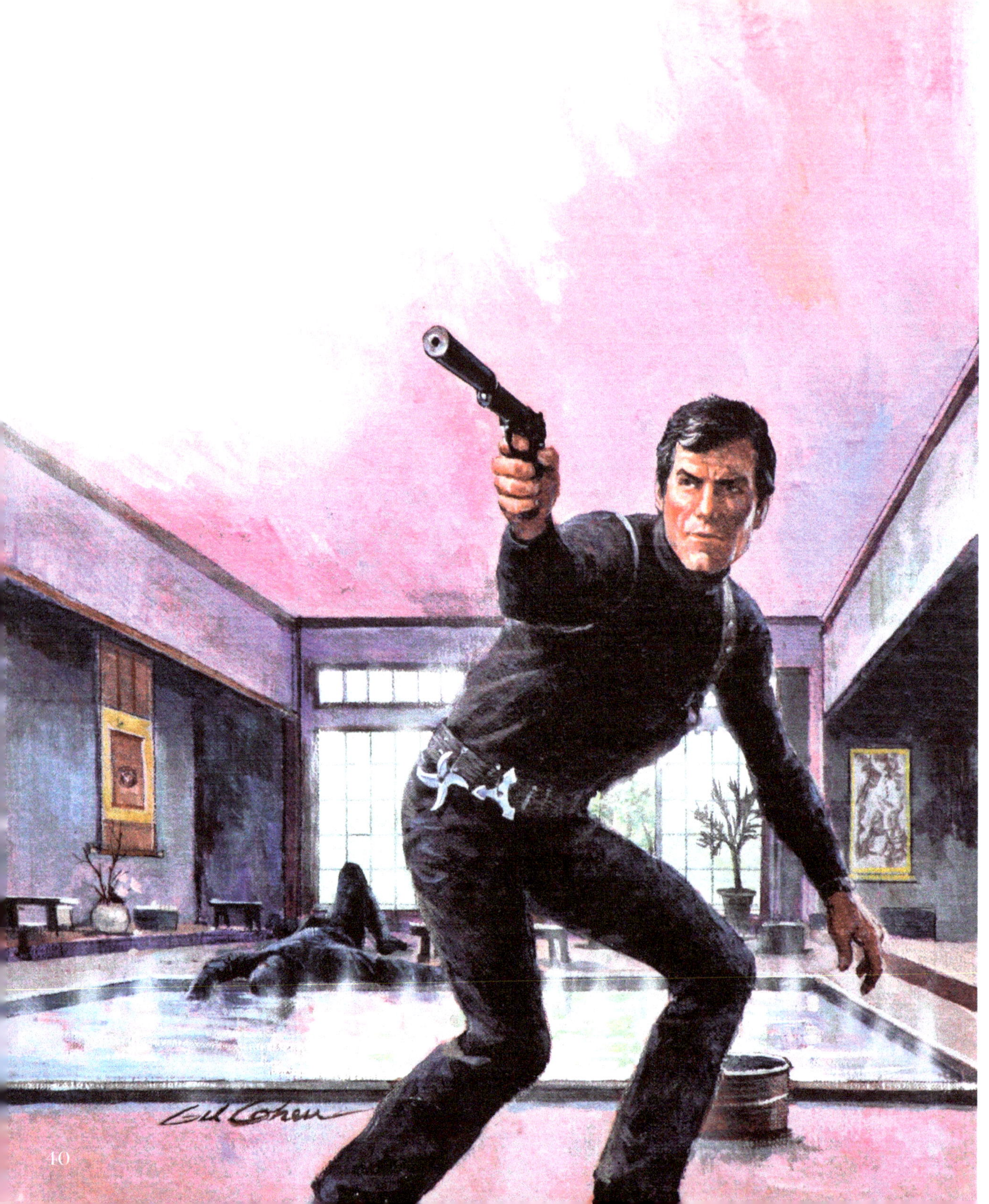

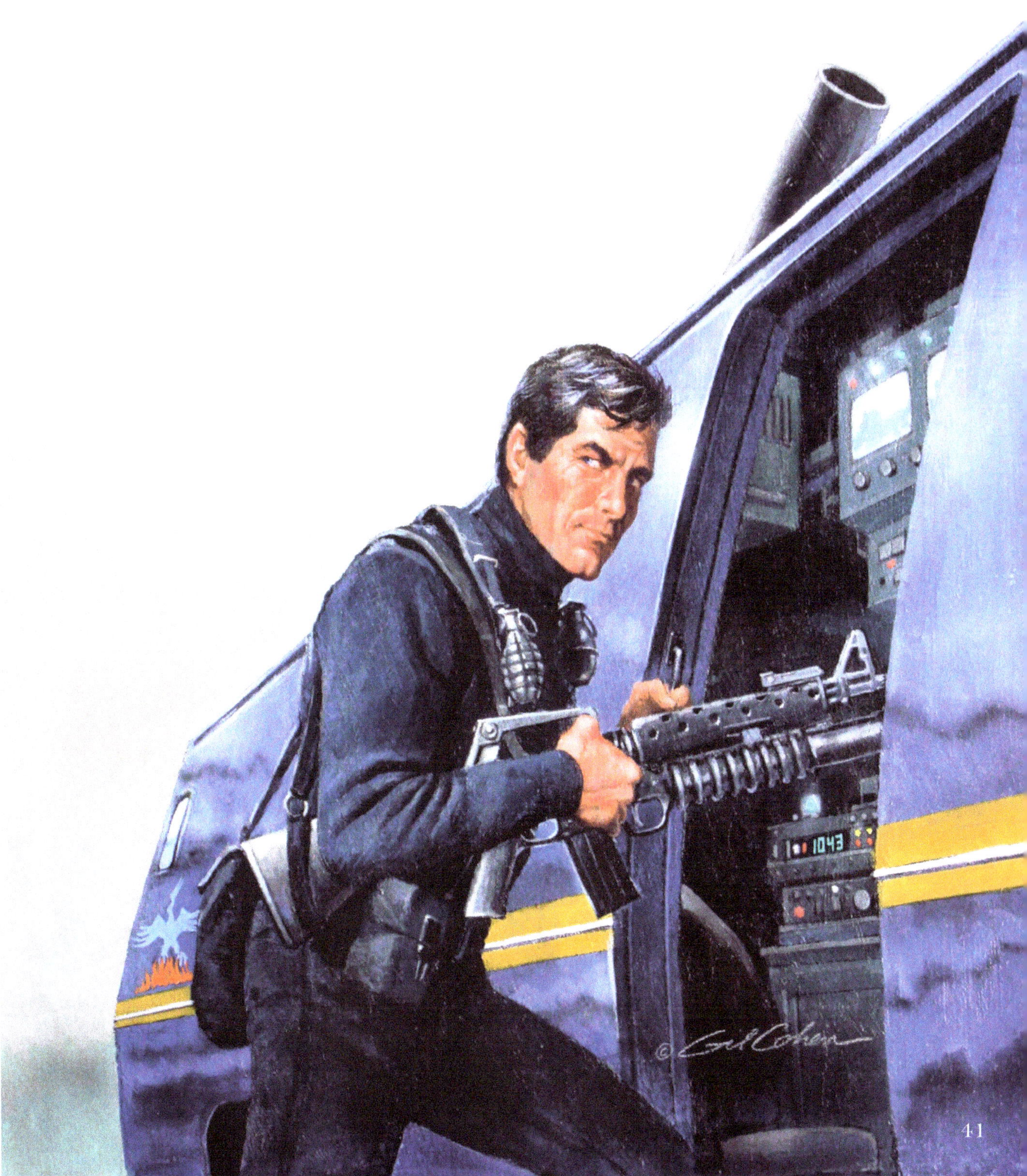

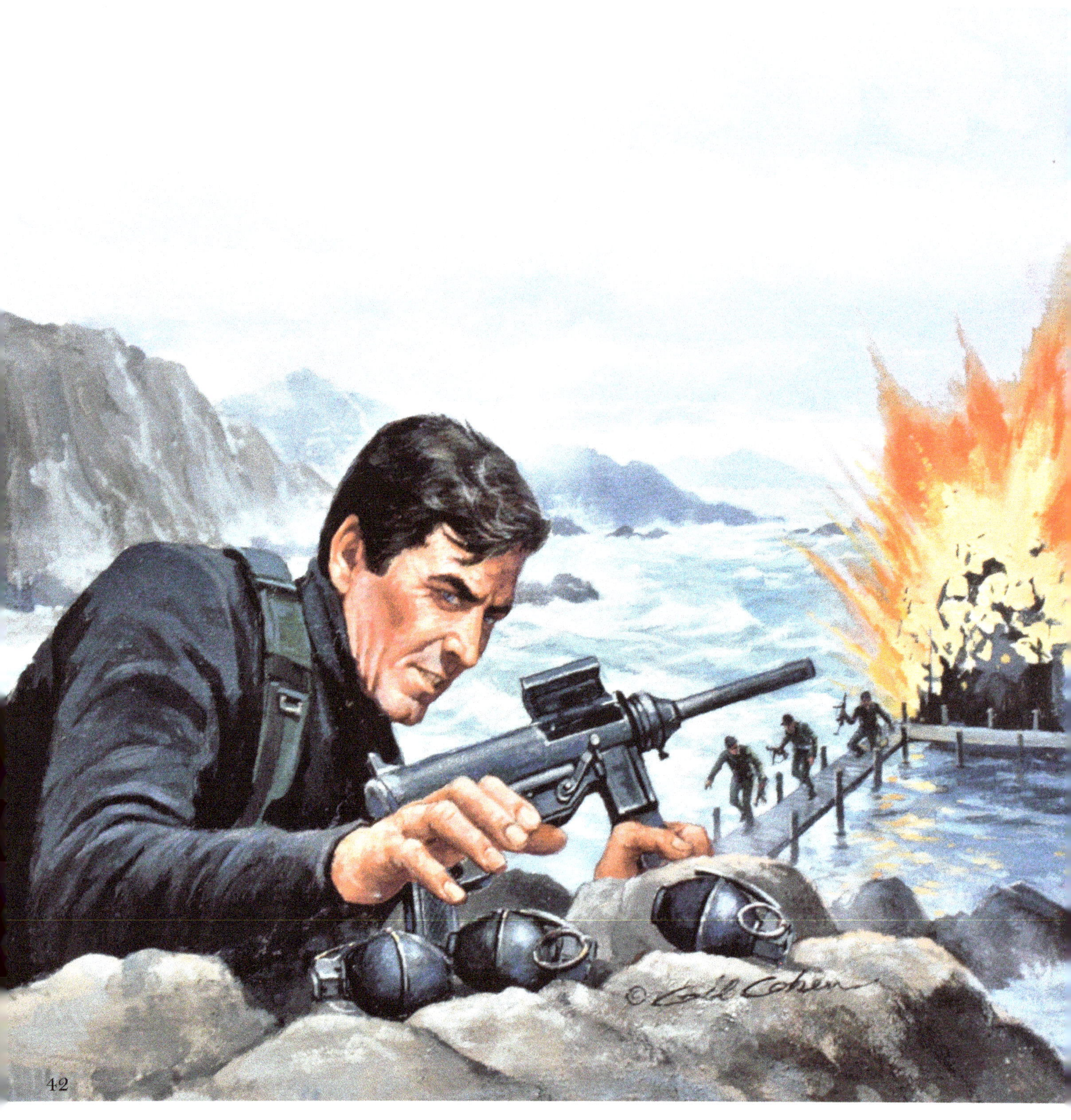

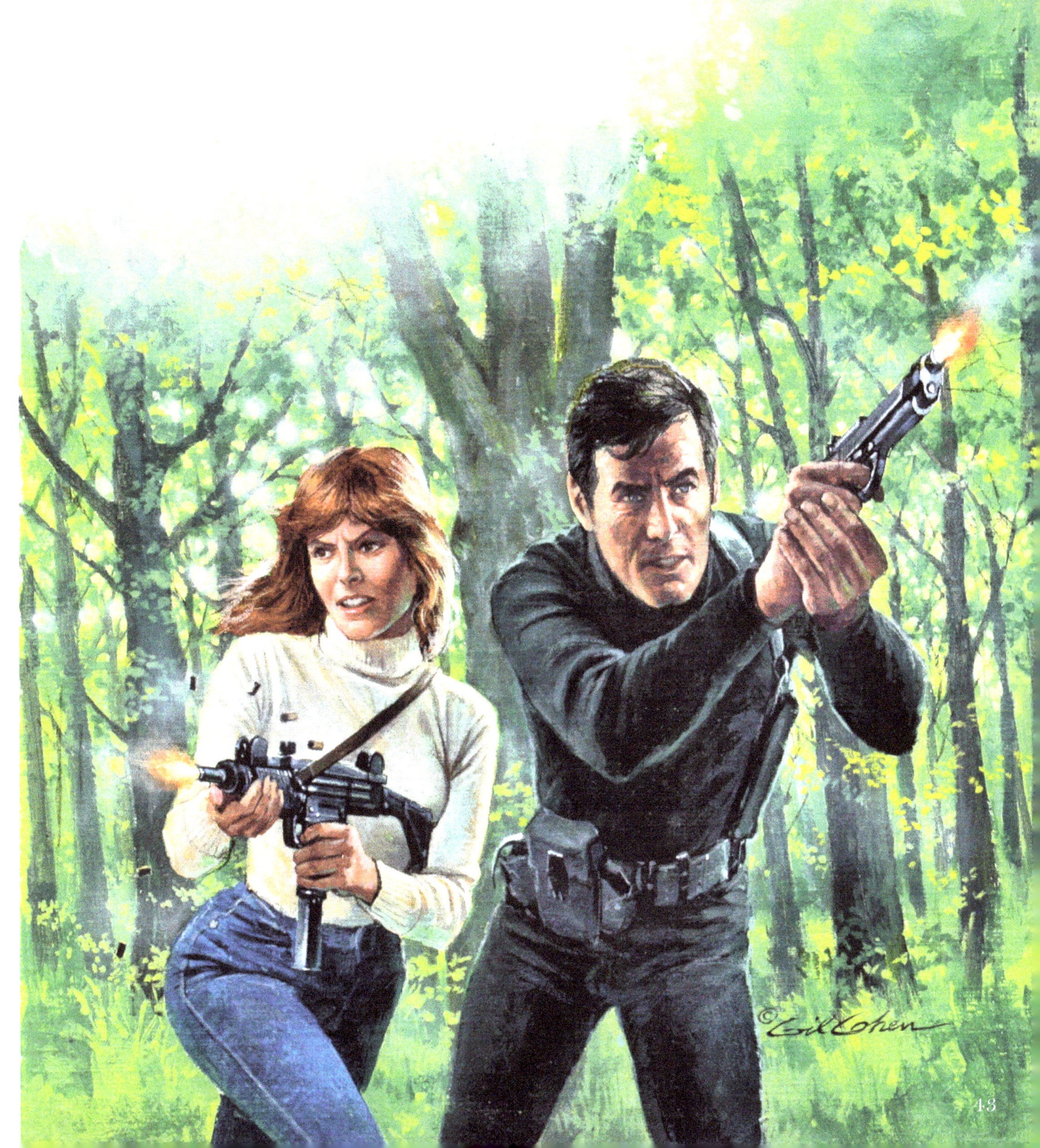

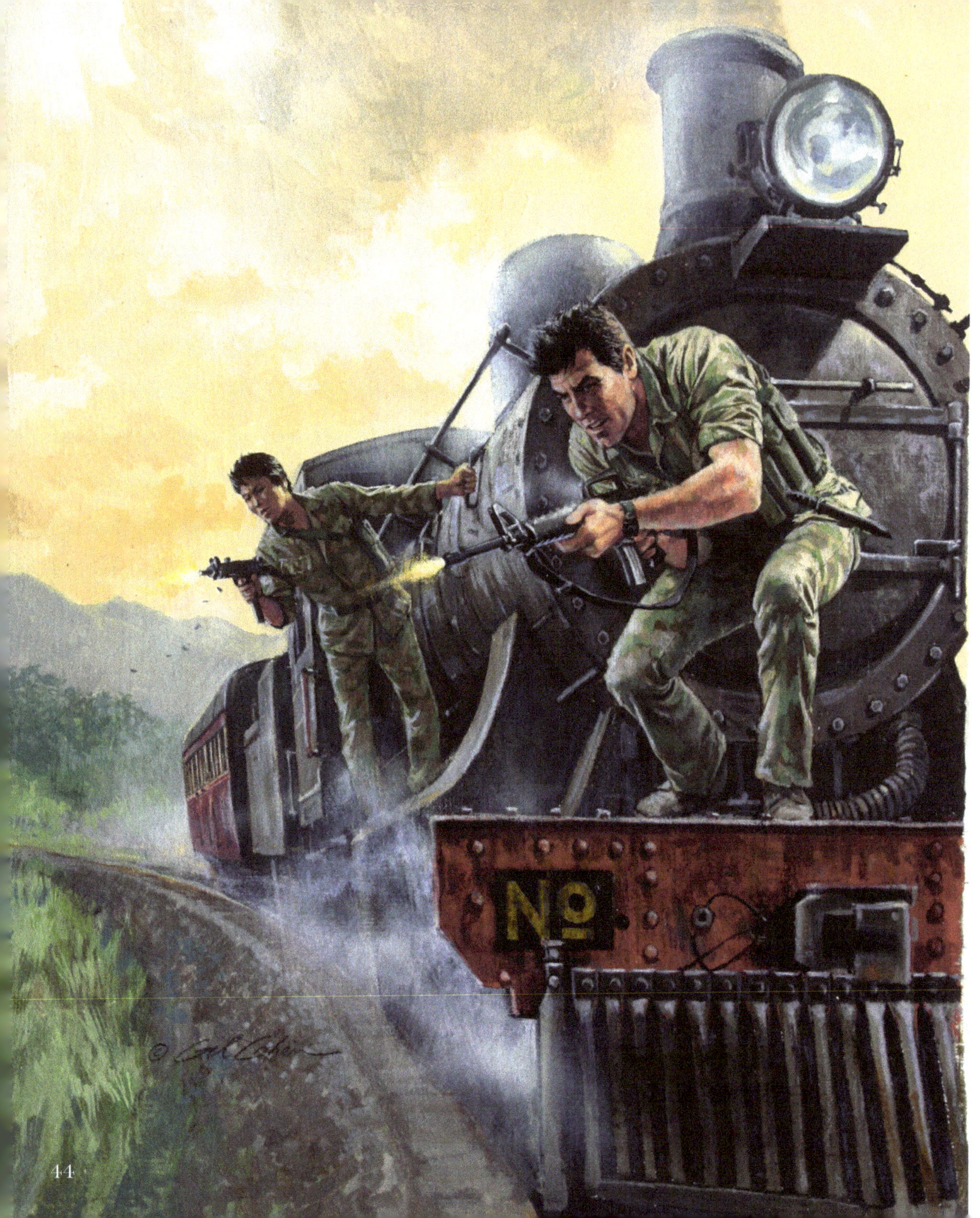
N⁰

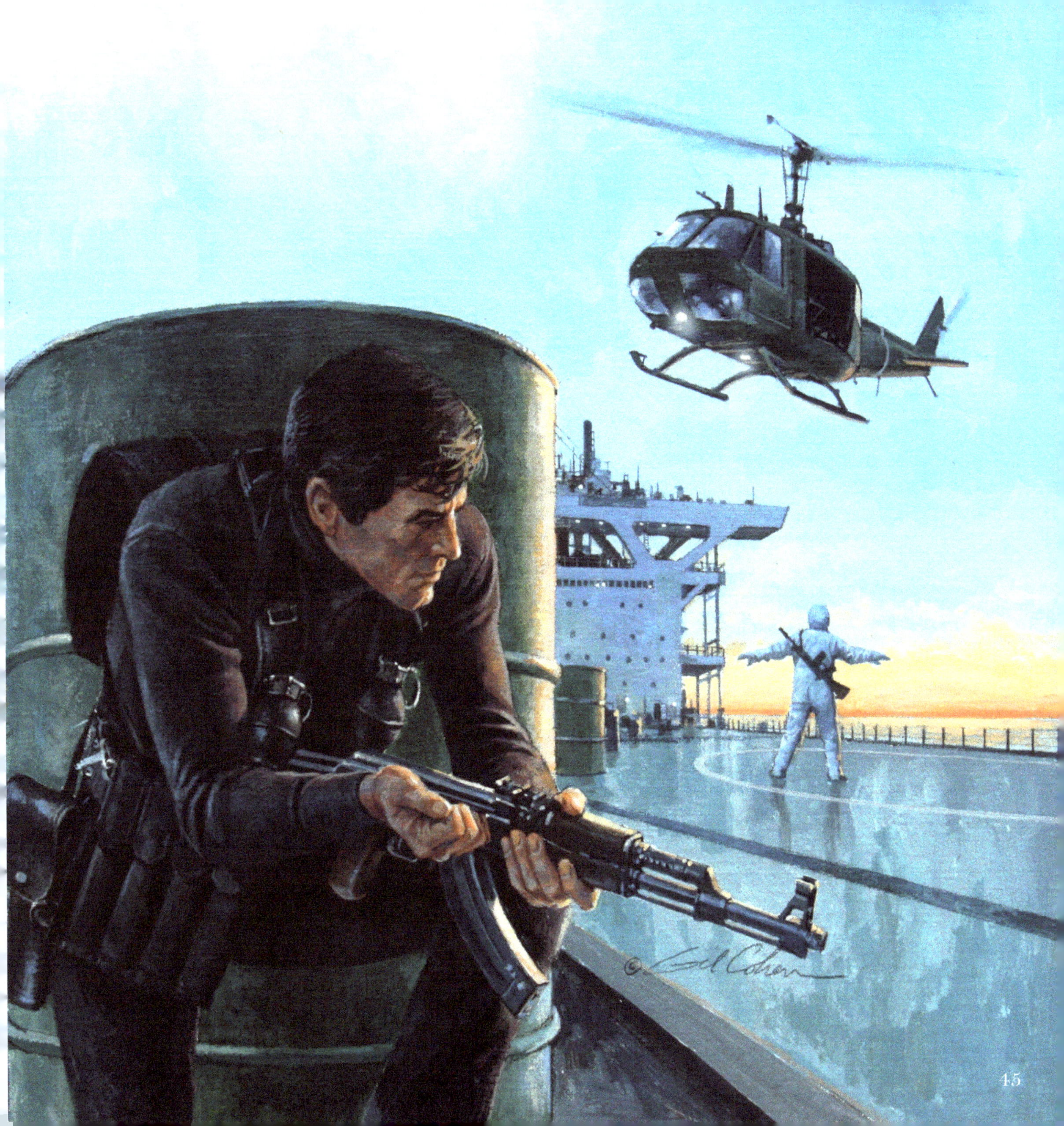

© Gil Cohen

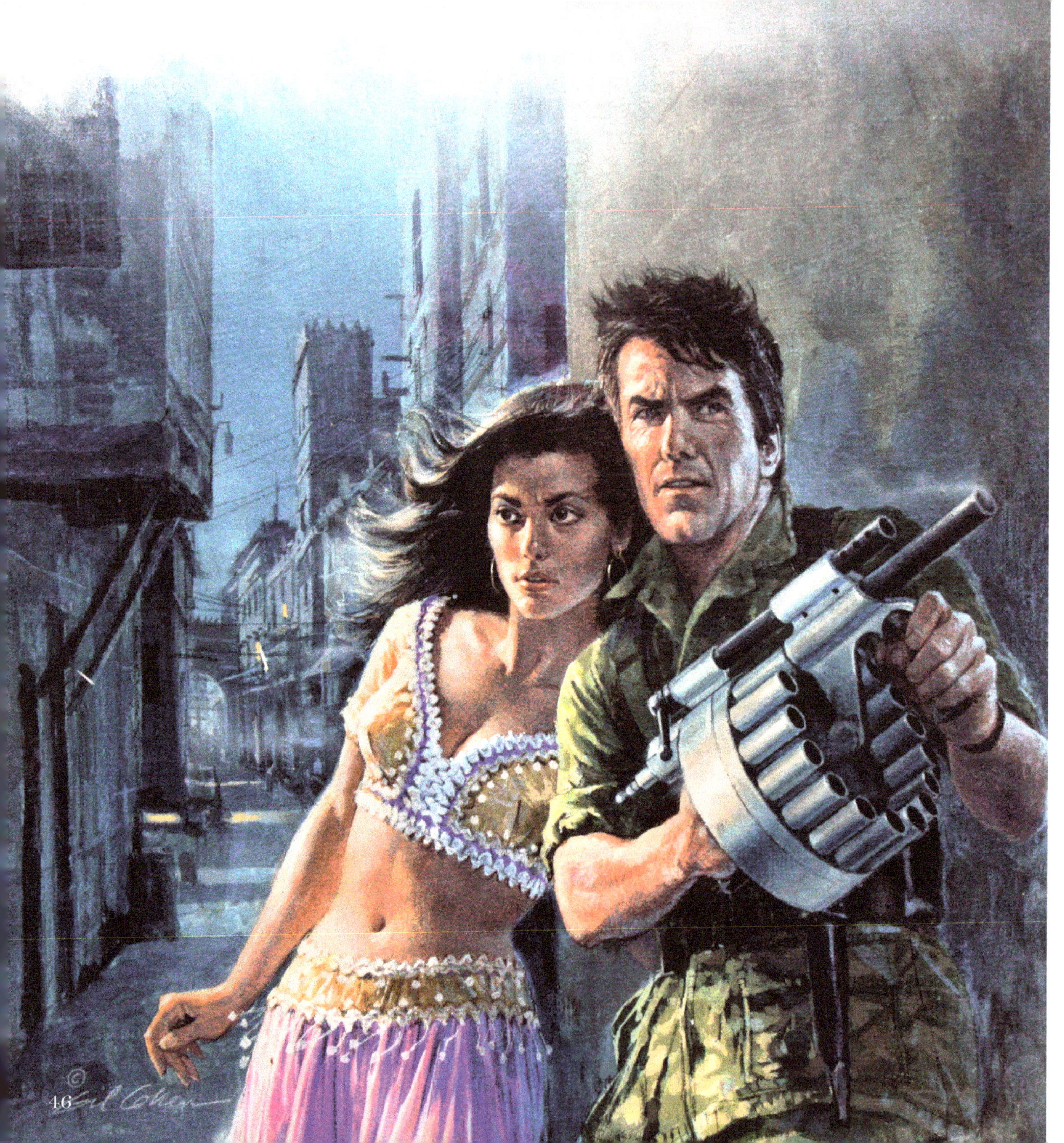
46

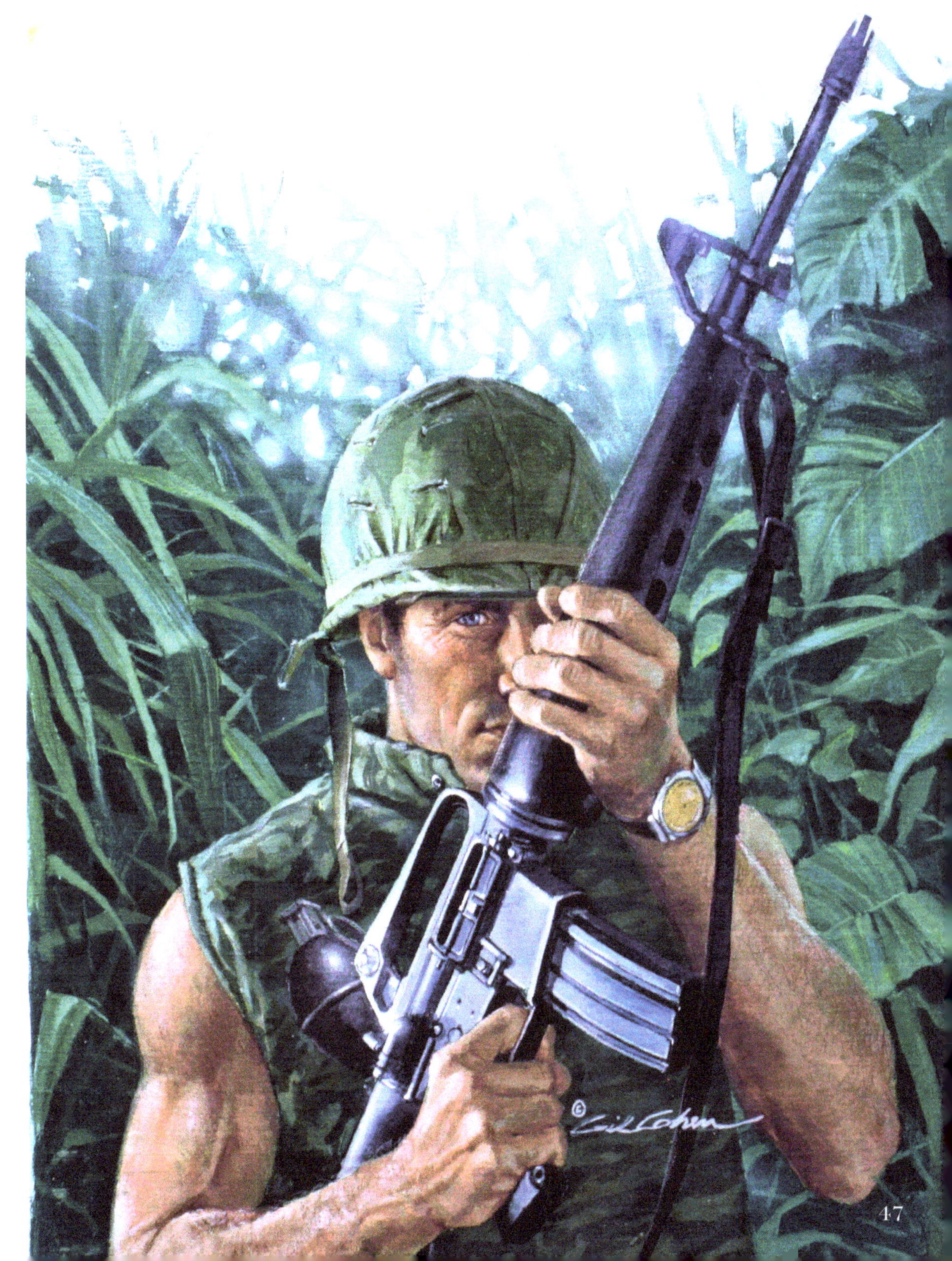

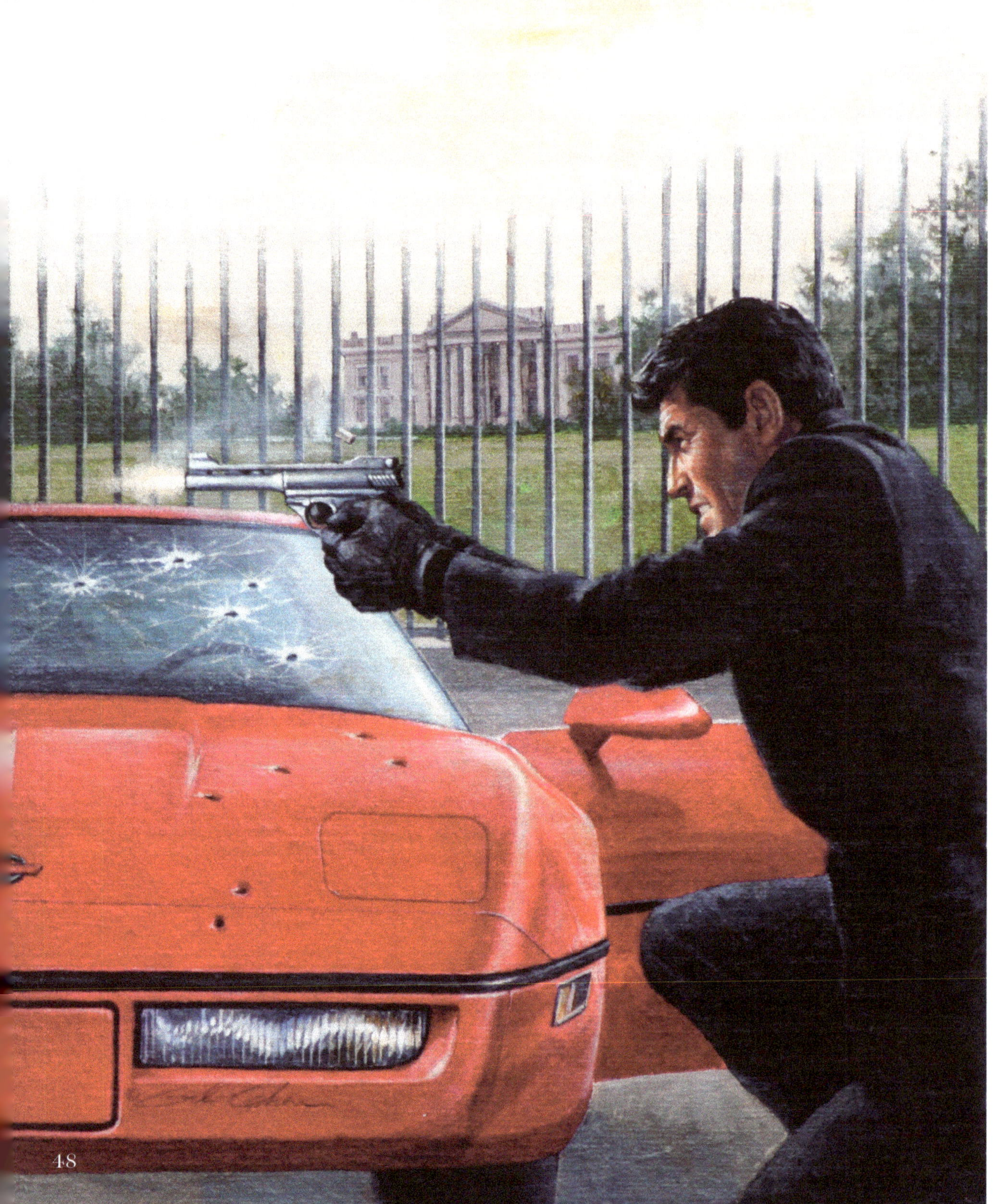

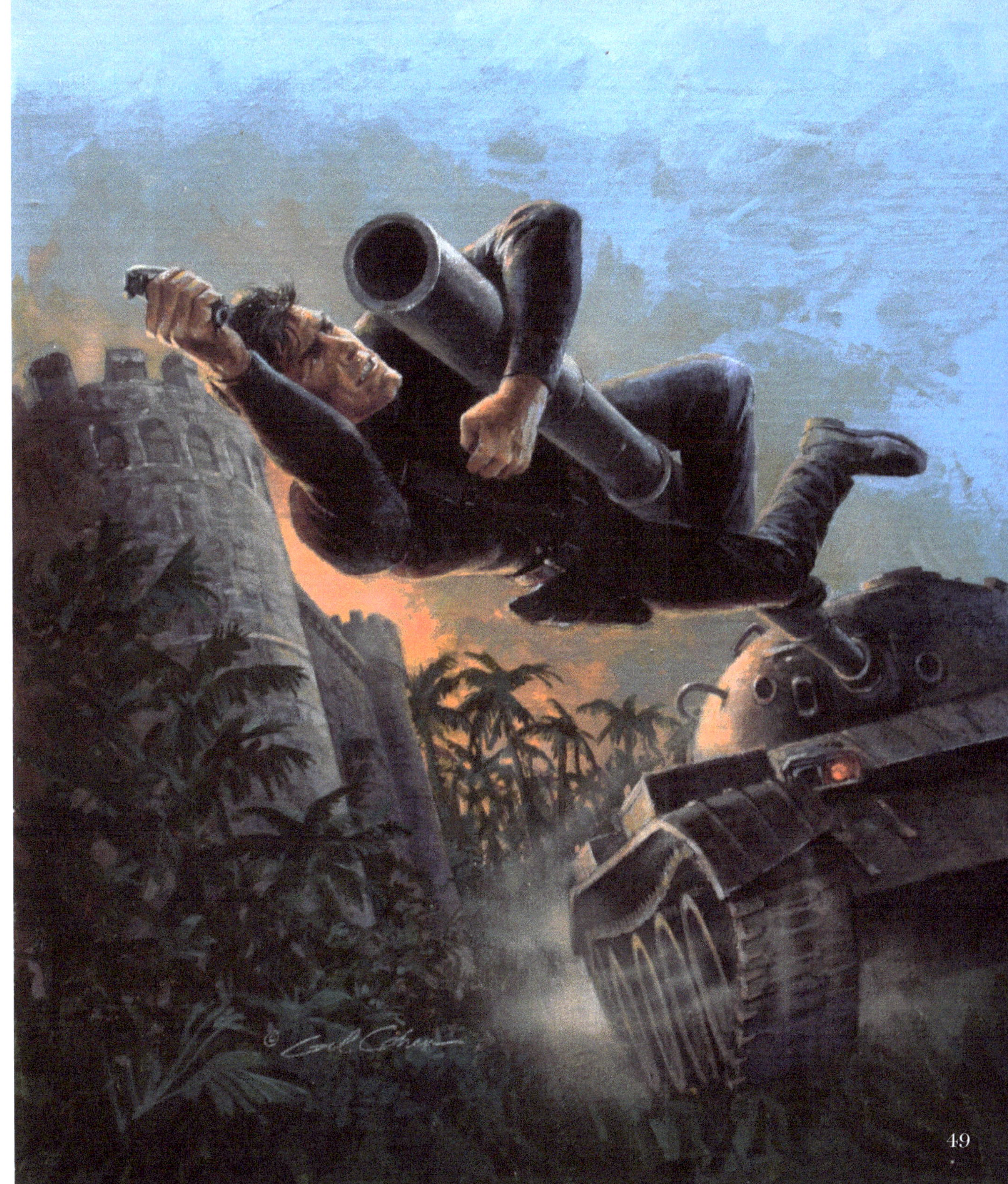

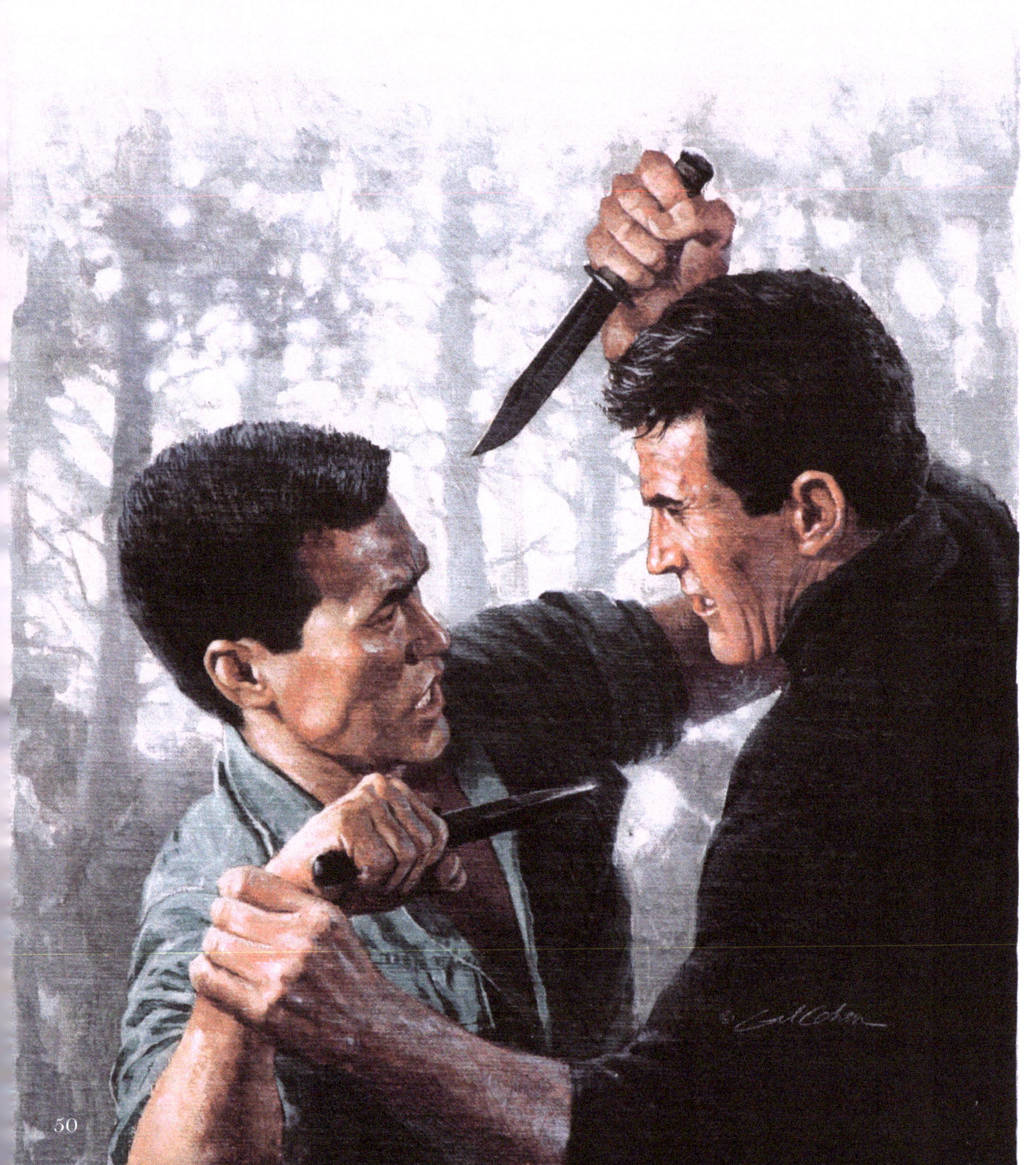

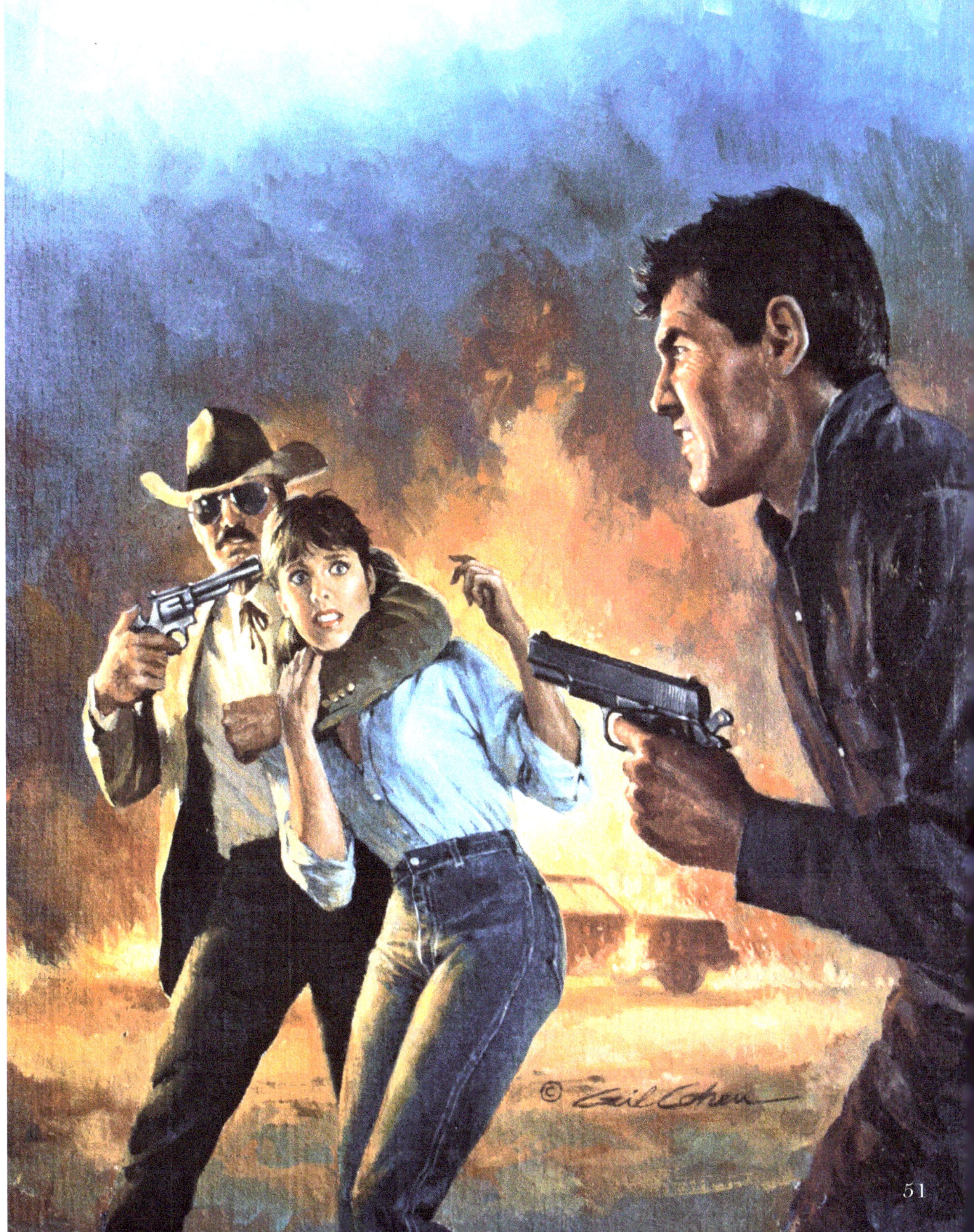

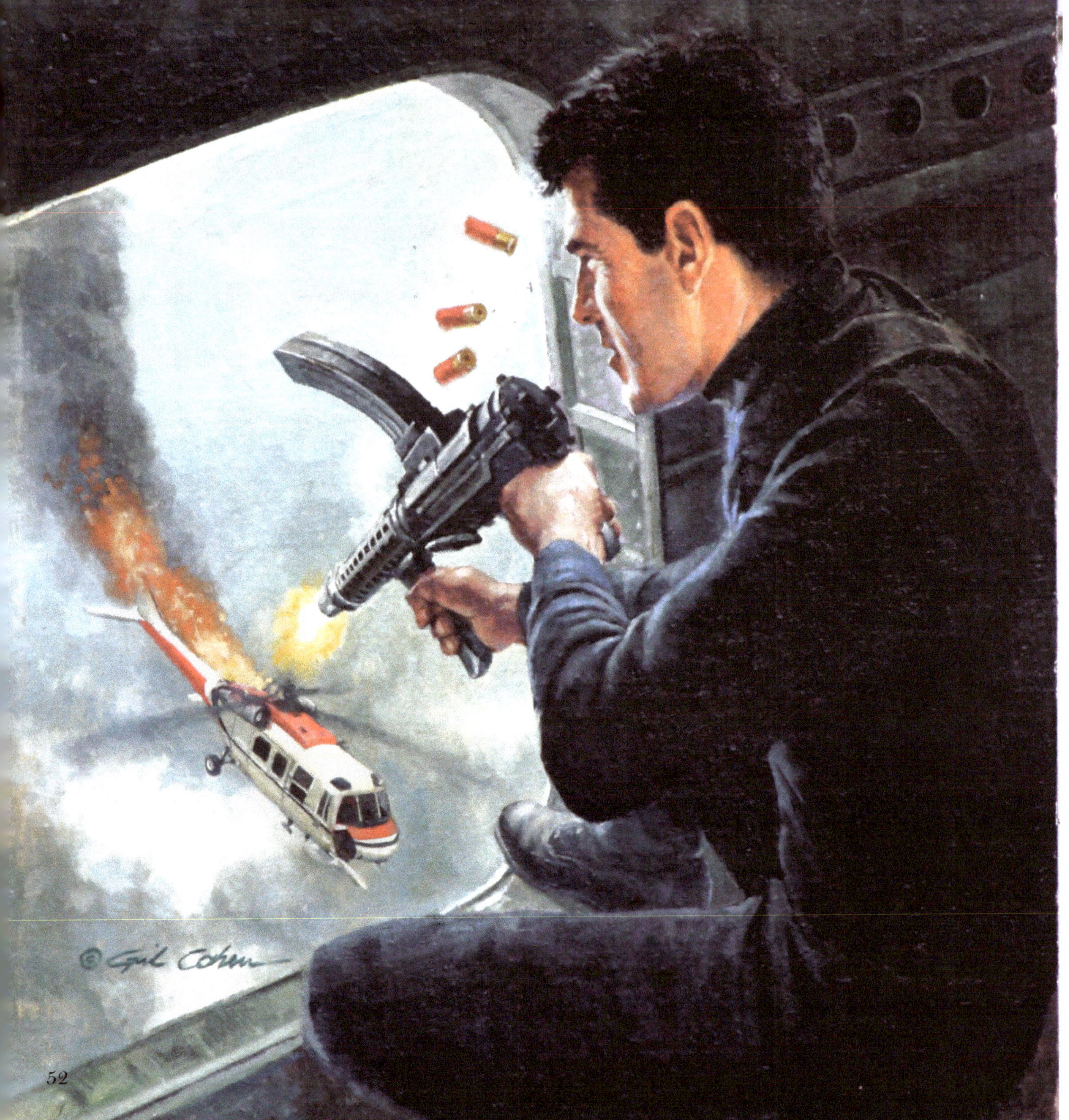

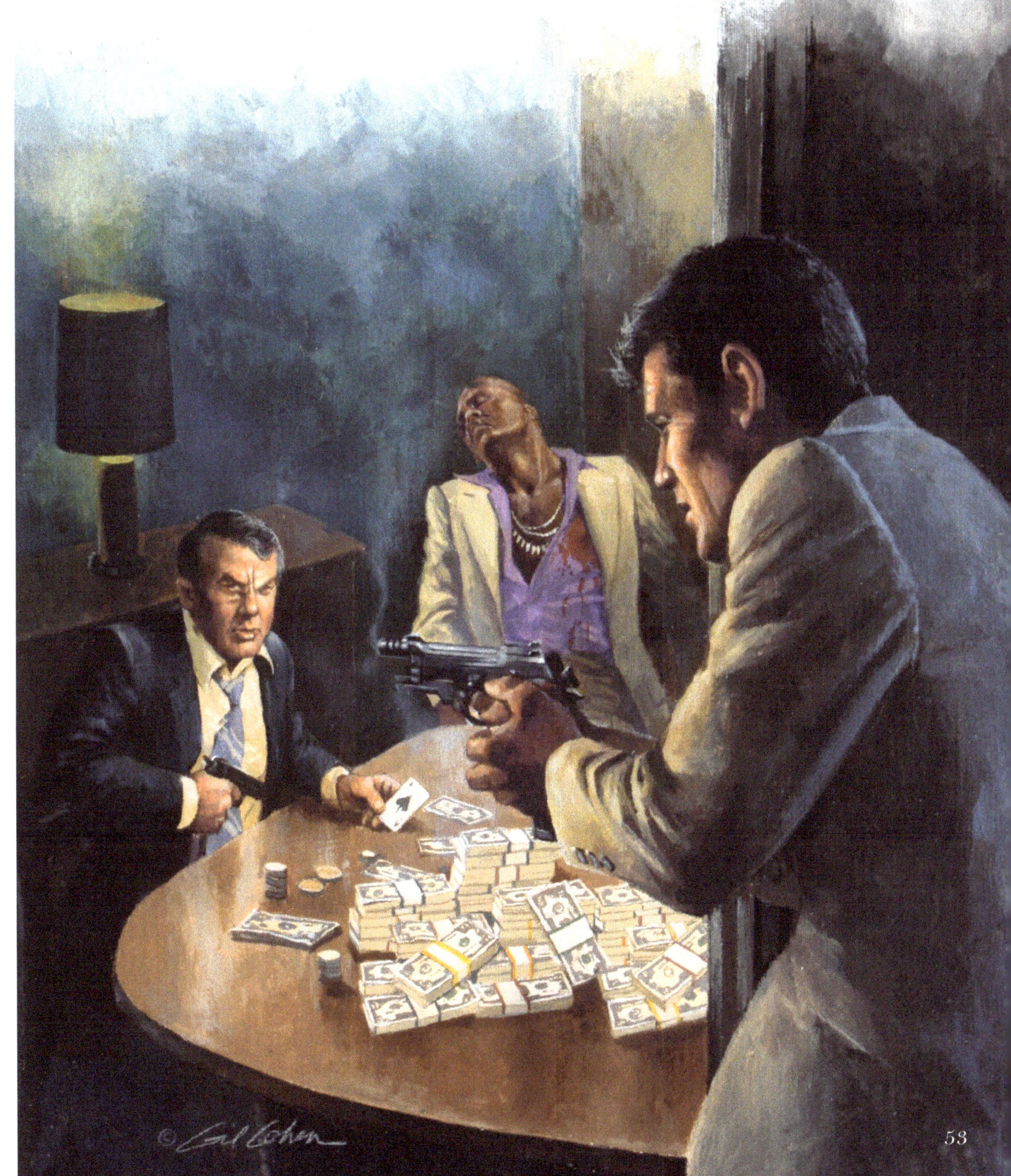

53

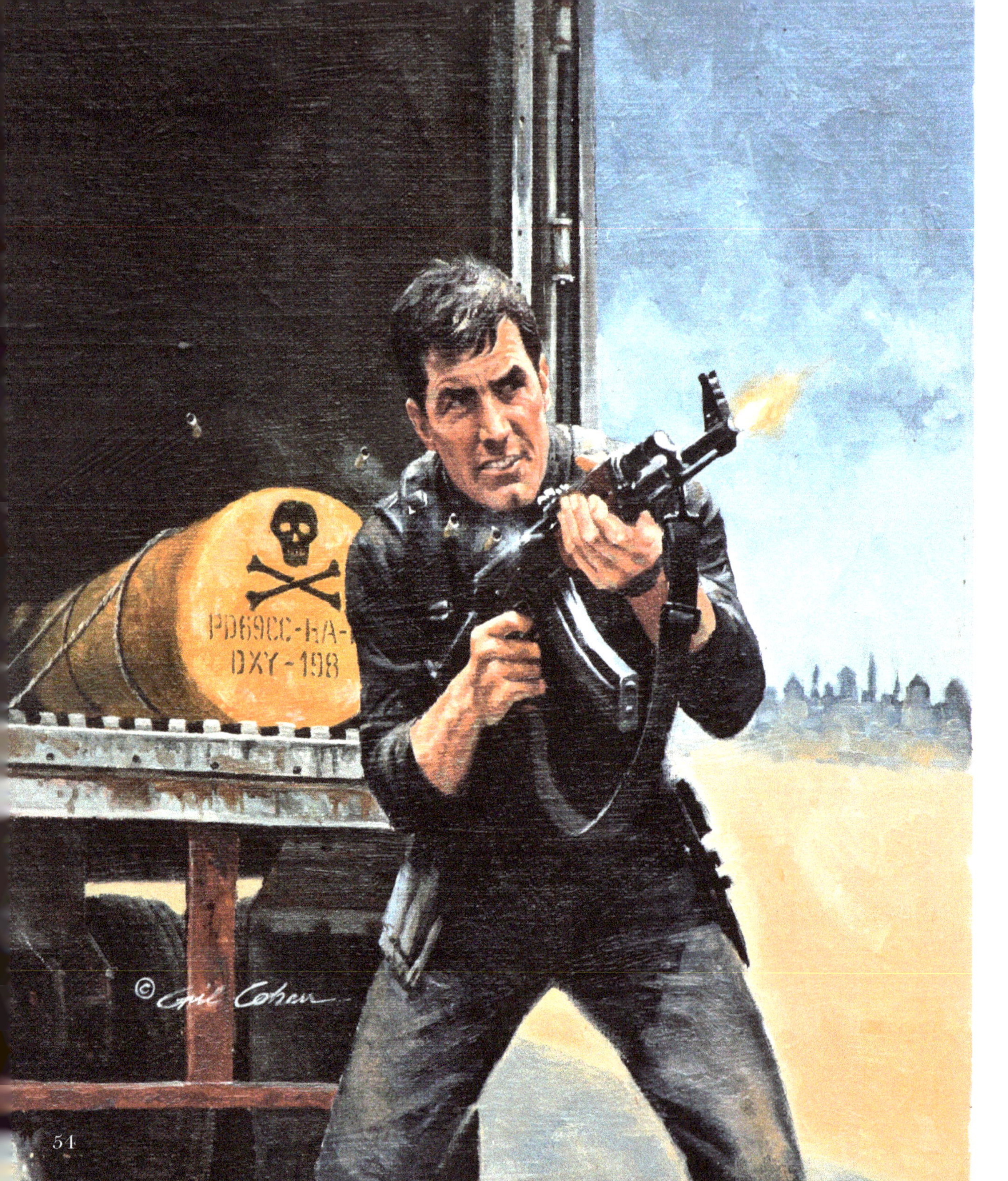

PD69CC-HA-
DXY-198
© Gil Cohen

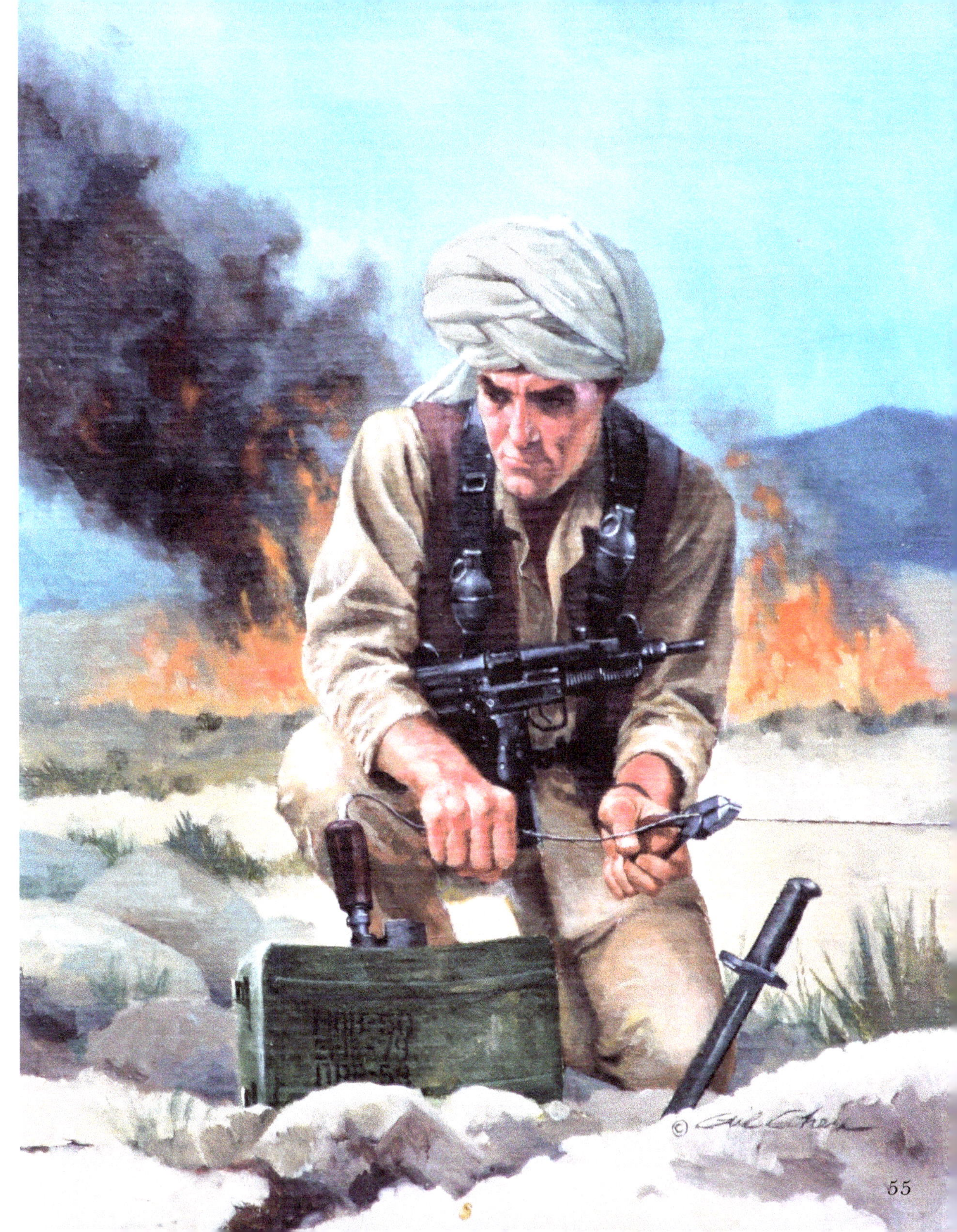

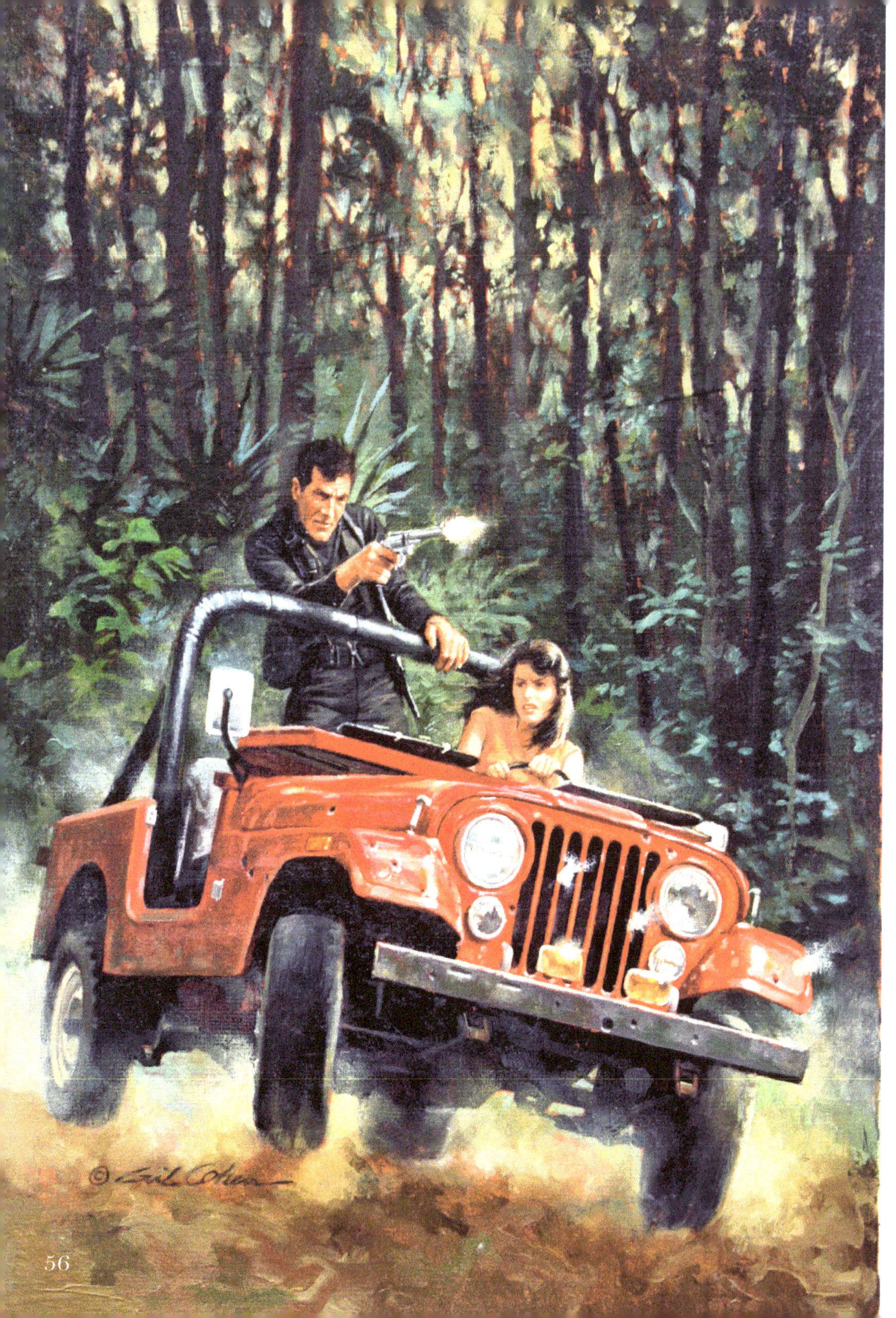

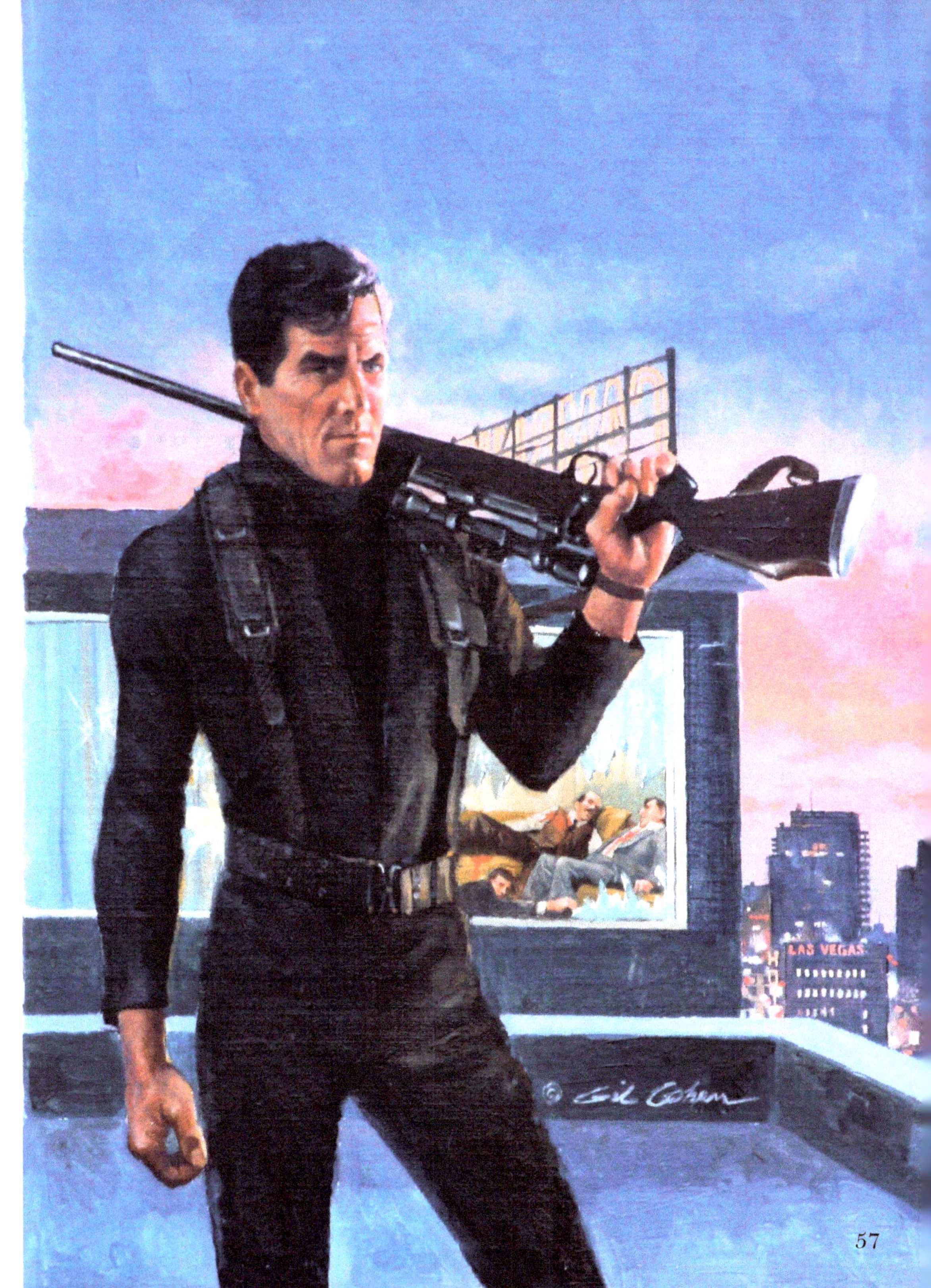

LAS VEGAS

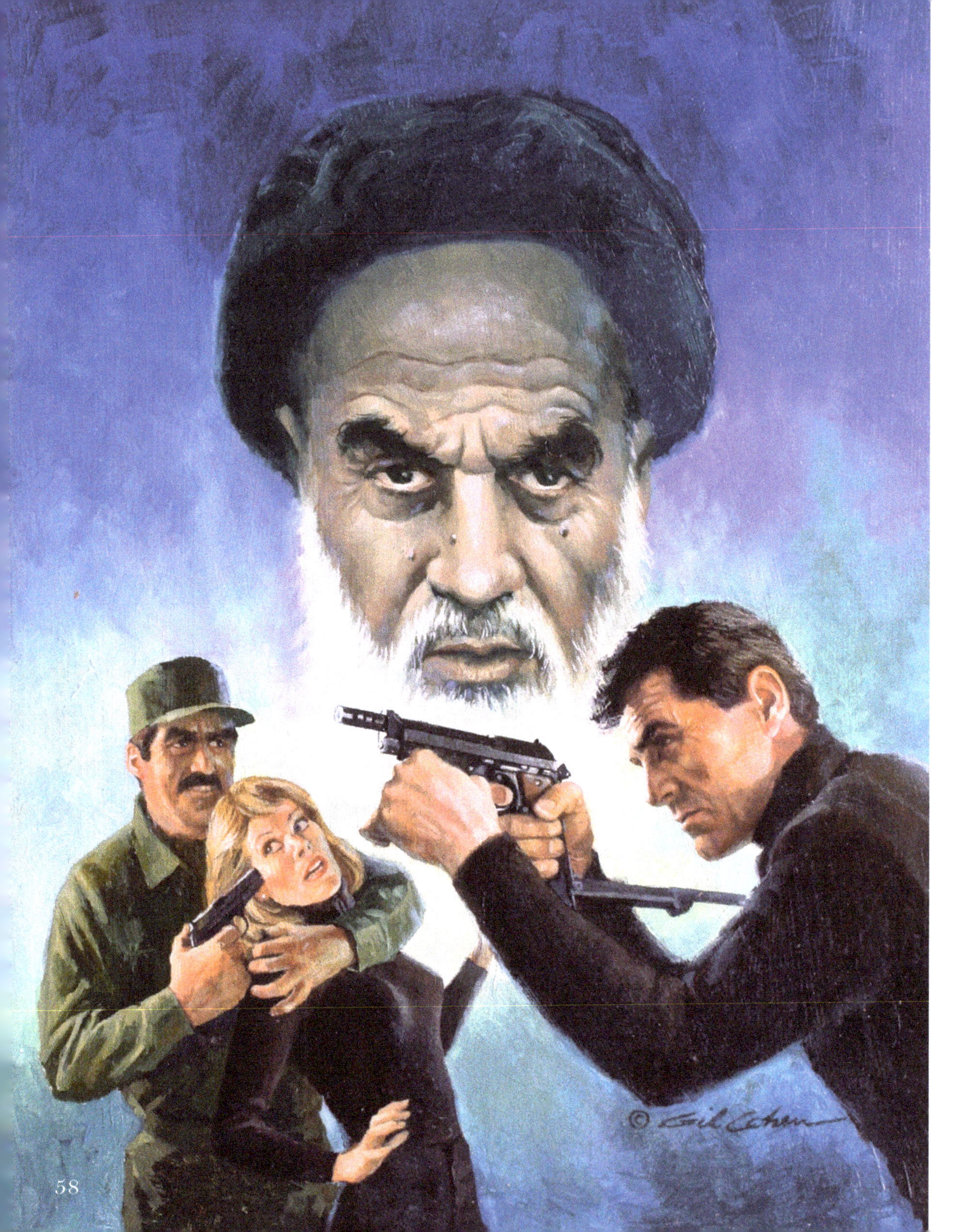

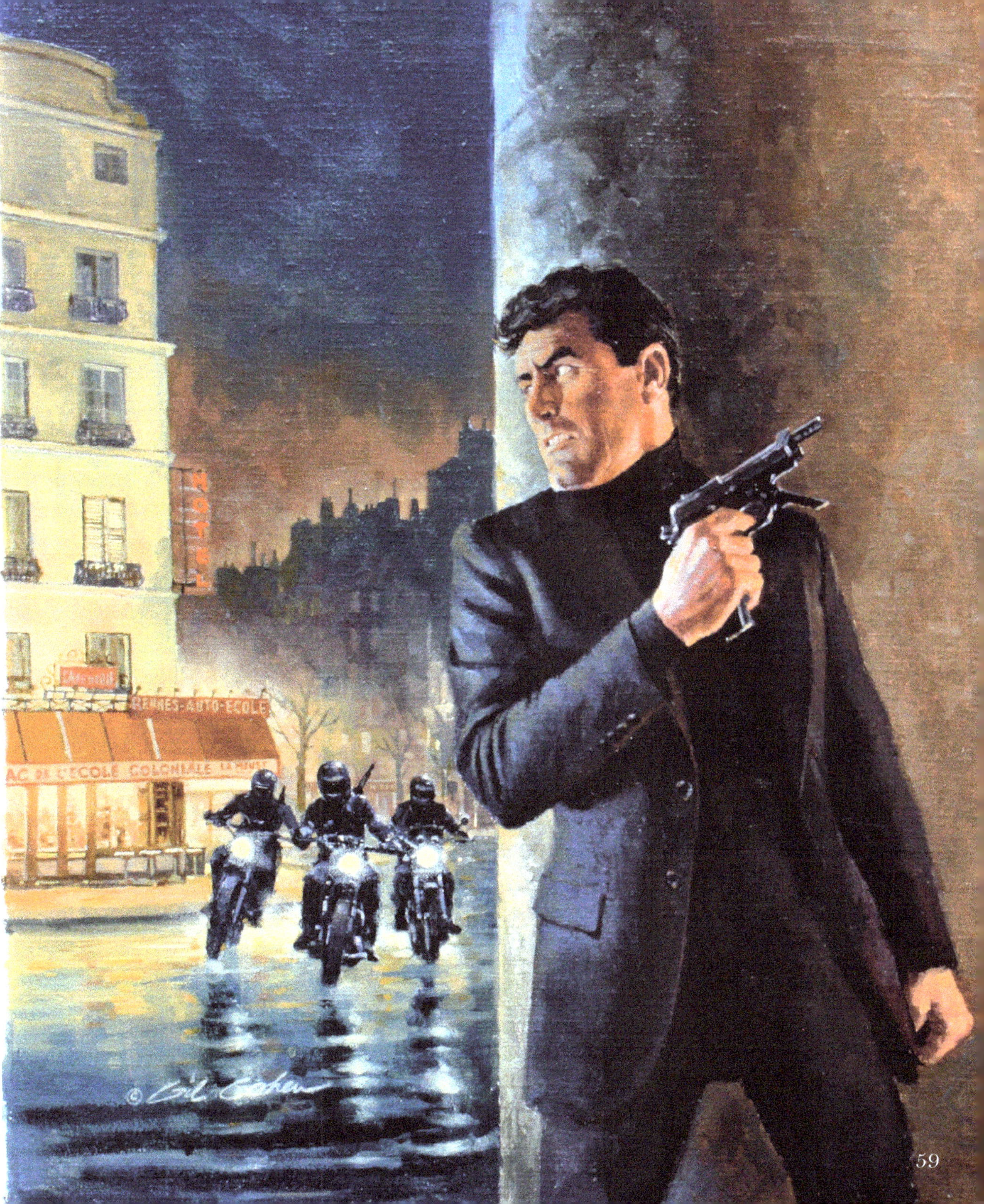
RENNES-AUTO-ECOLE
© Gil Cohen

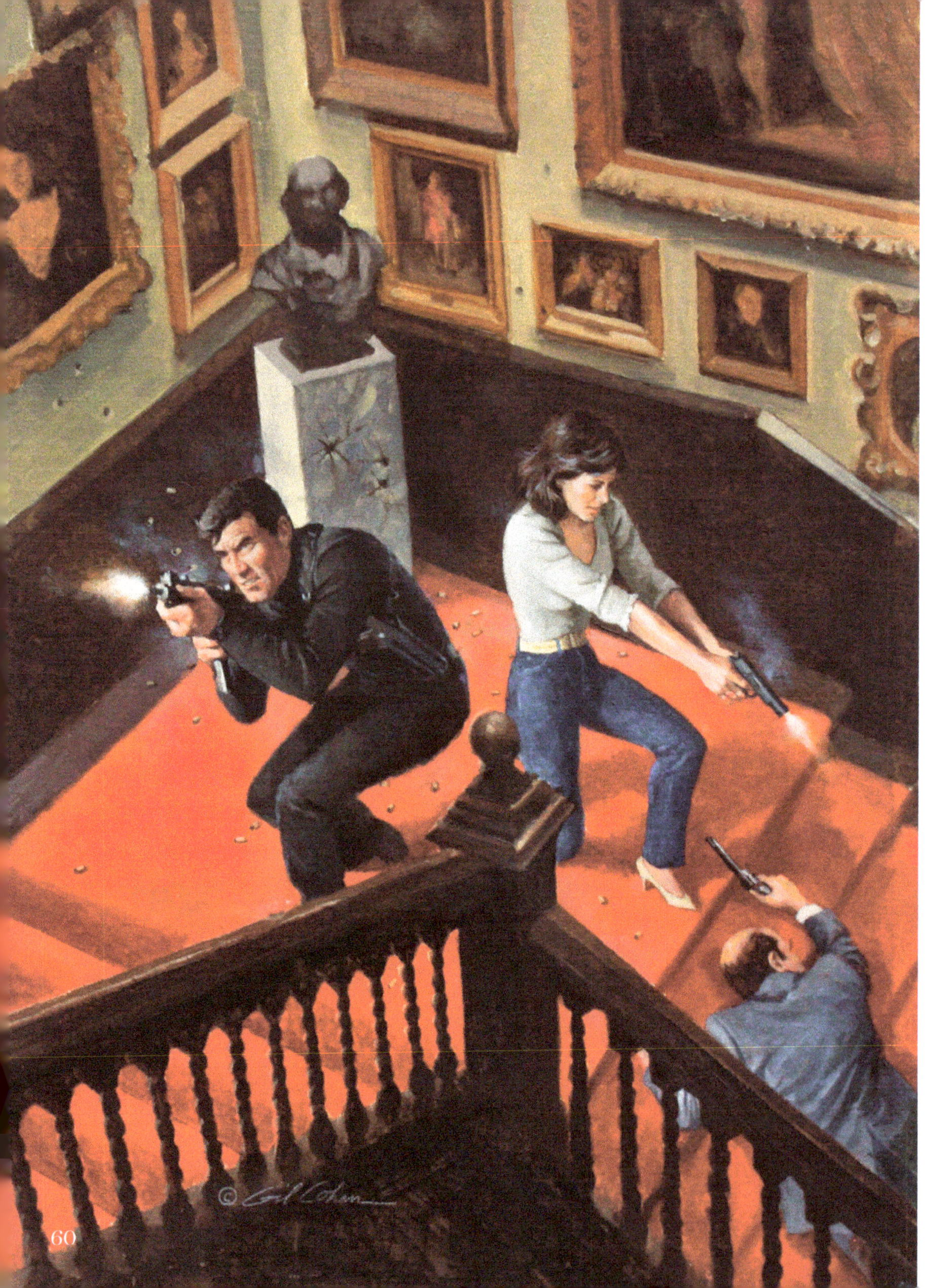

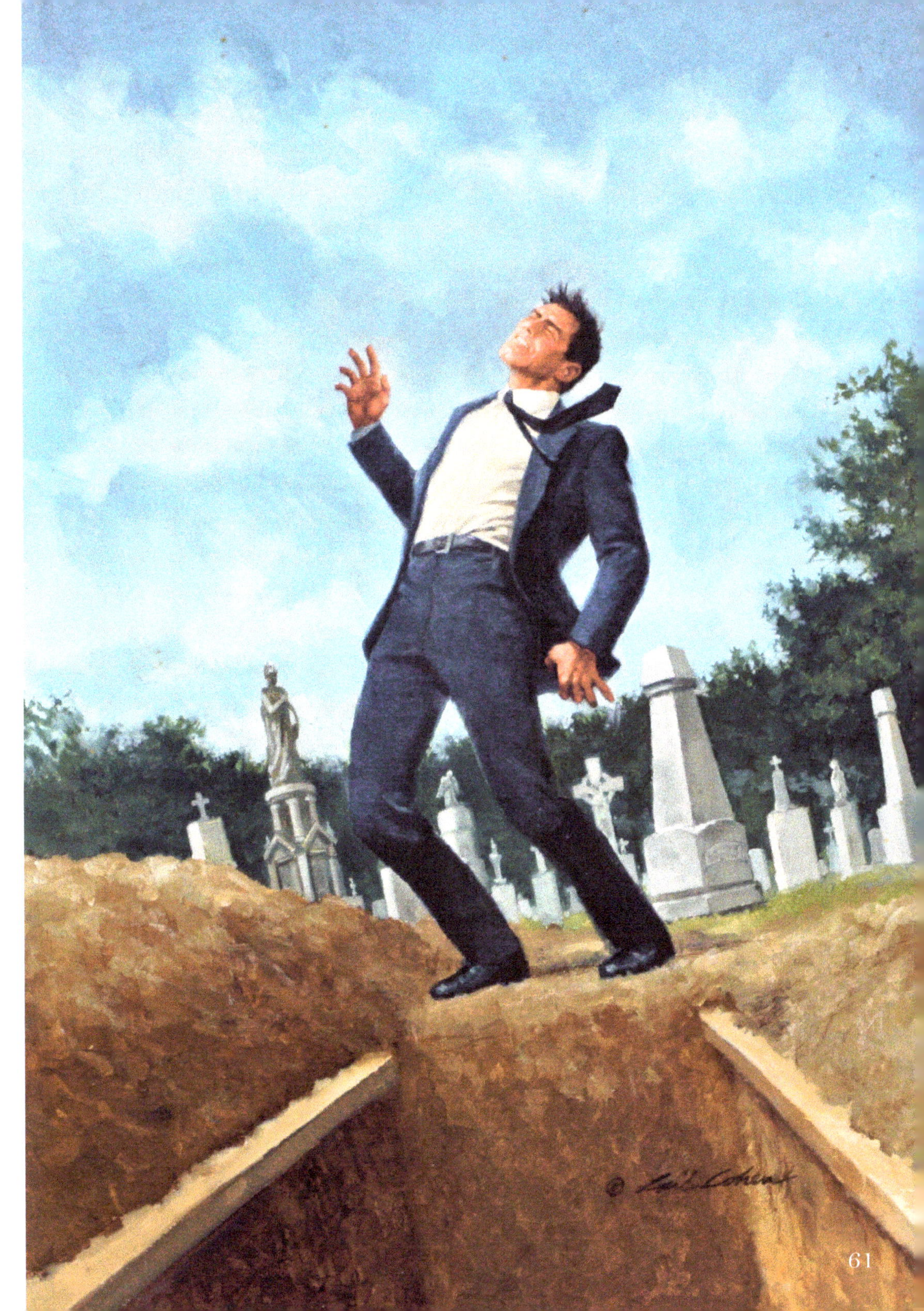

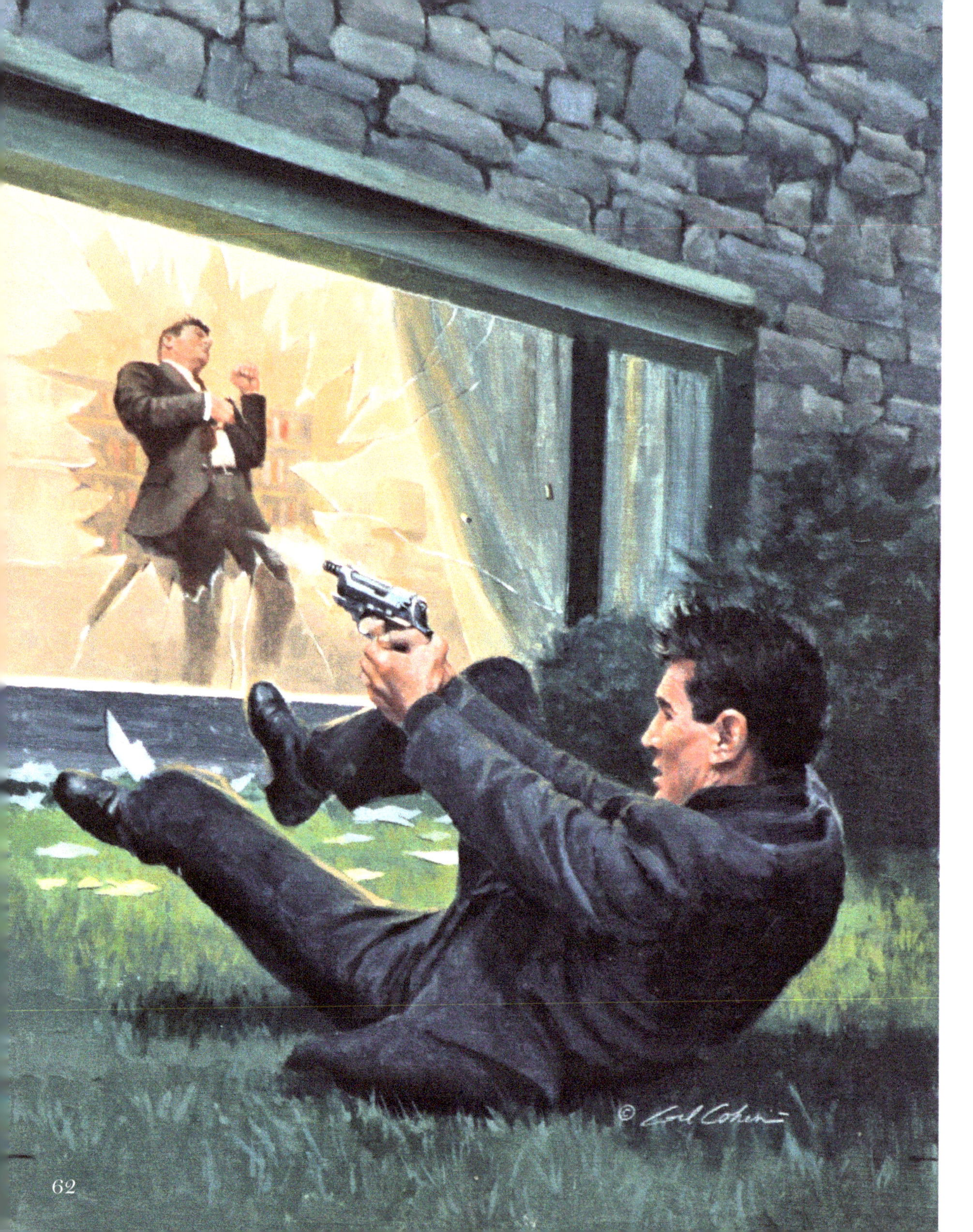

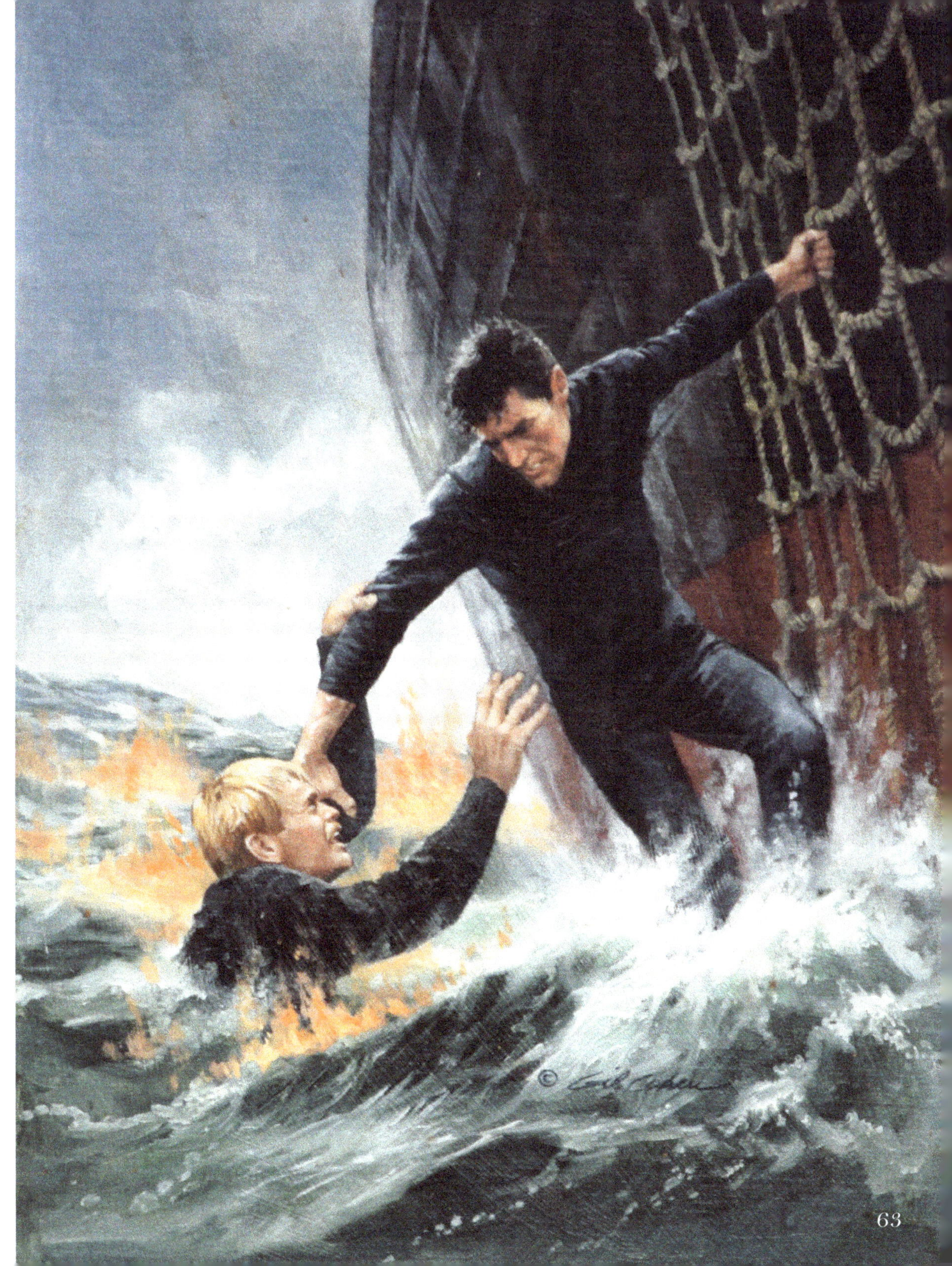

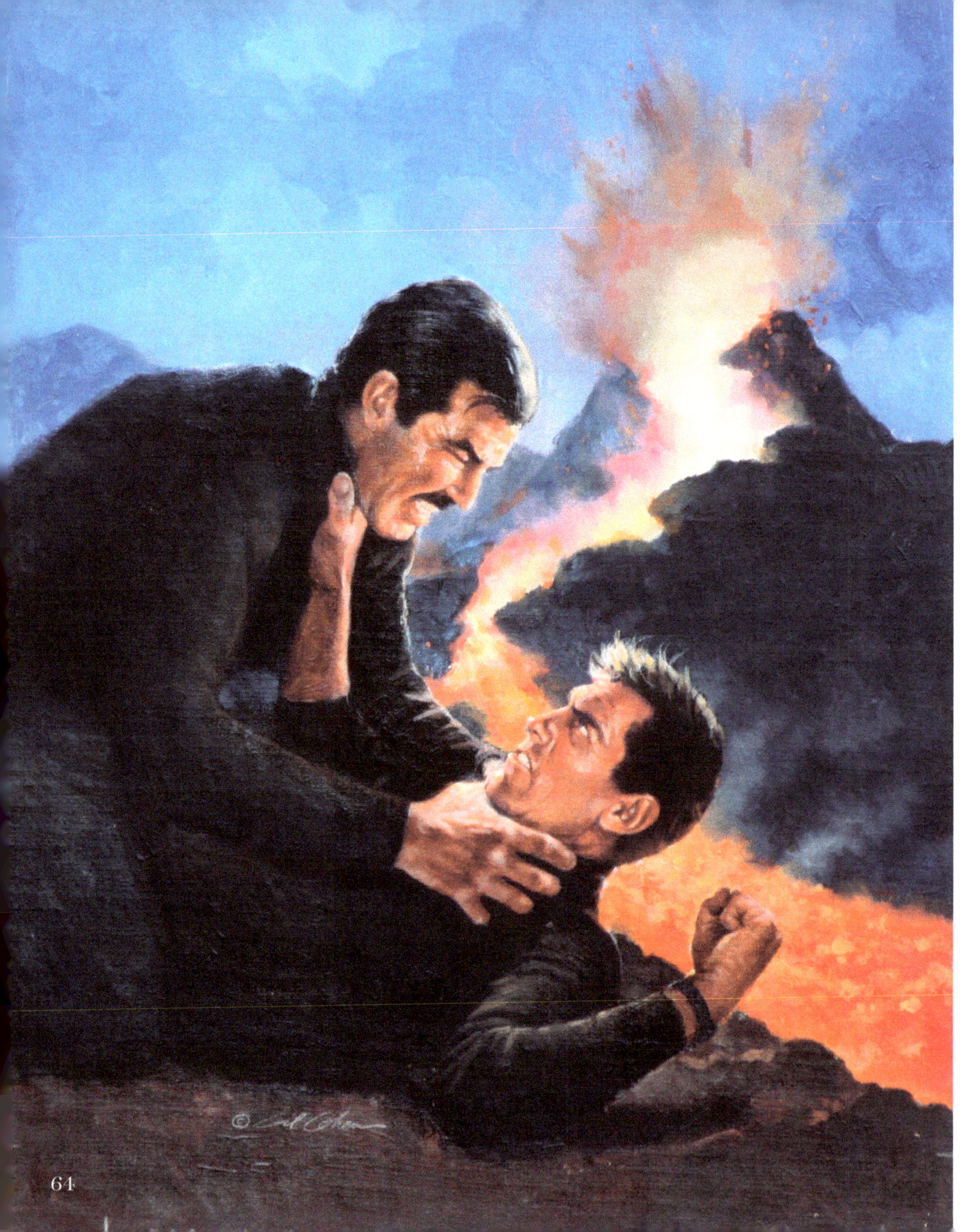

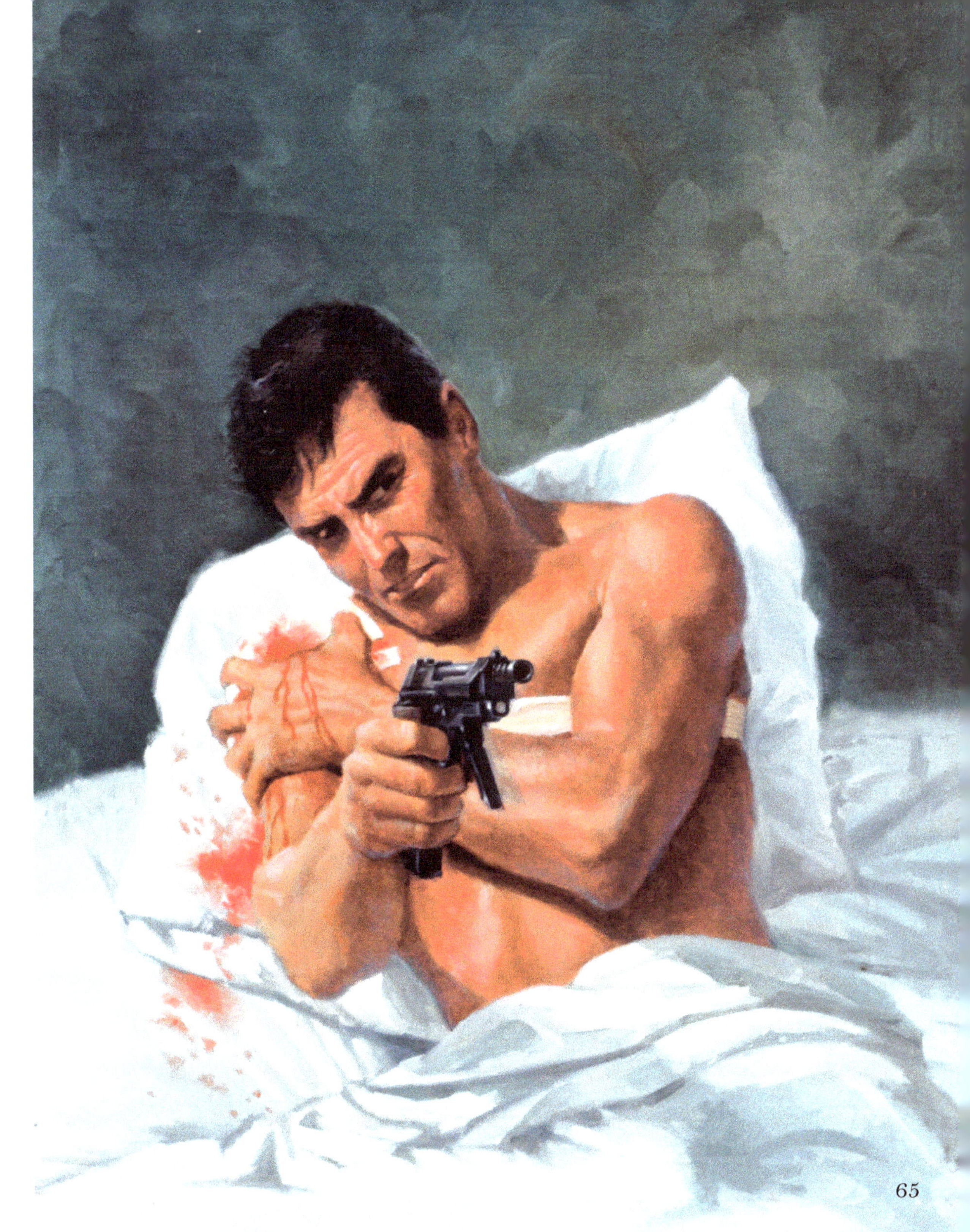

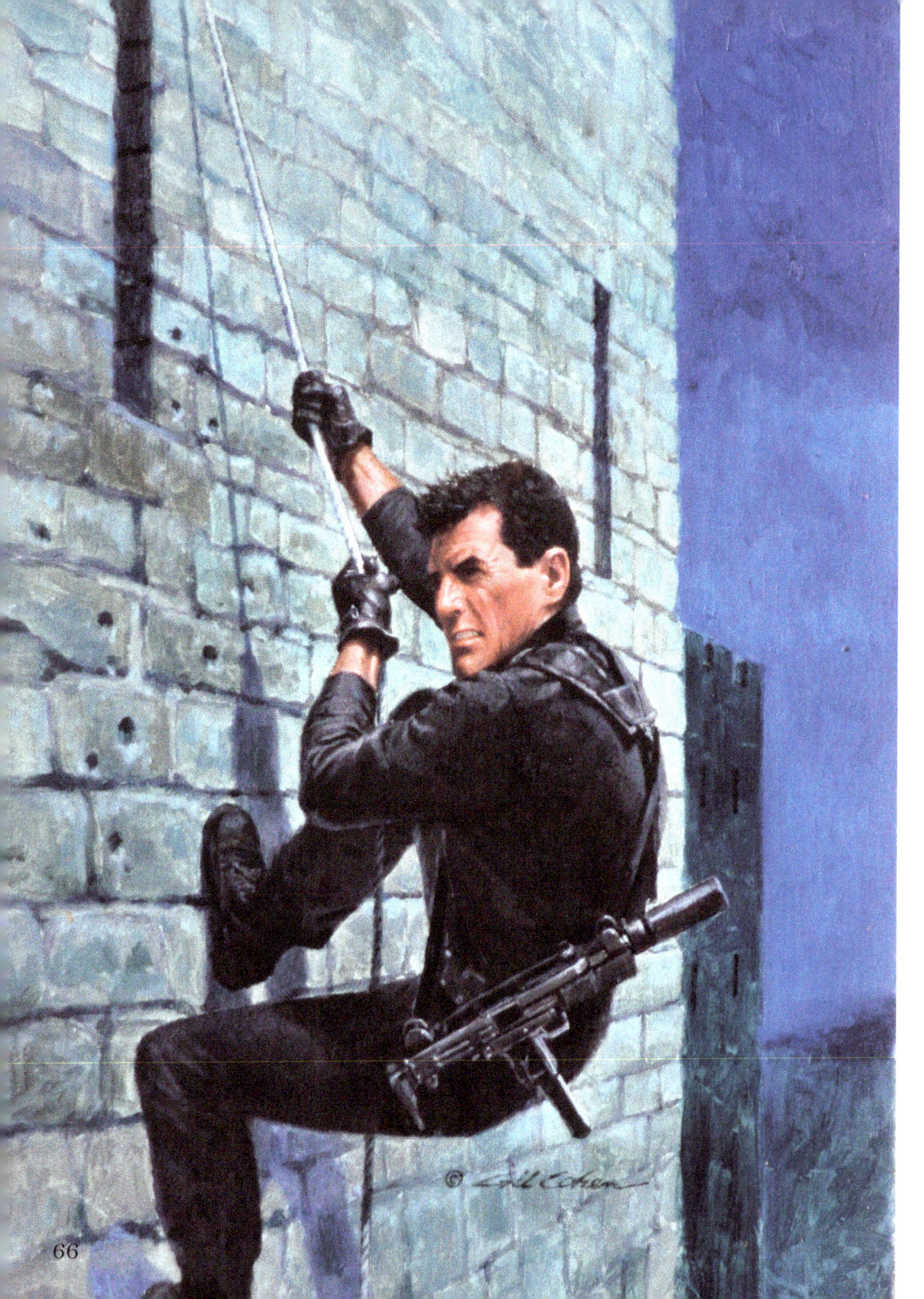

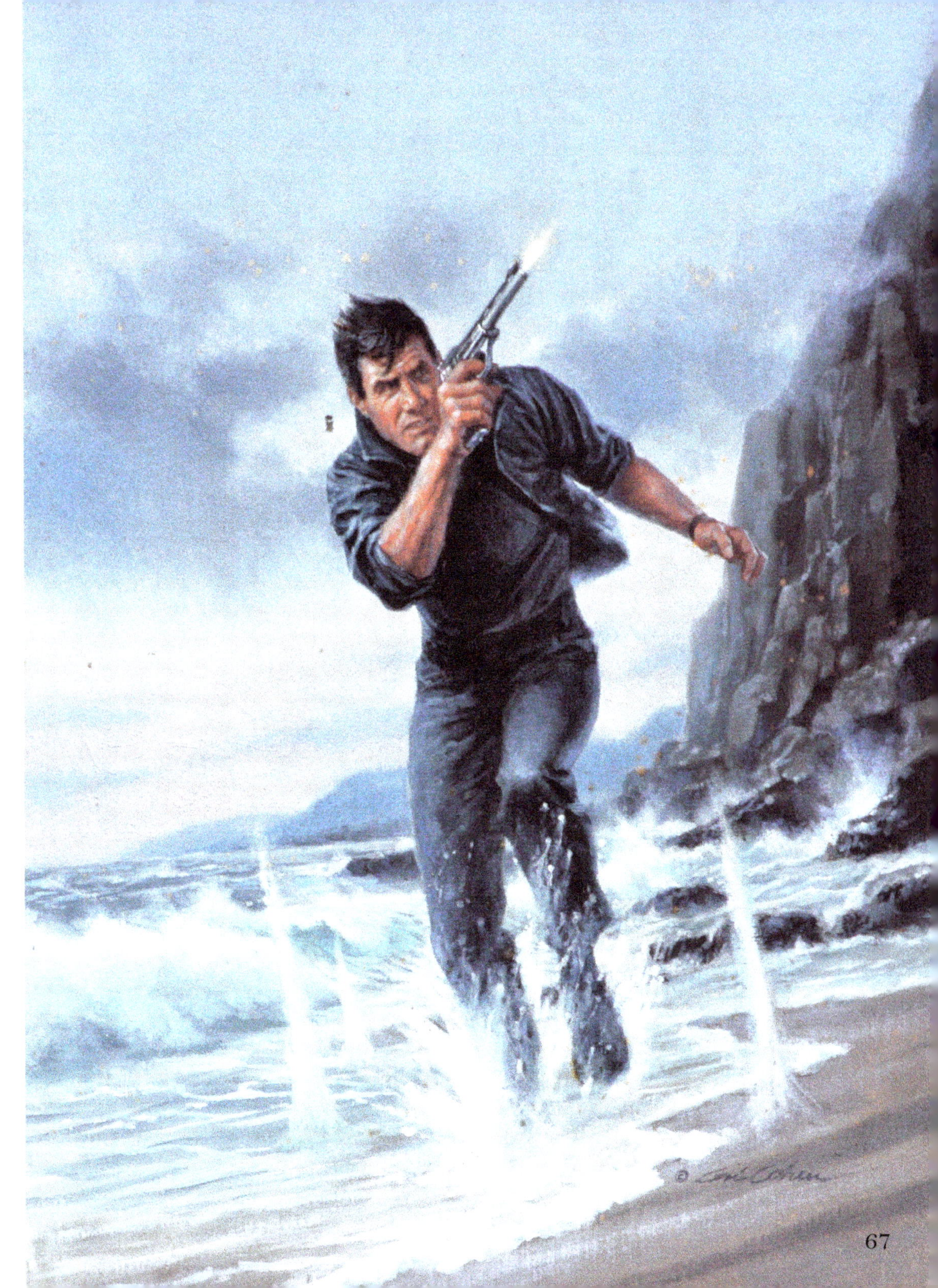

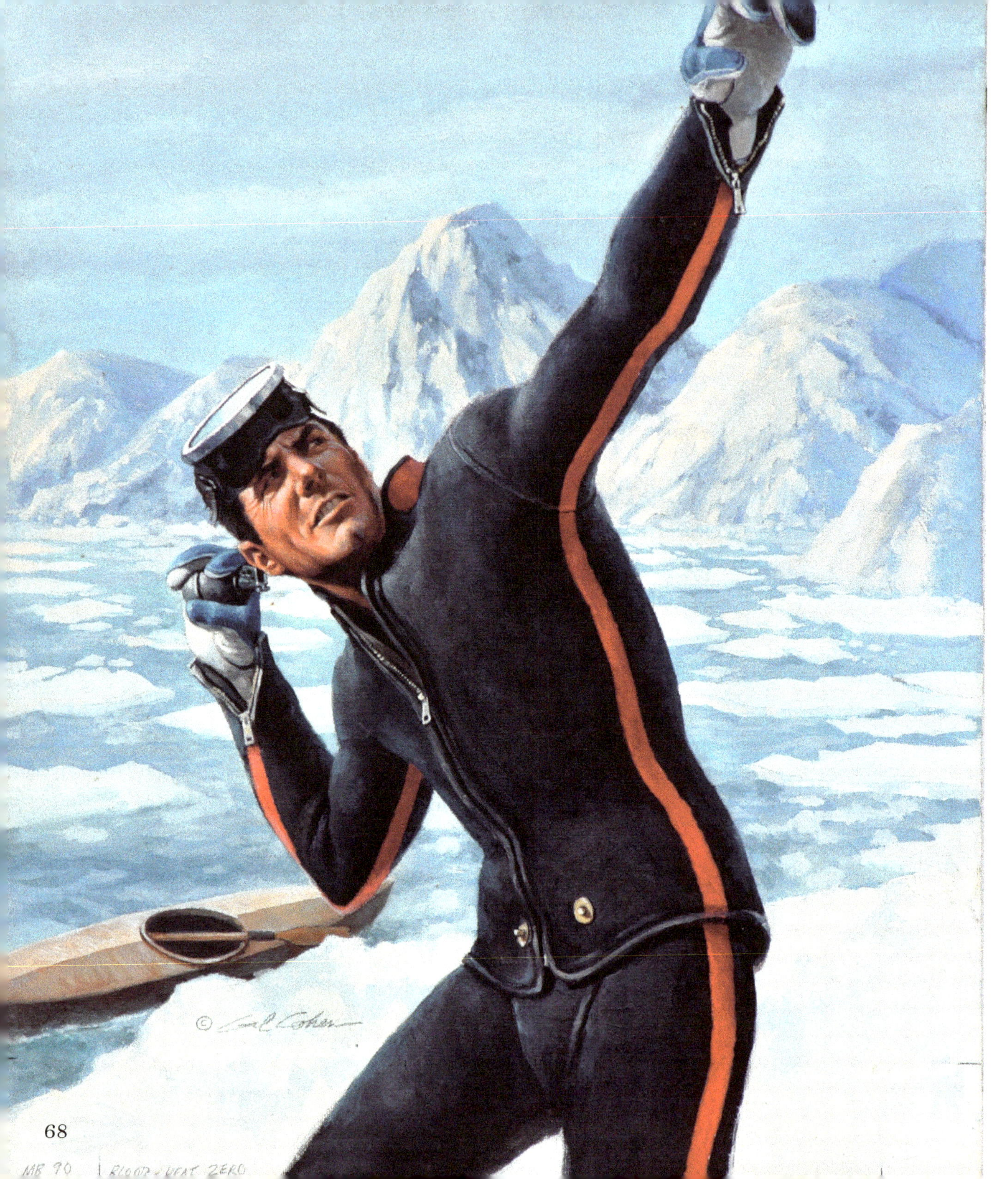

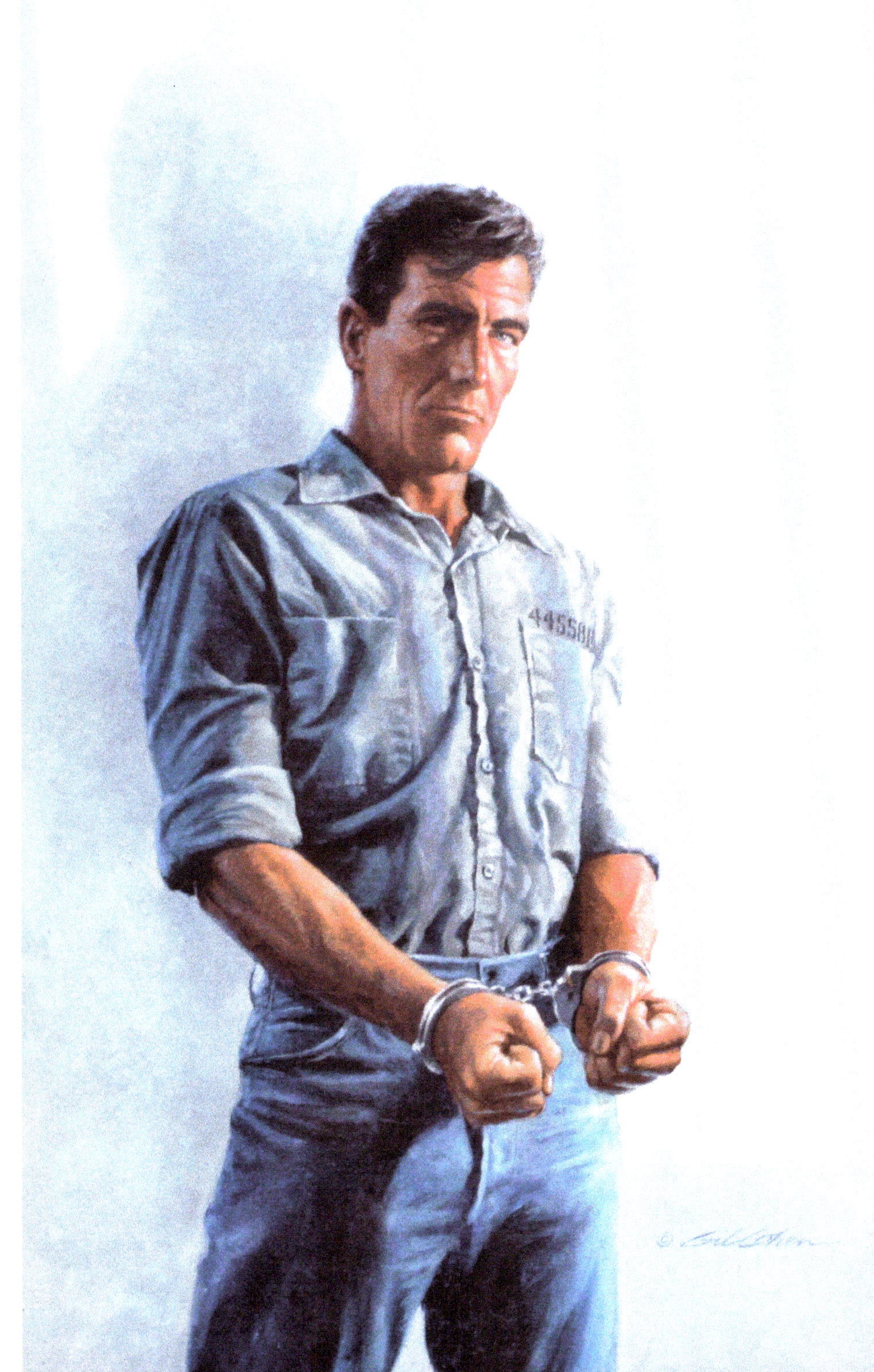

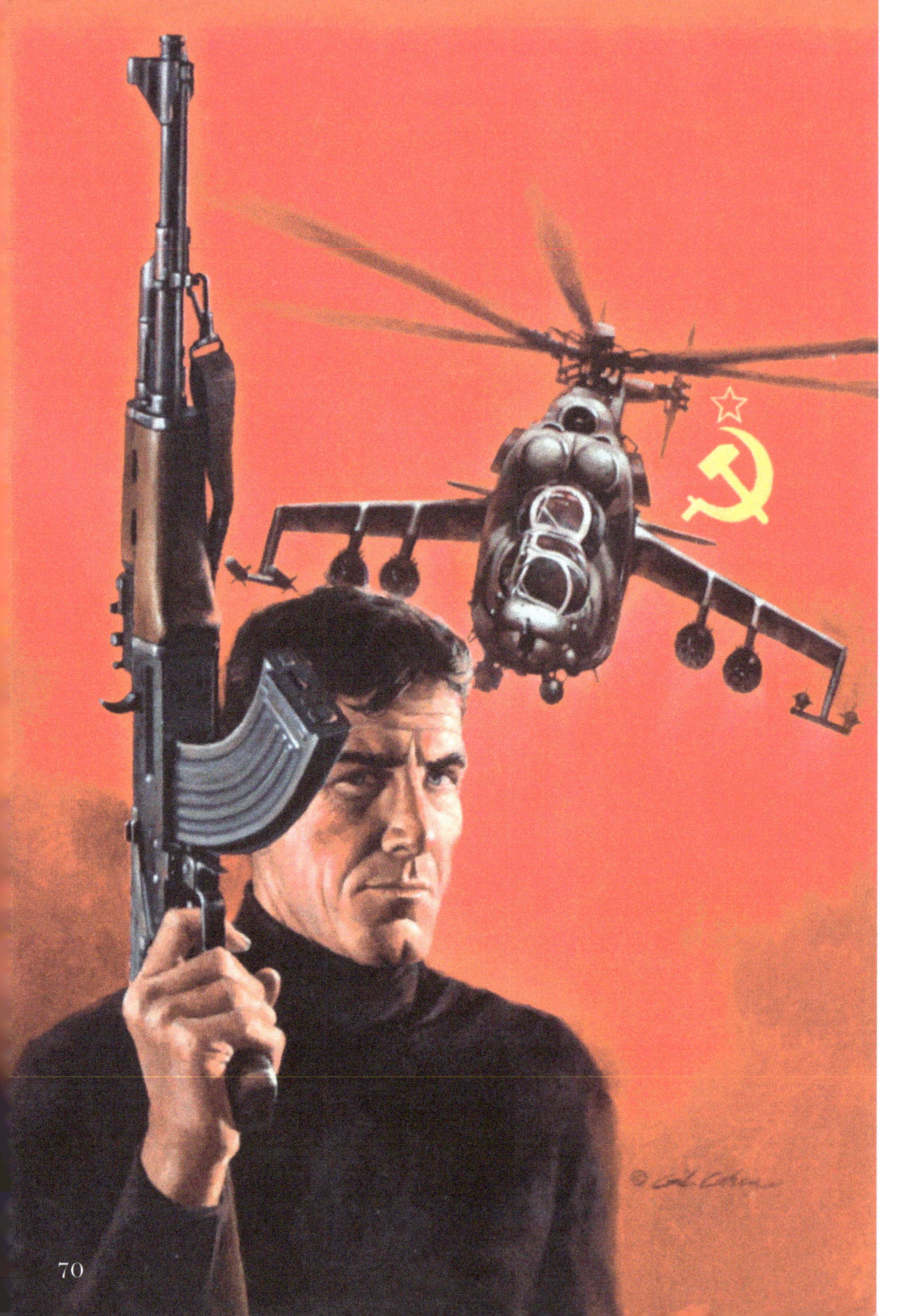

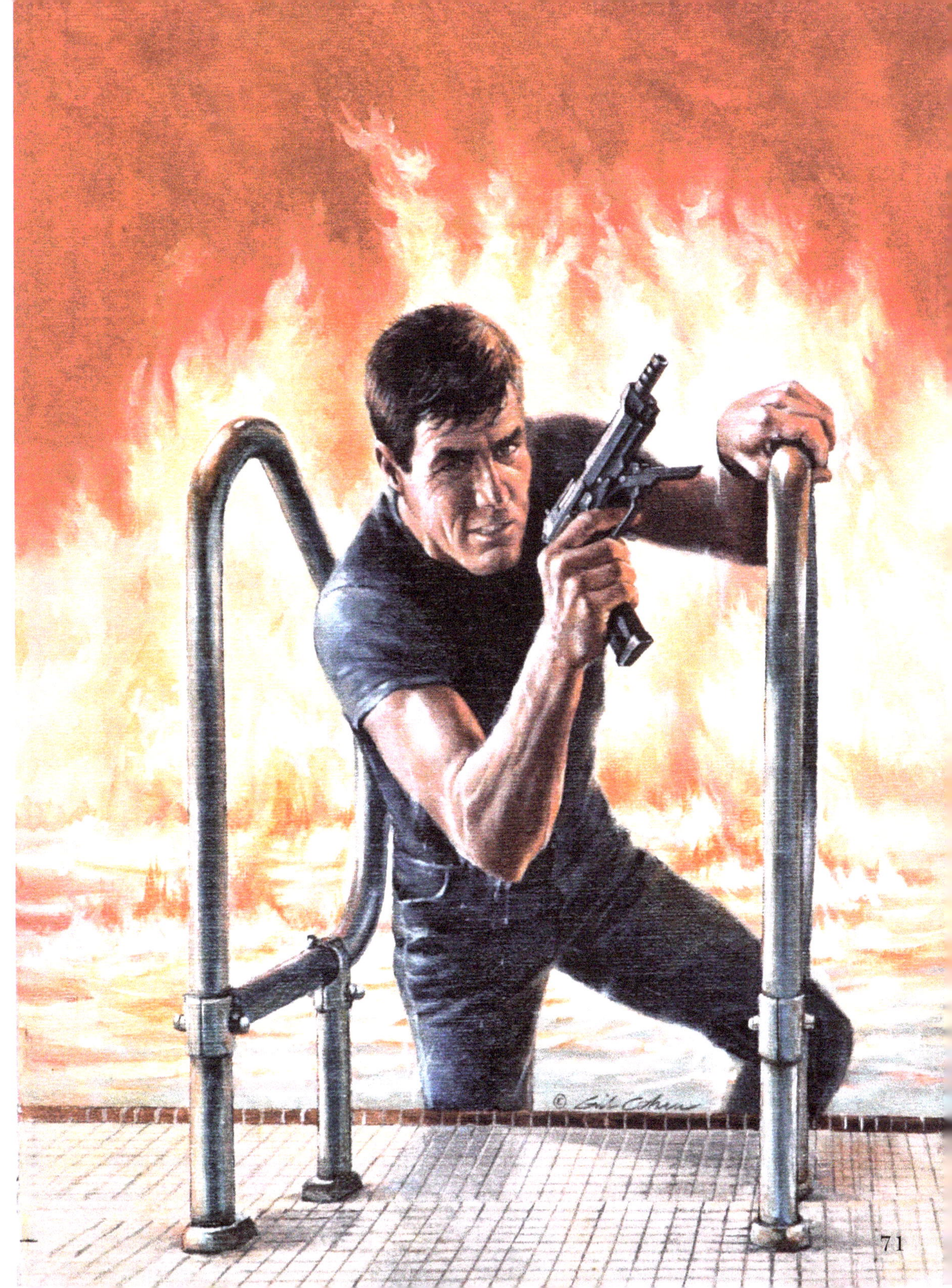

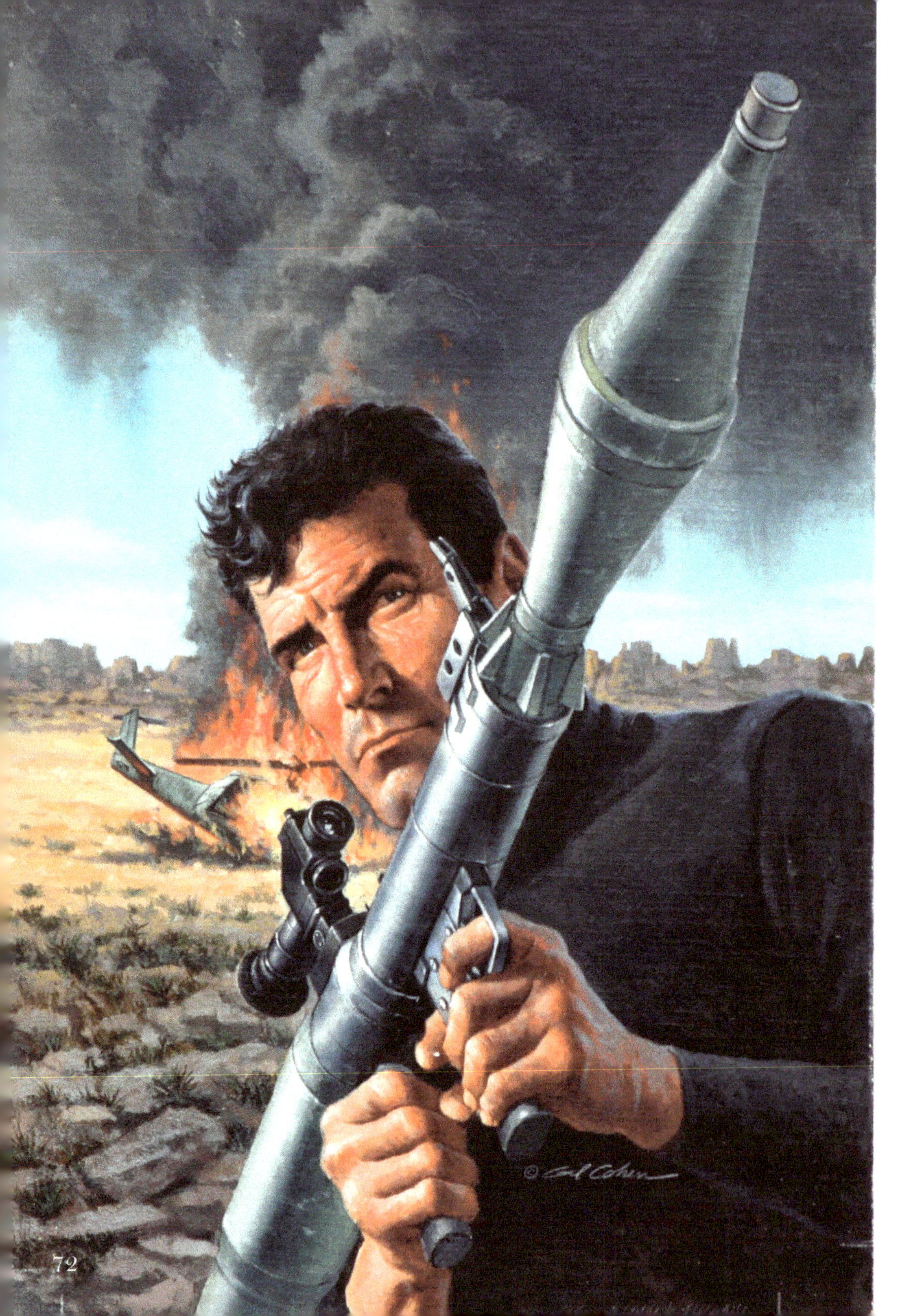

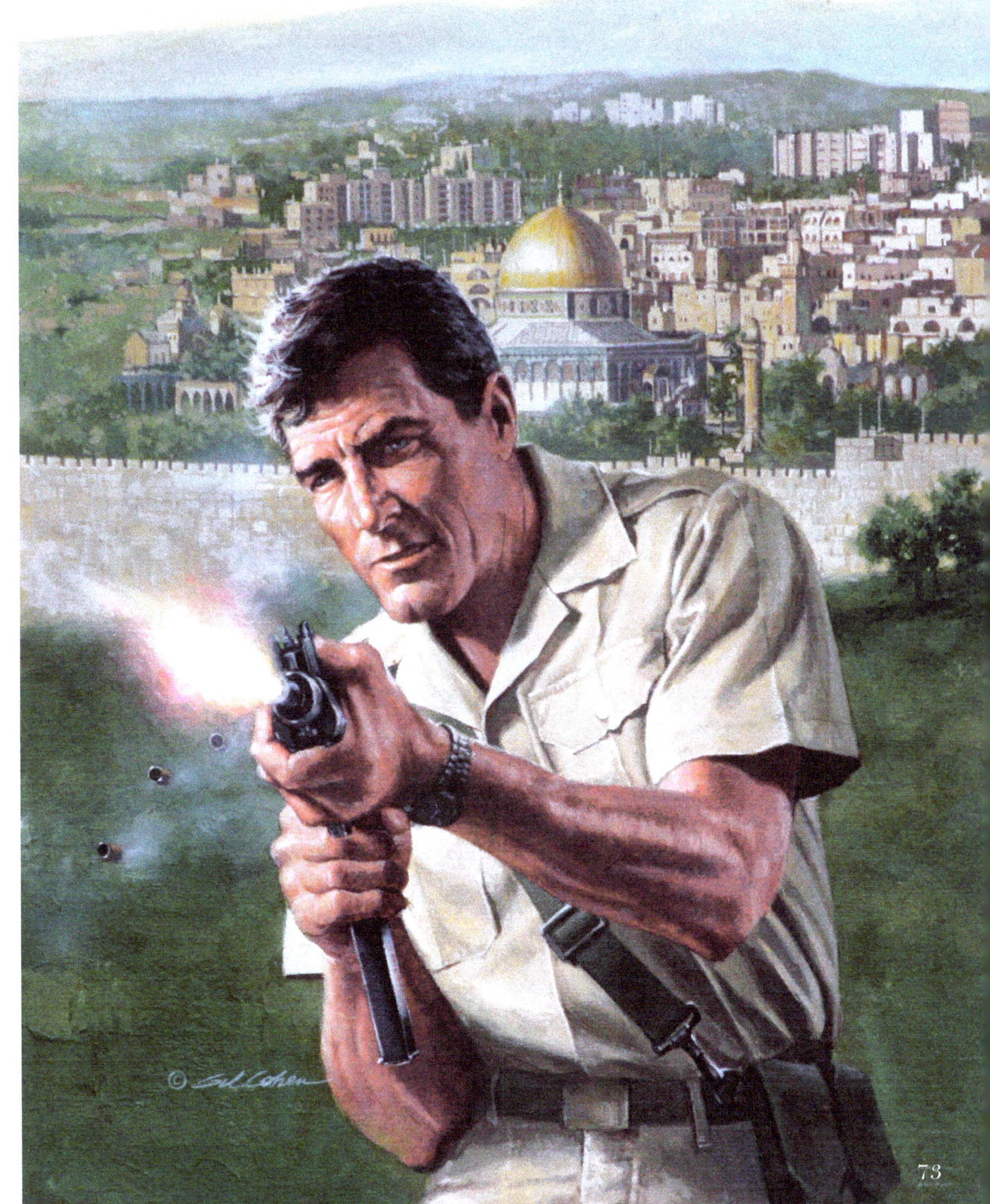

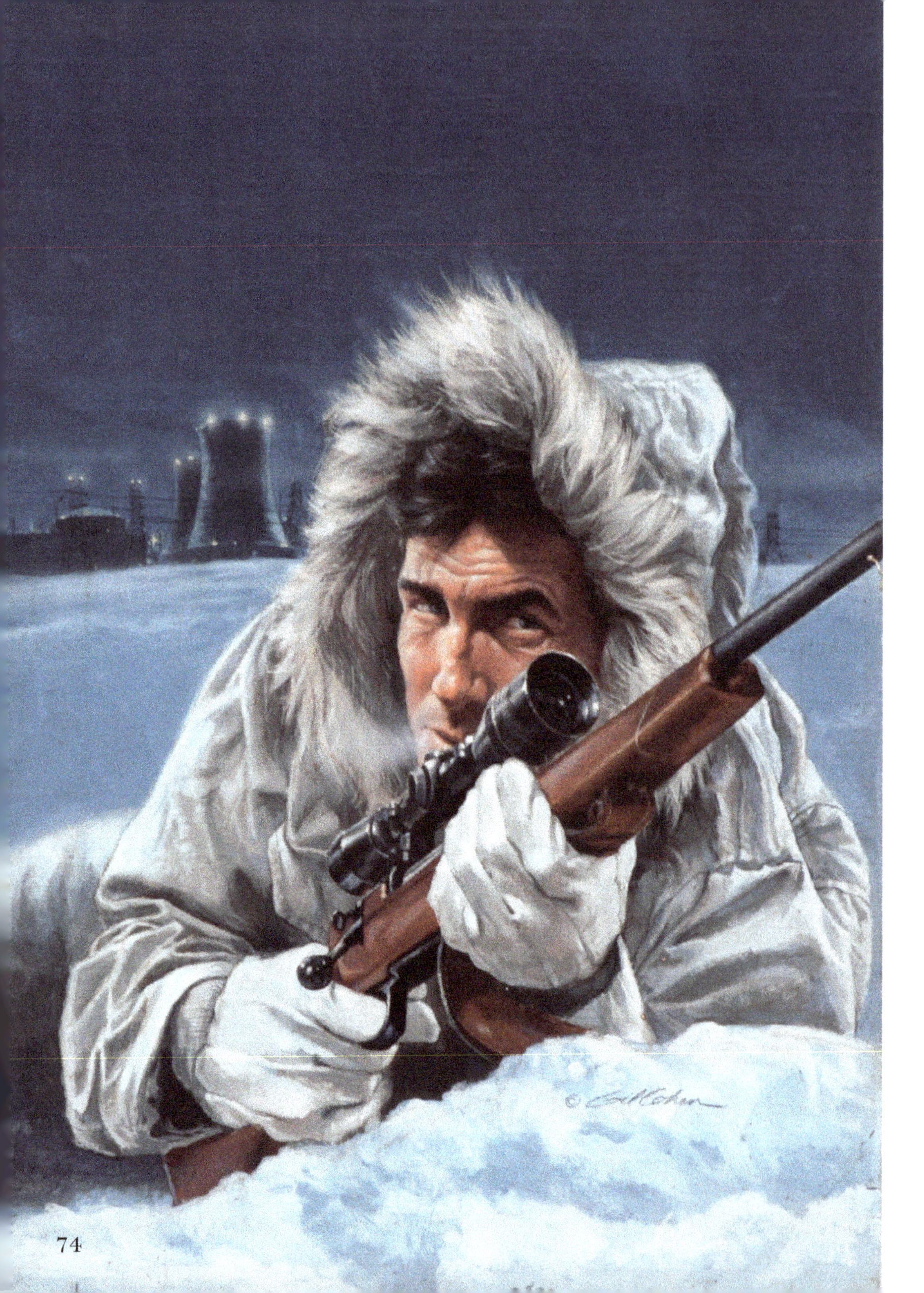

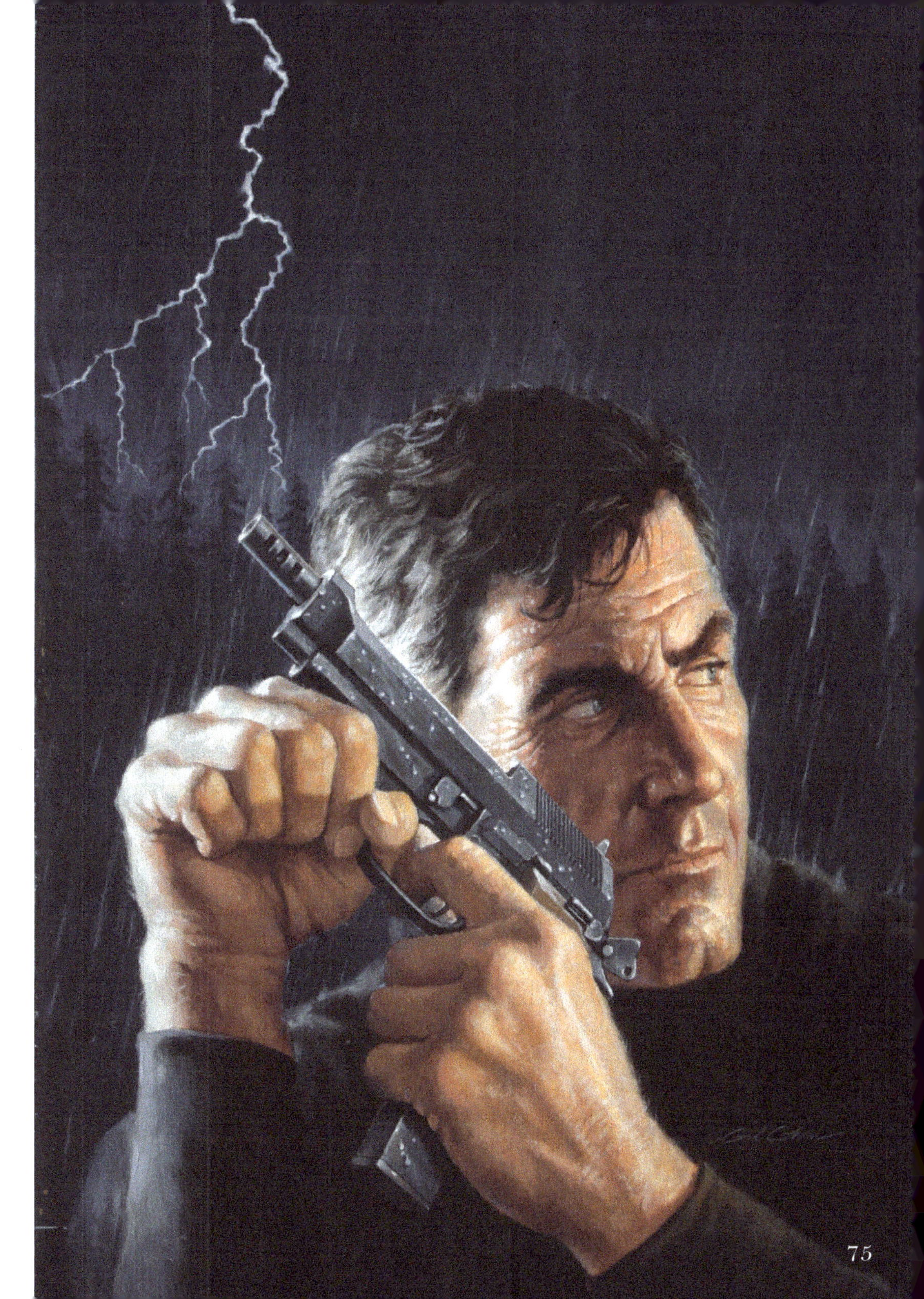

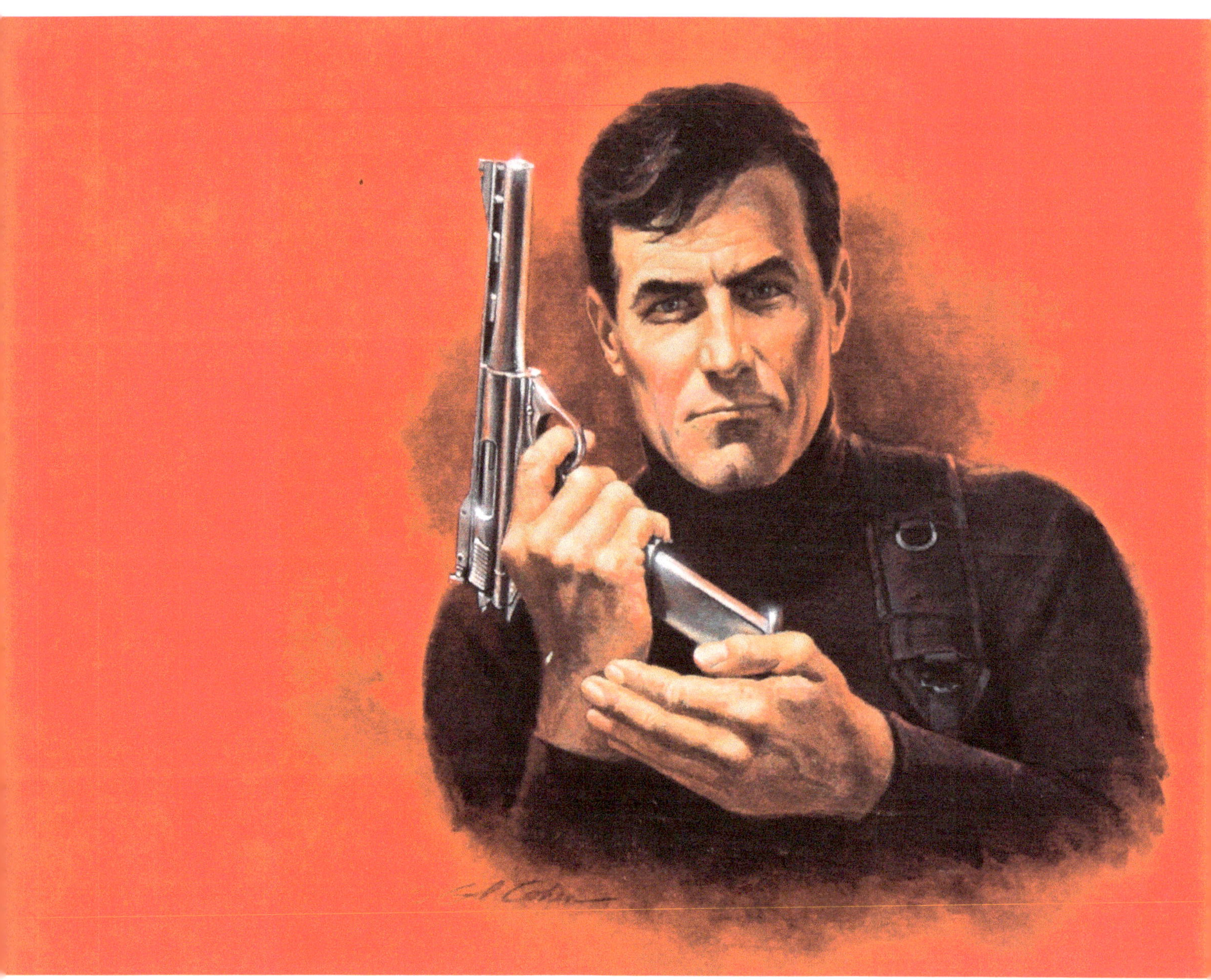

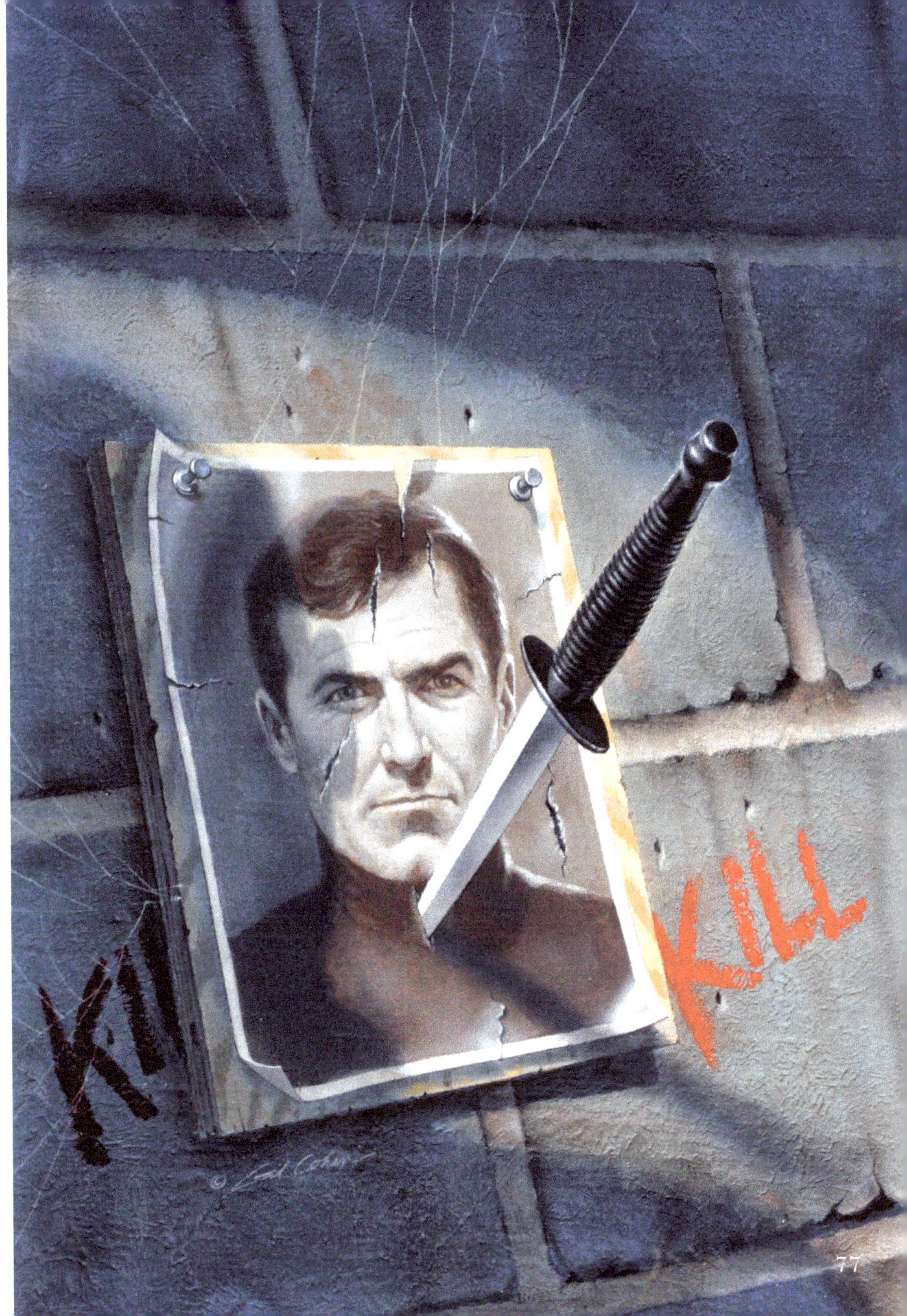

KILL
KILL

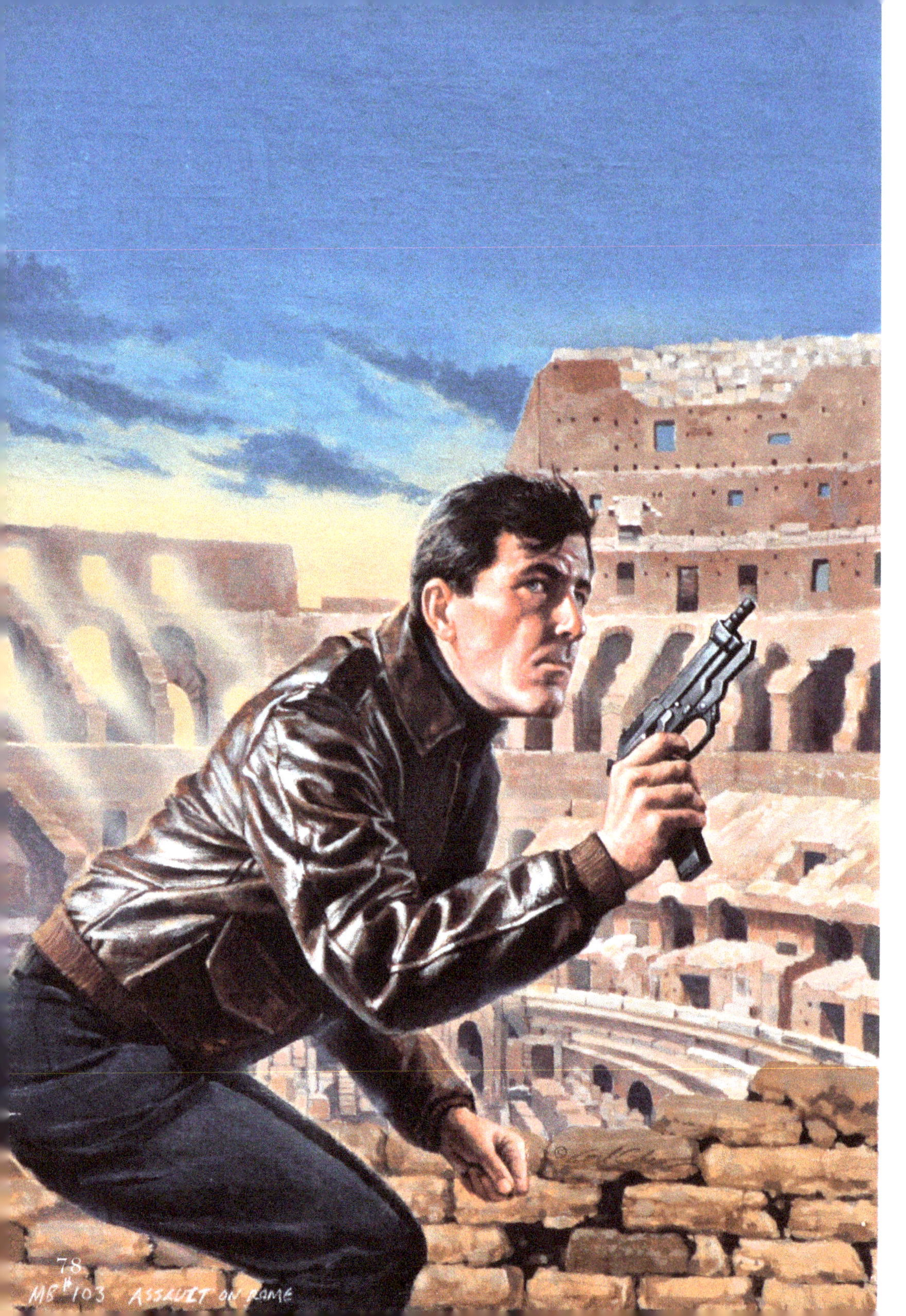

78
MS #103   ASSAULT ON ROME

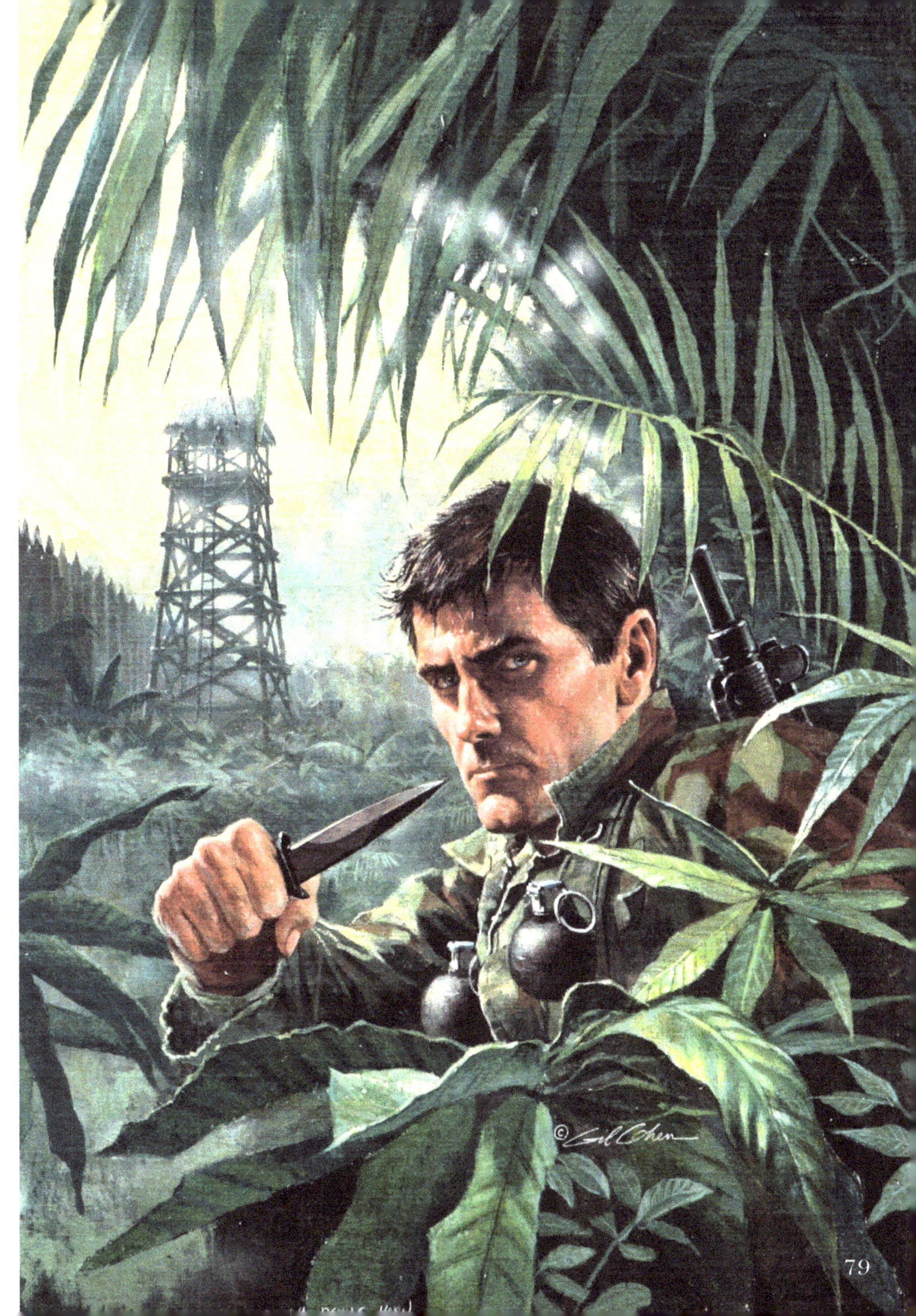

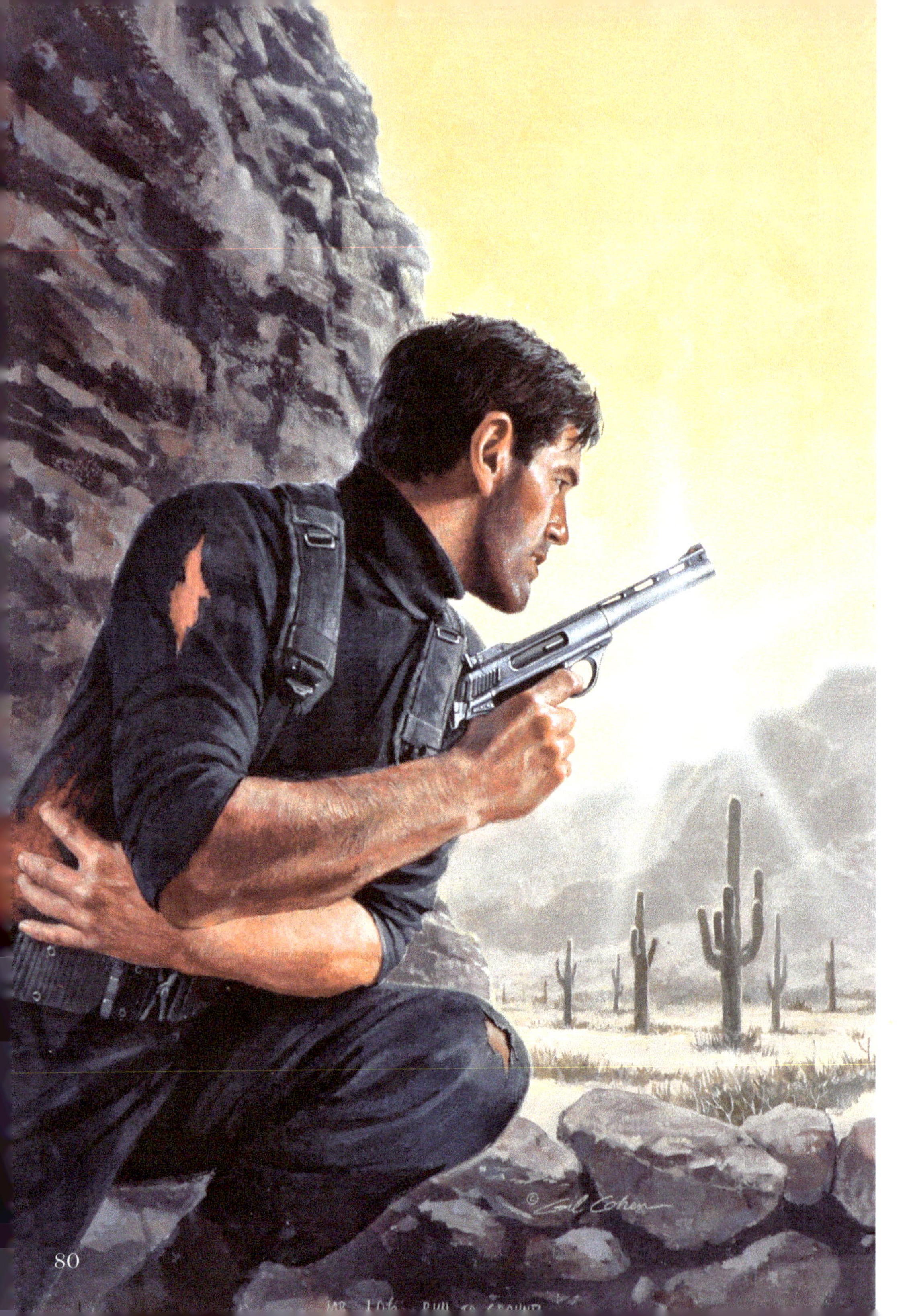

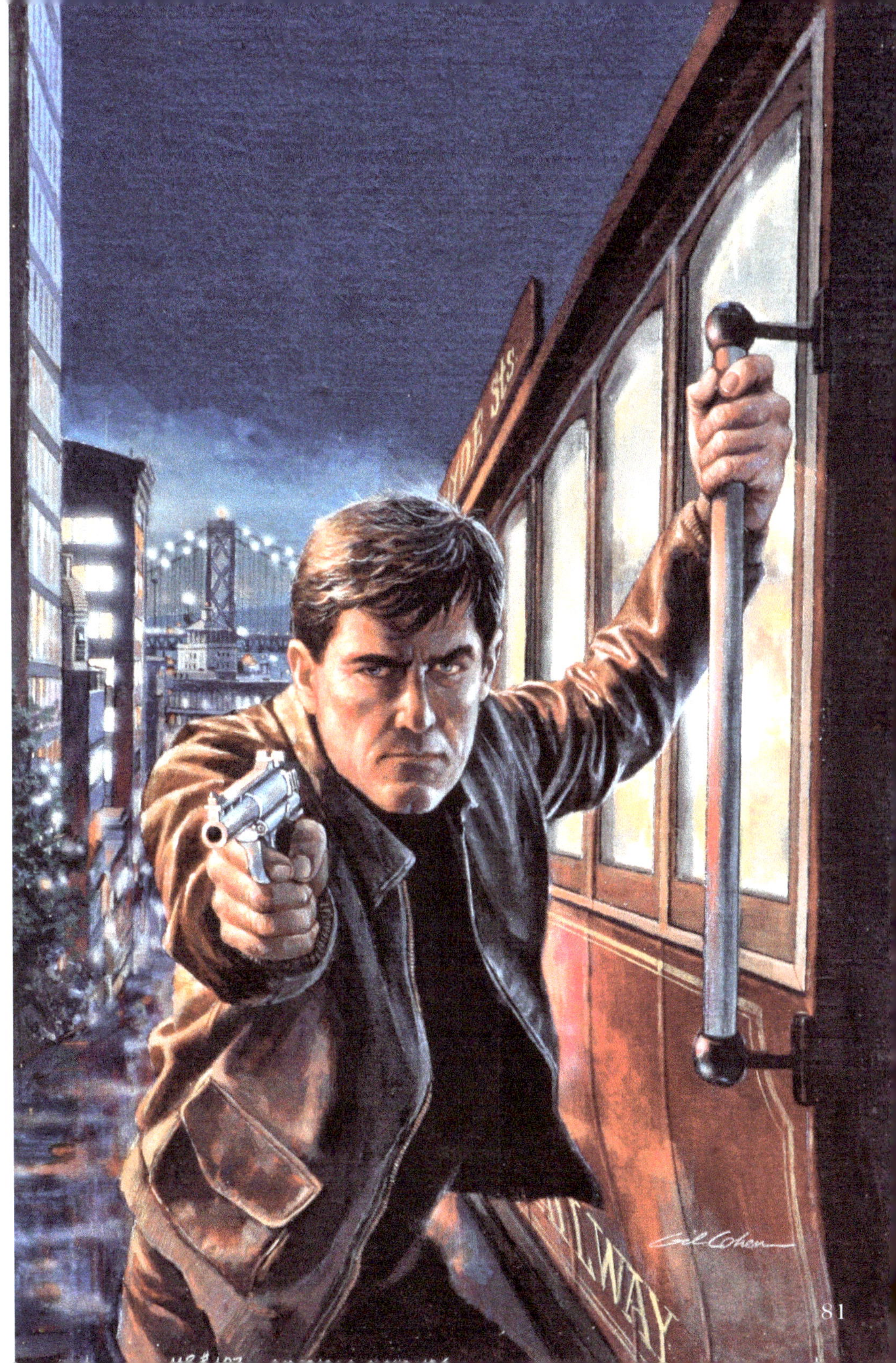

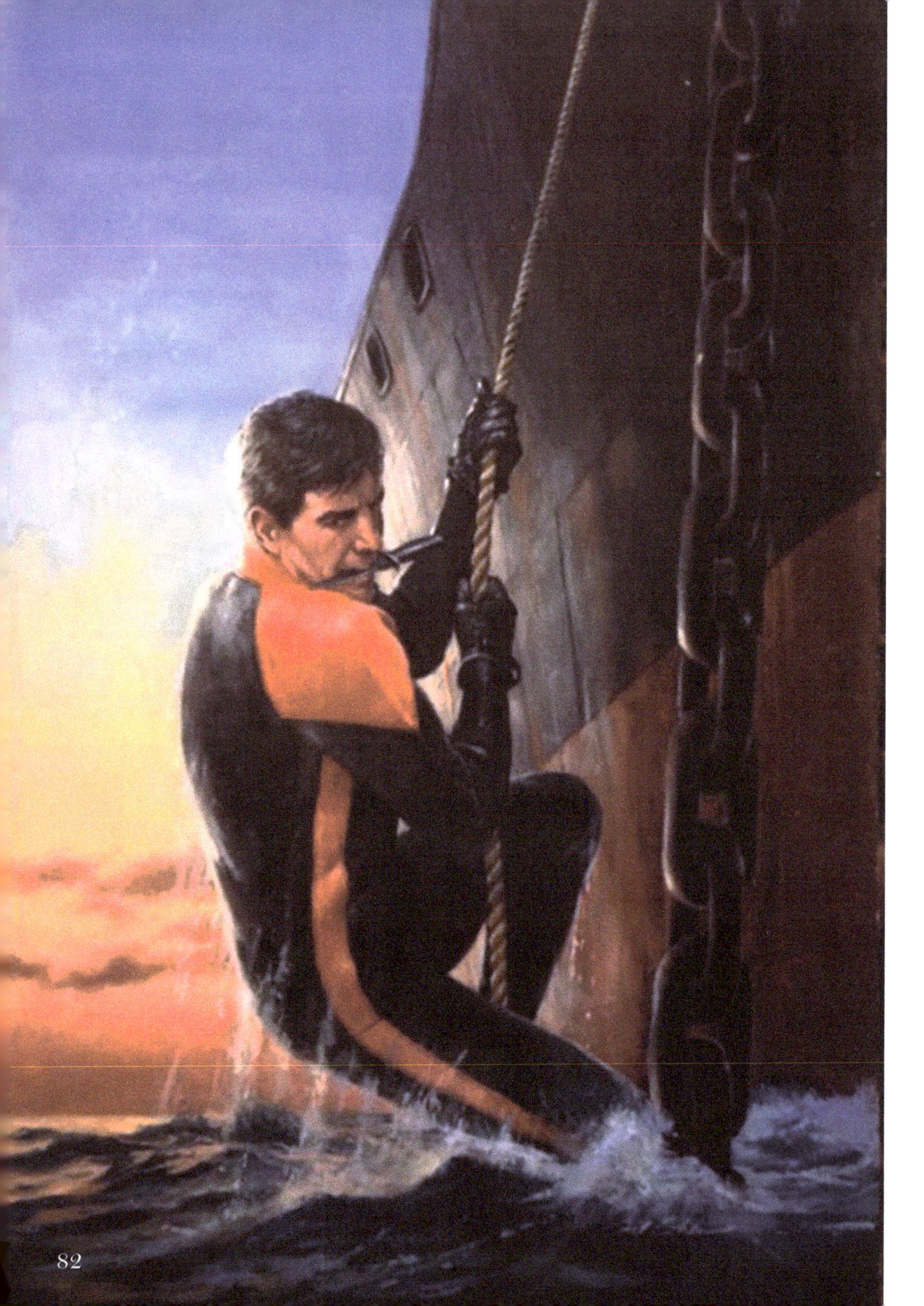

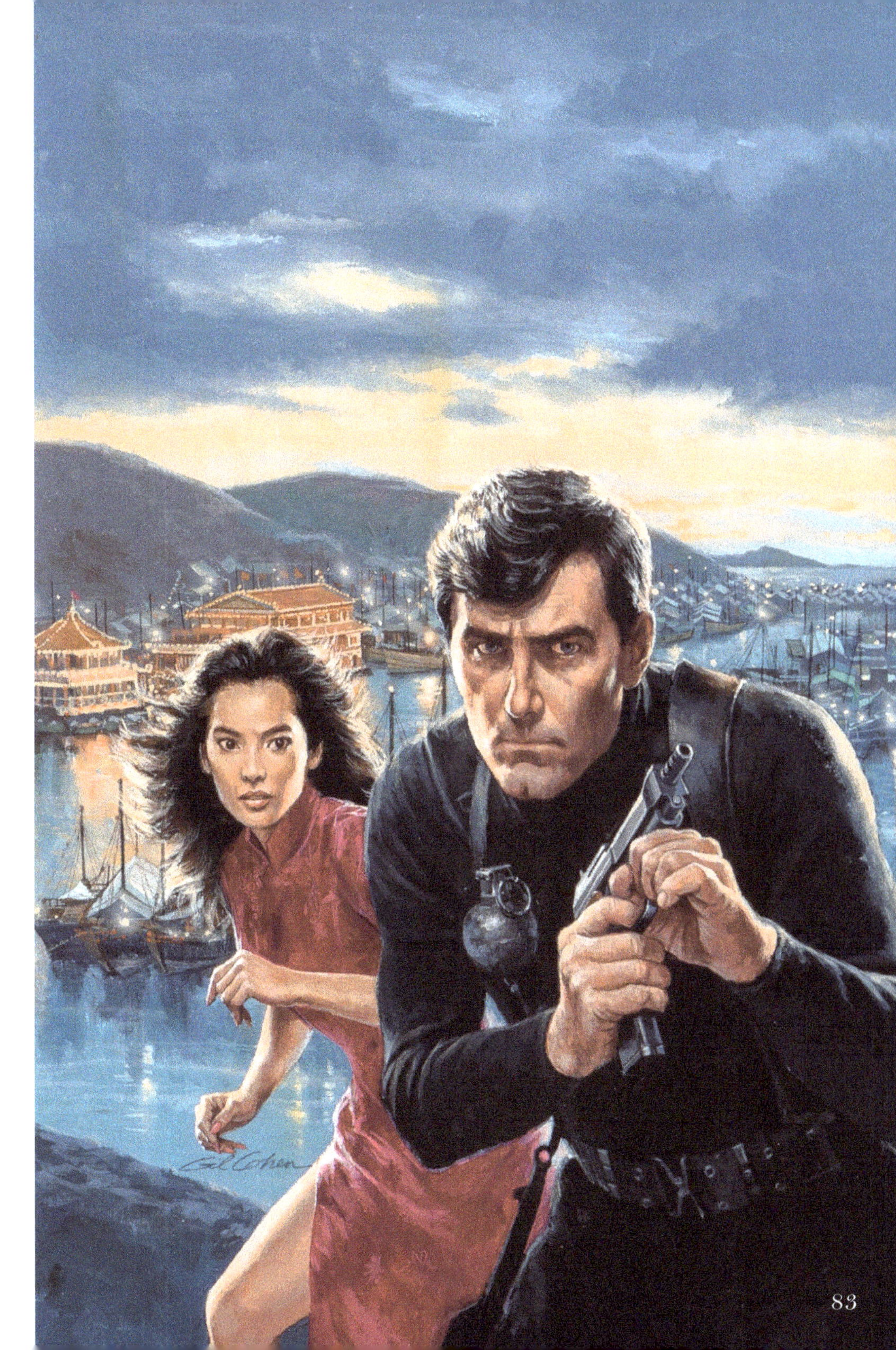

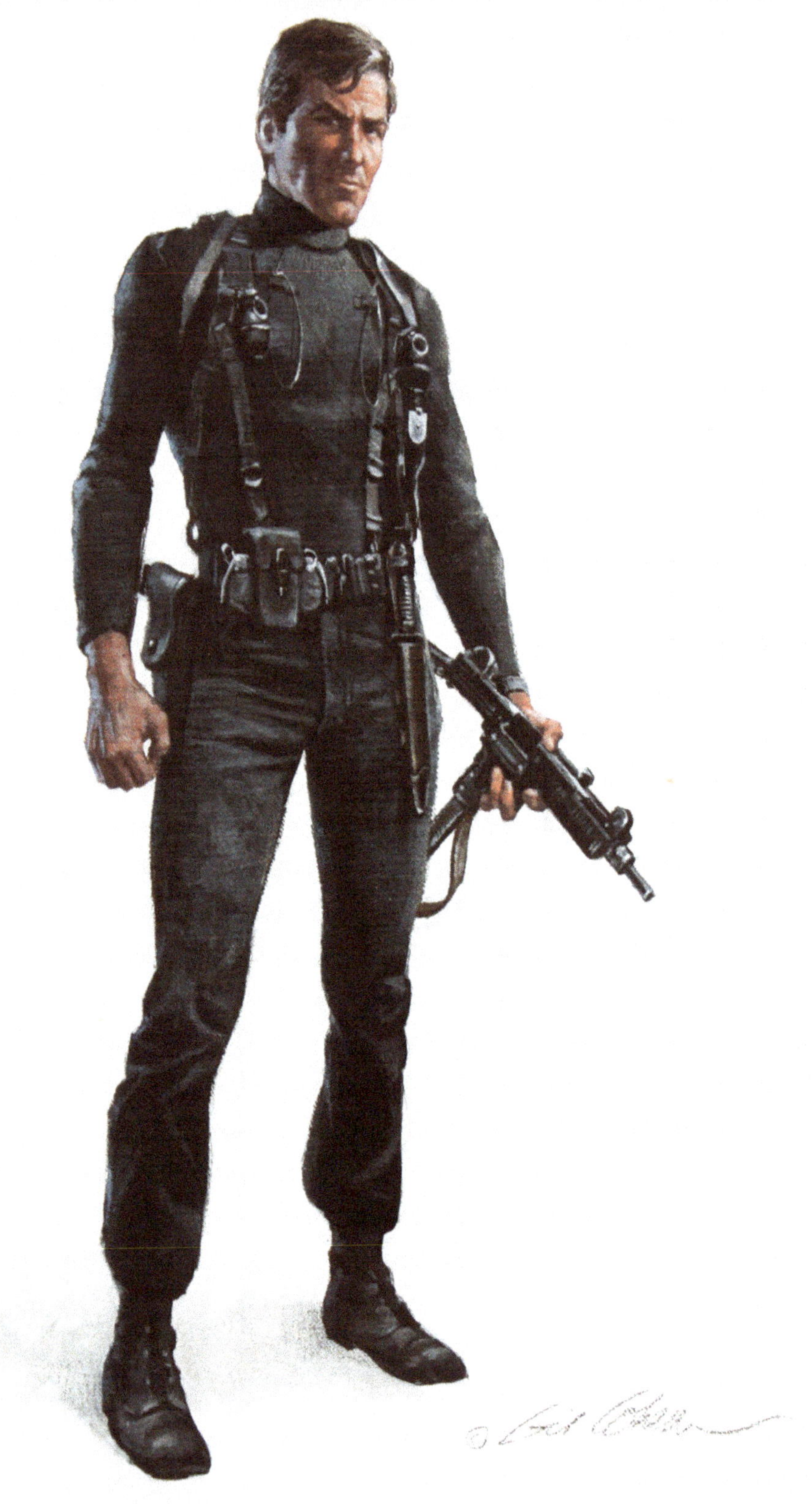

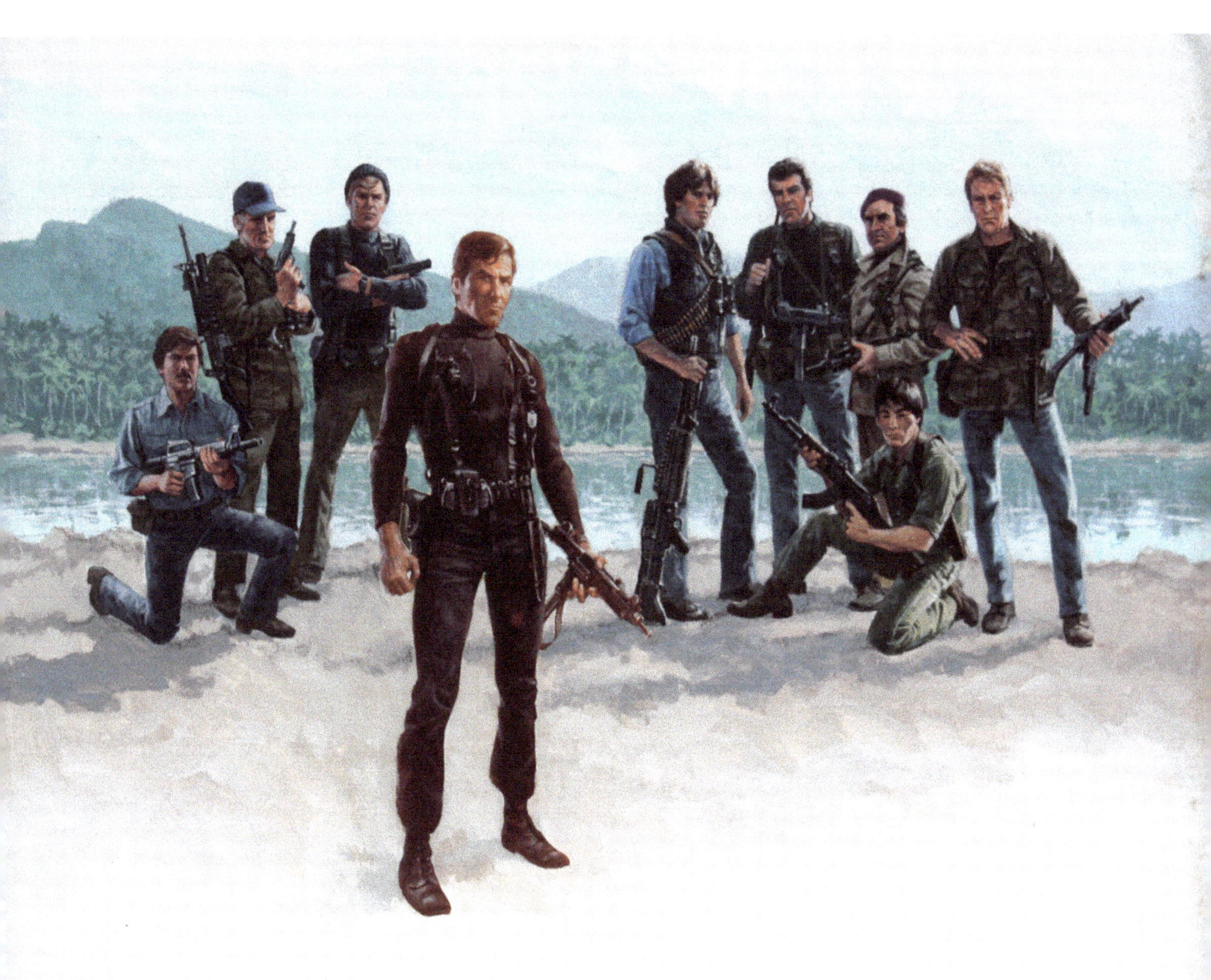

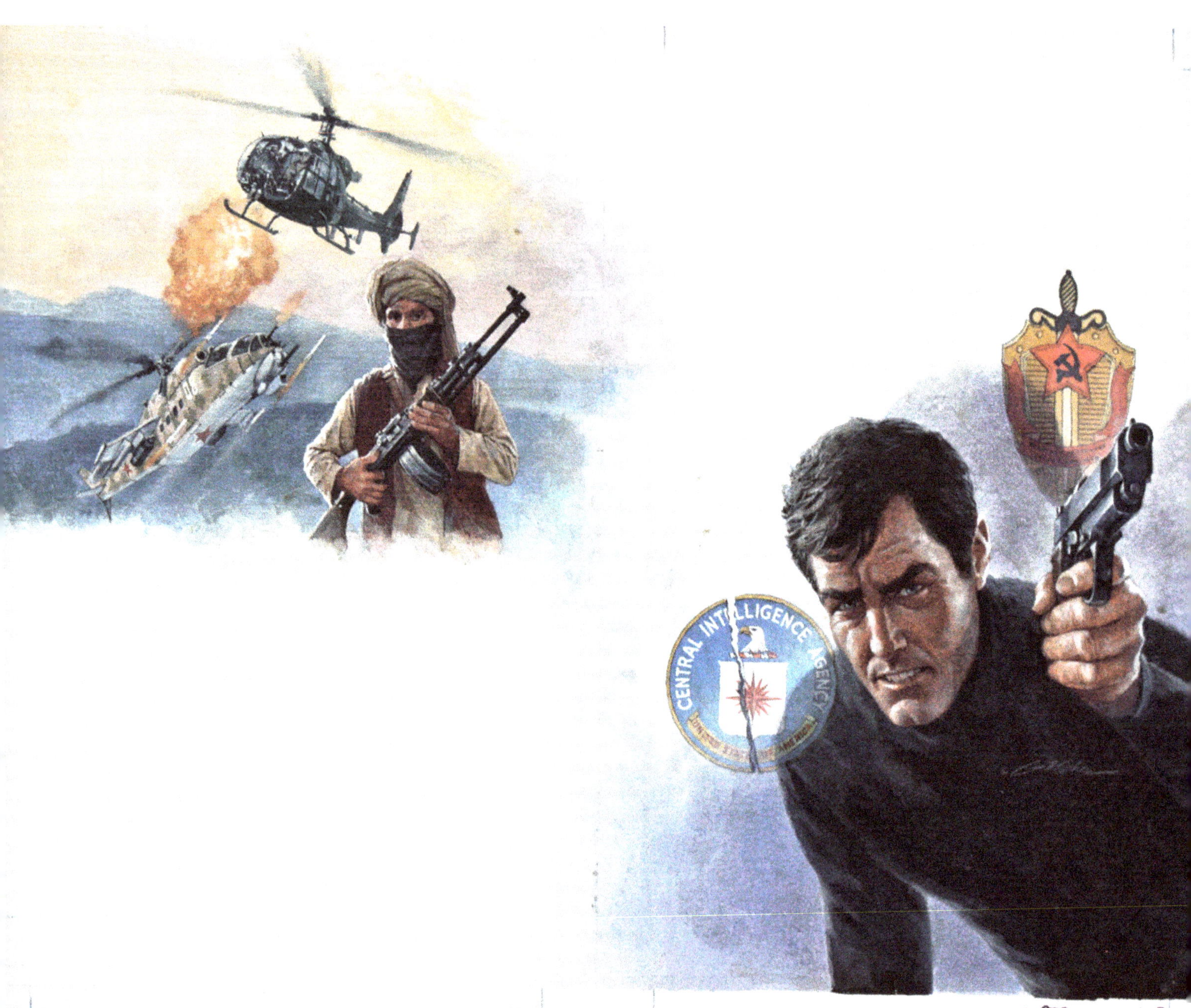
CENTRAL INTELLIGENCE AGENCY
SUPER BOLAN 2

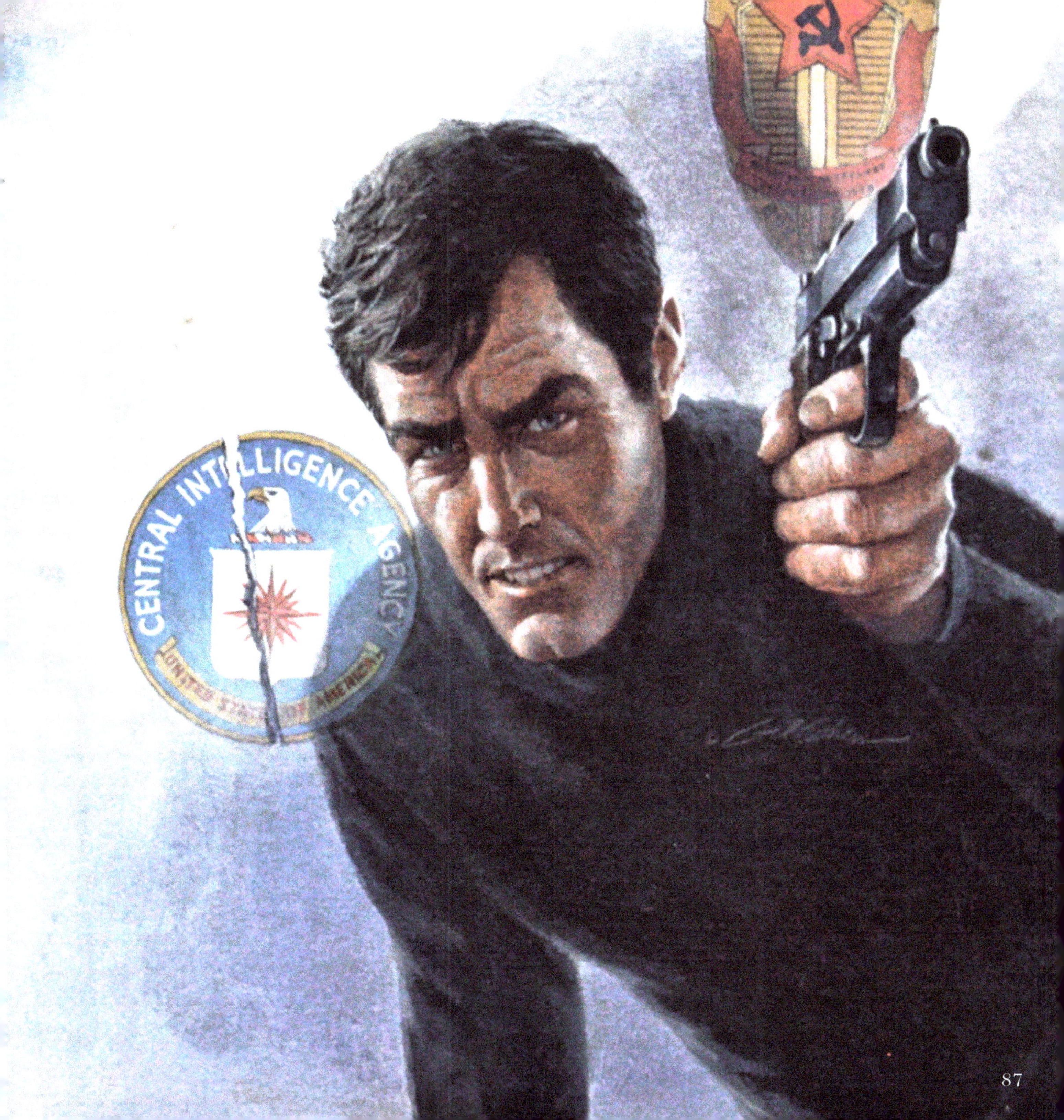
CENTRAL INTELLIGENCE AGENCY
UNITED STATES OF AMERICA

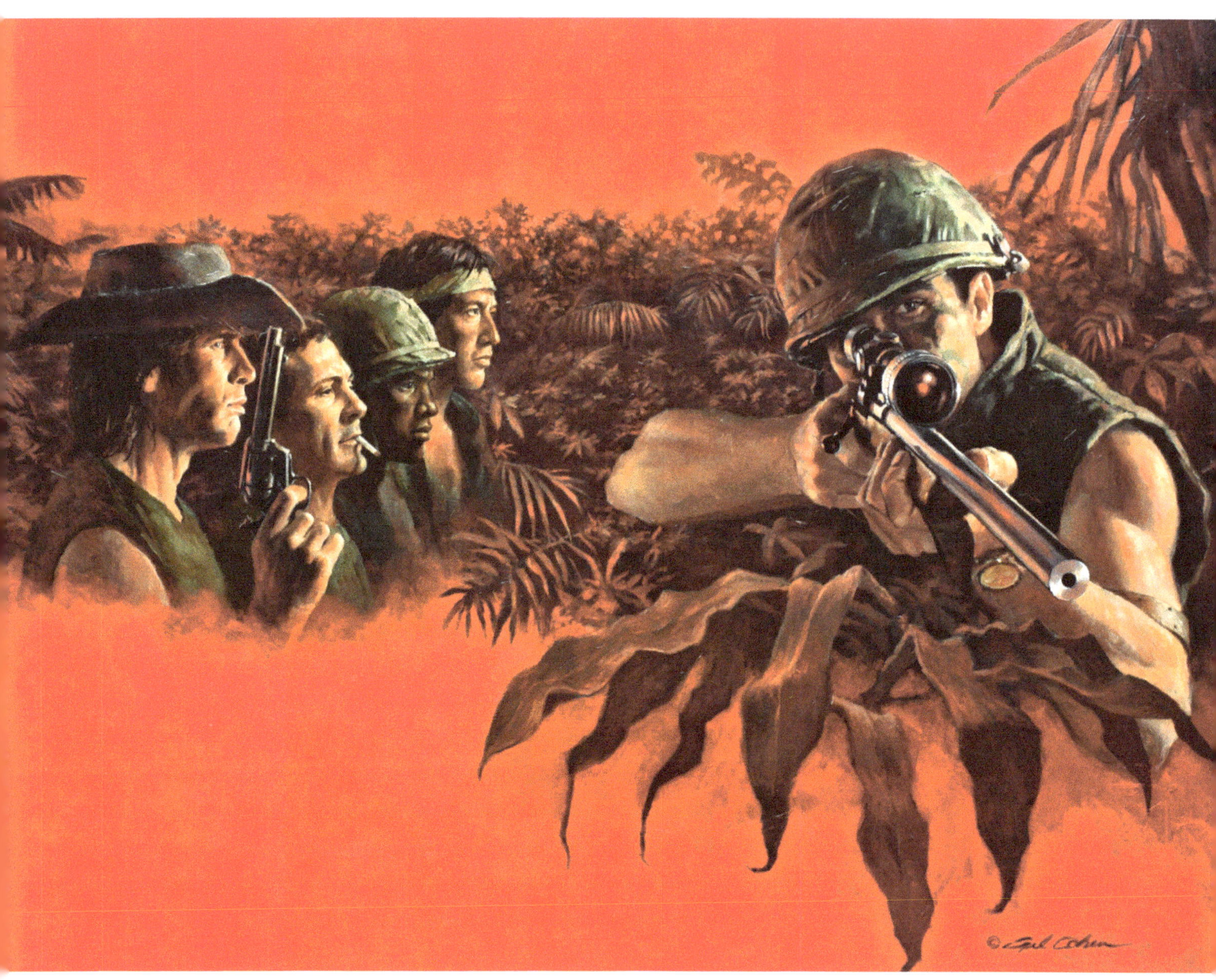

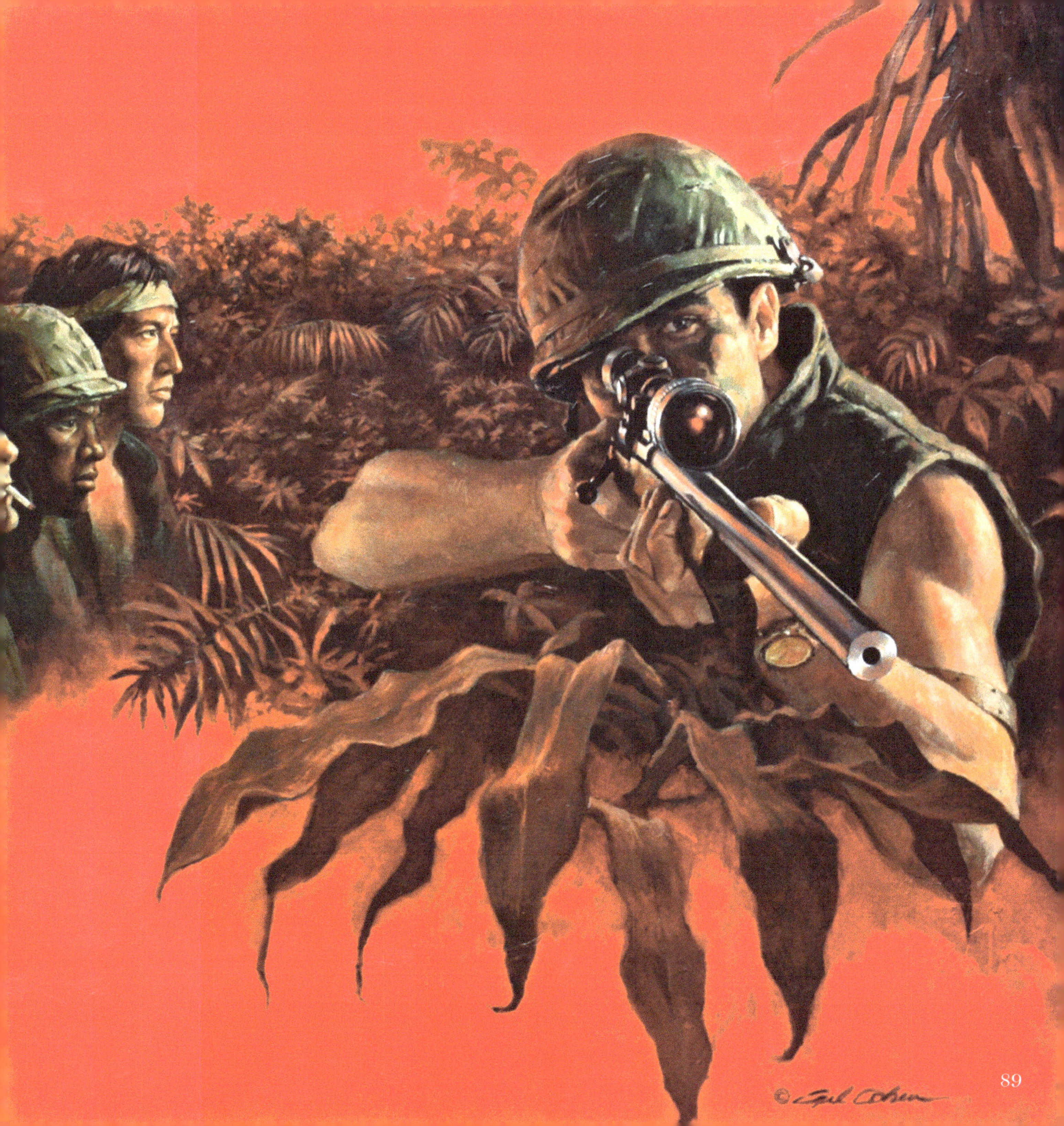

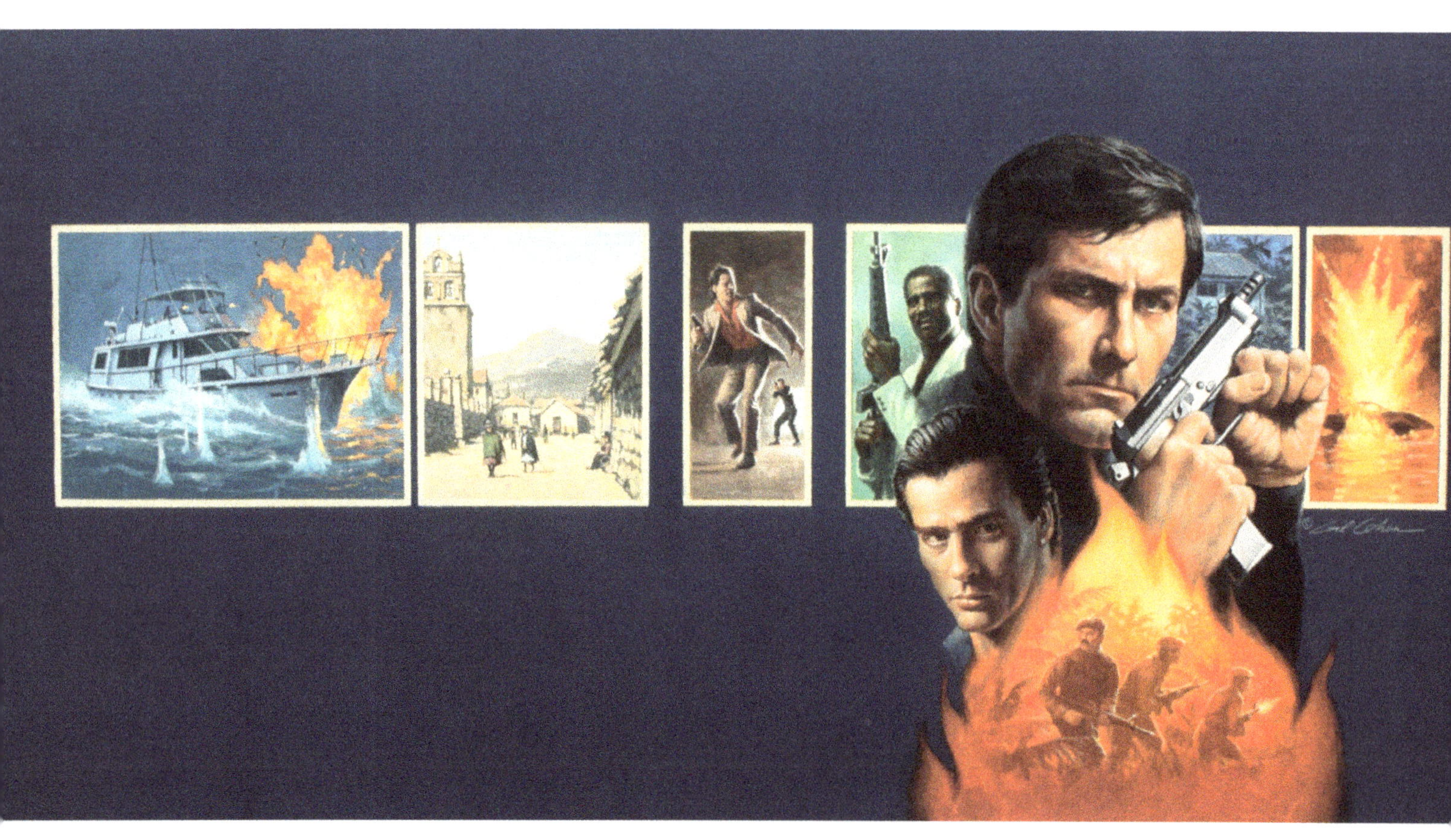

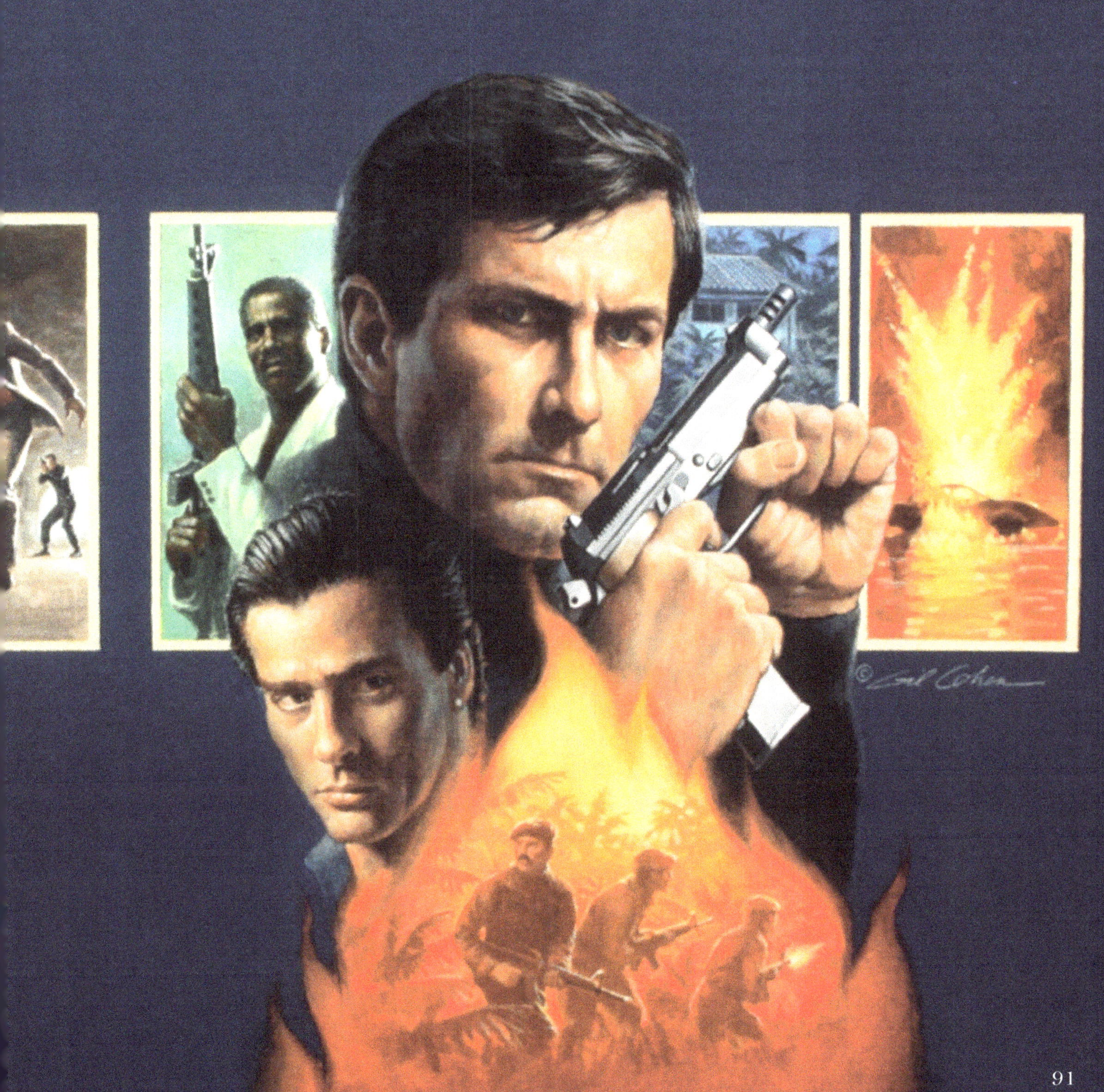

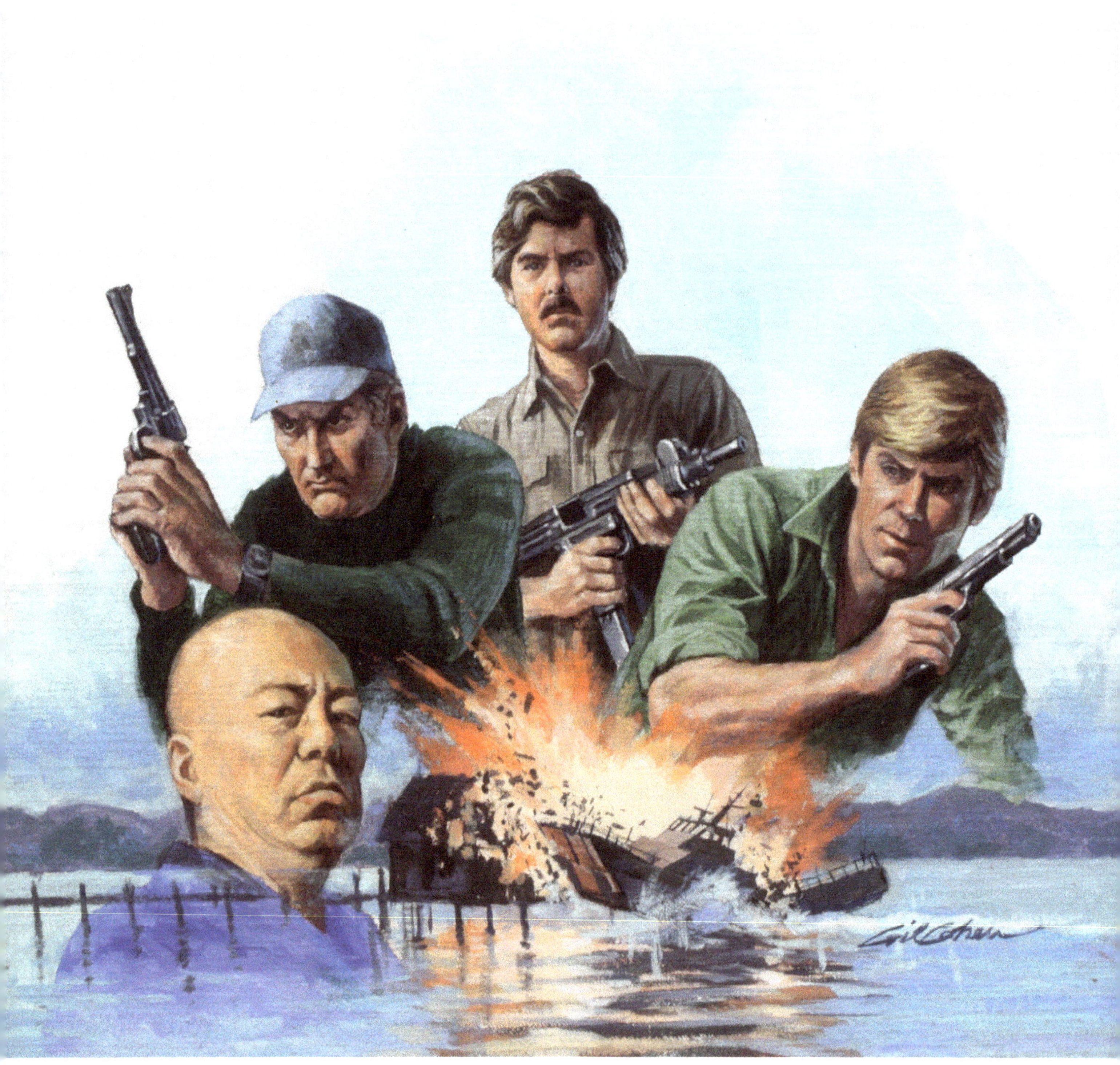

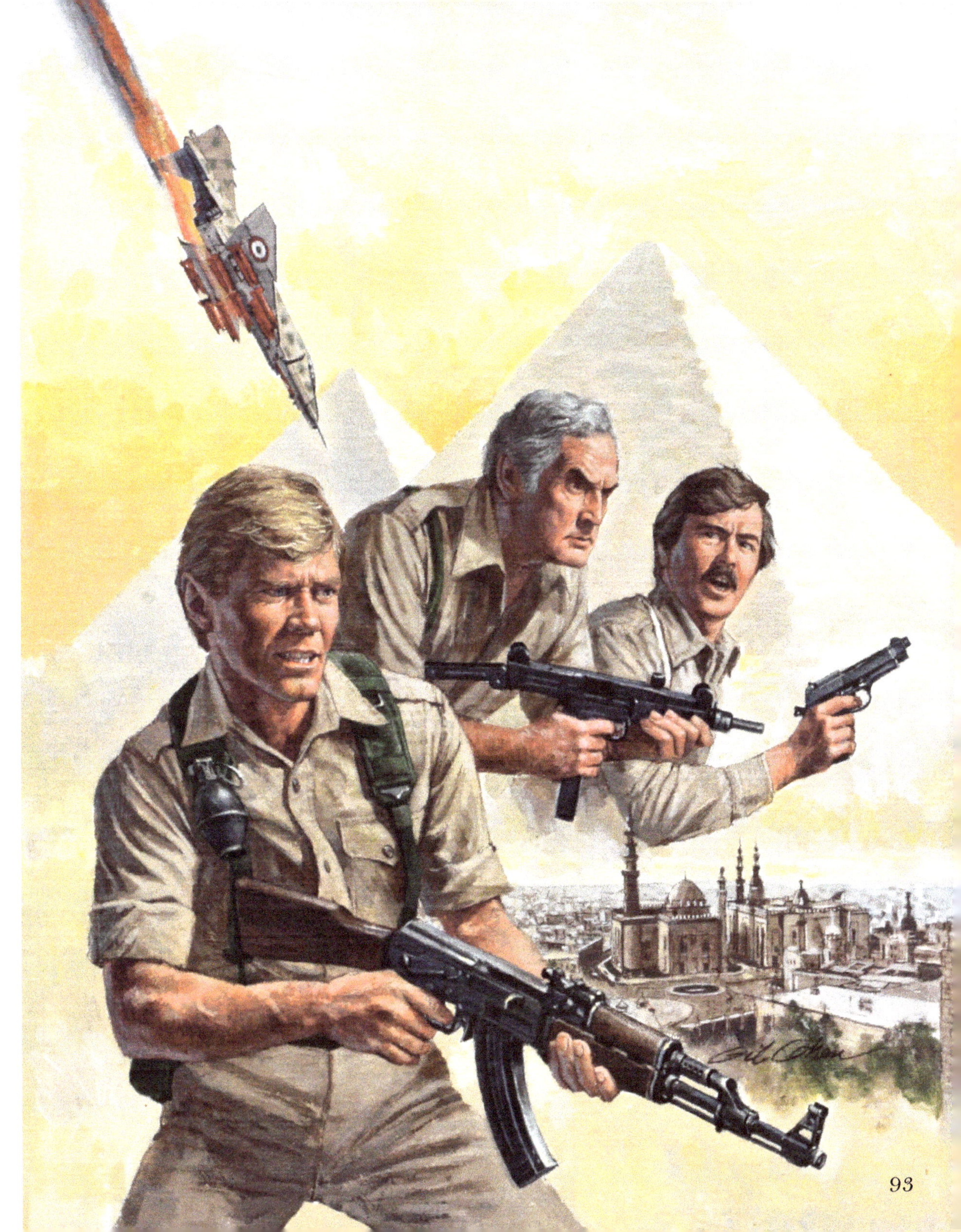

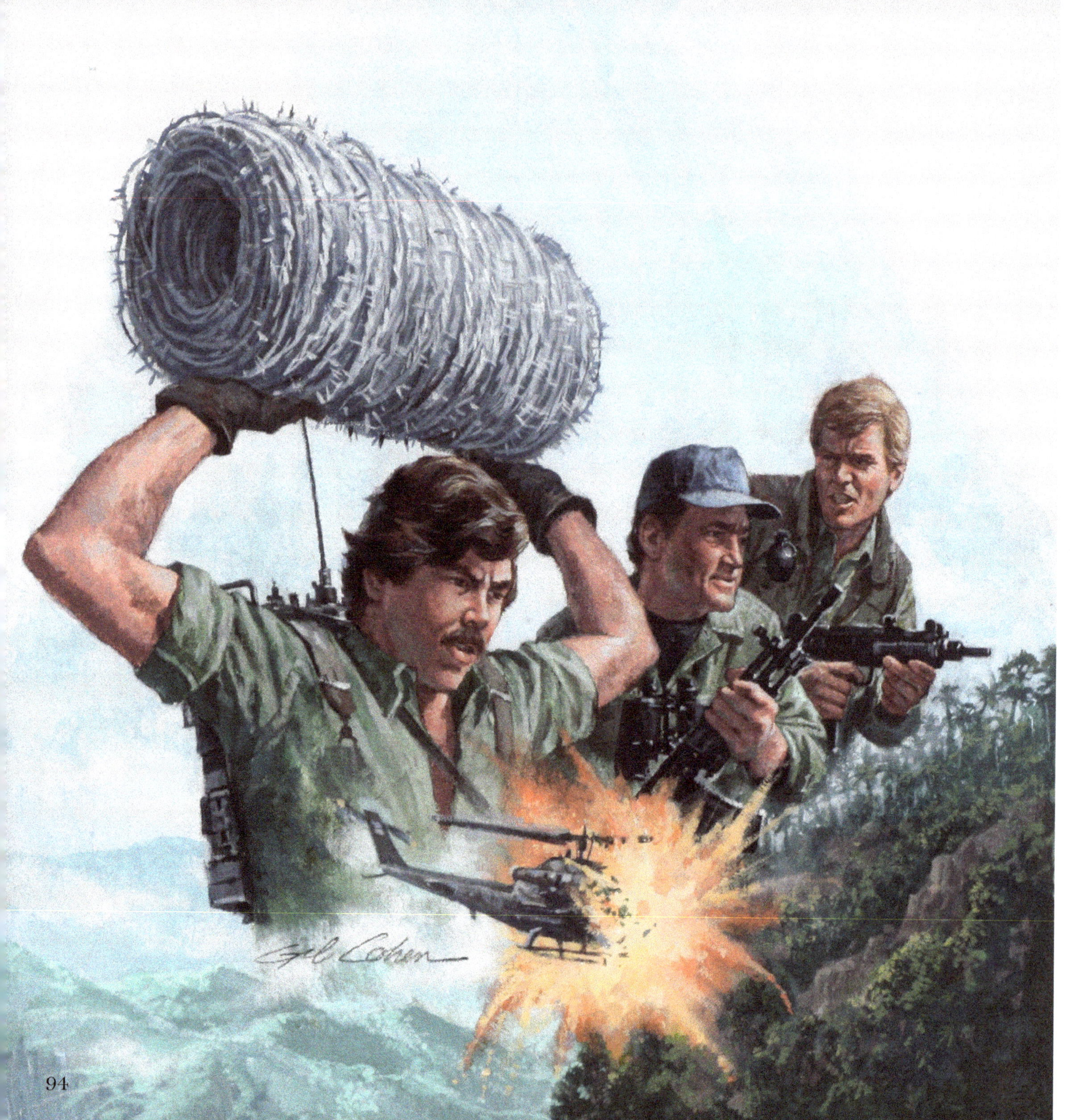

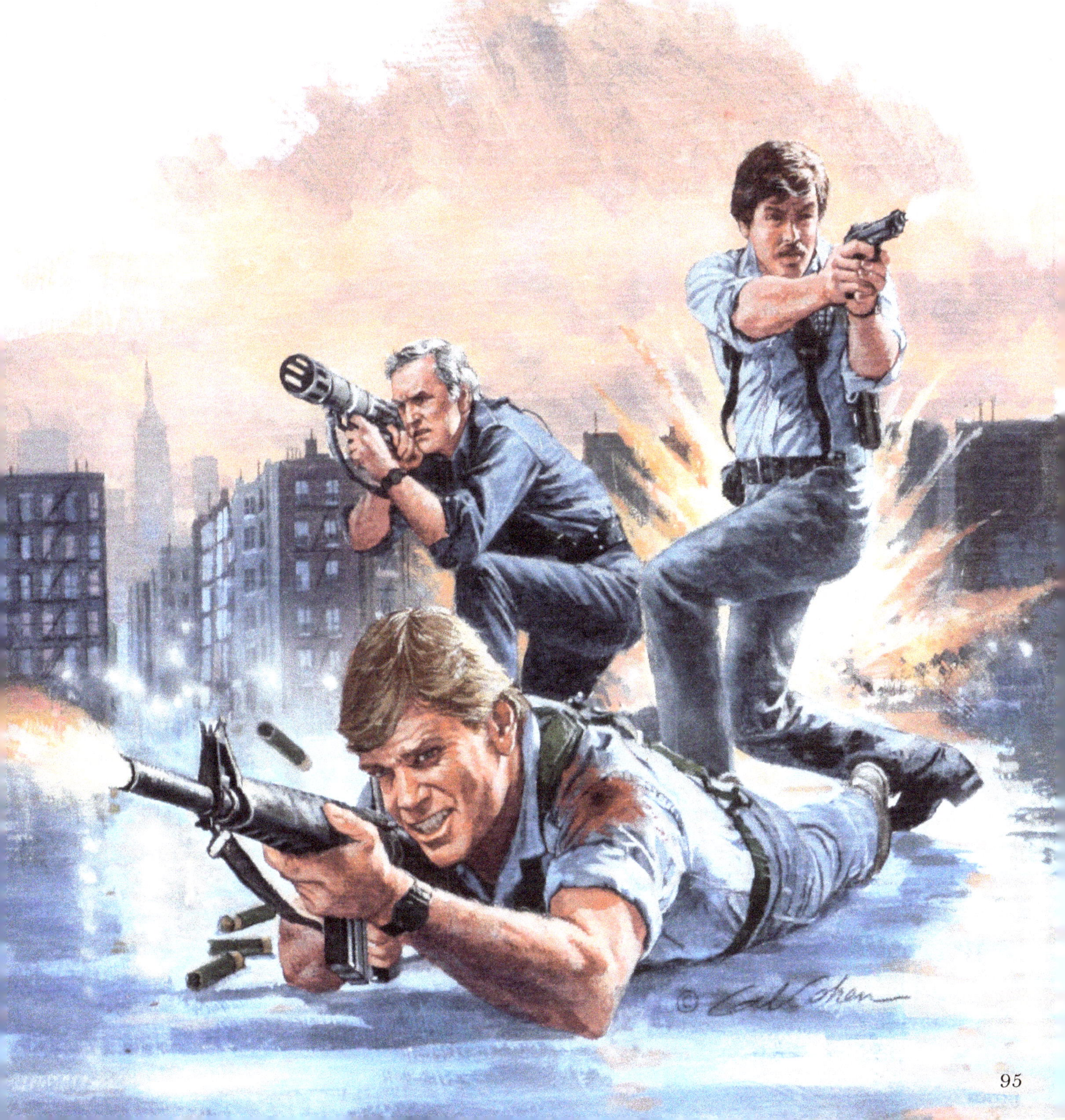

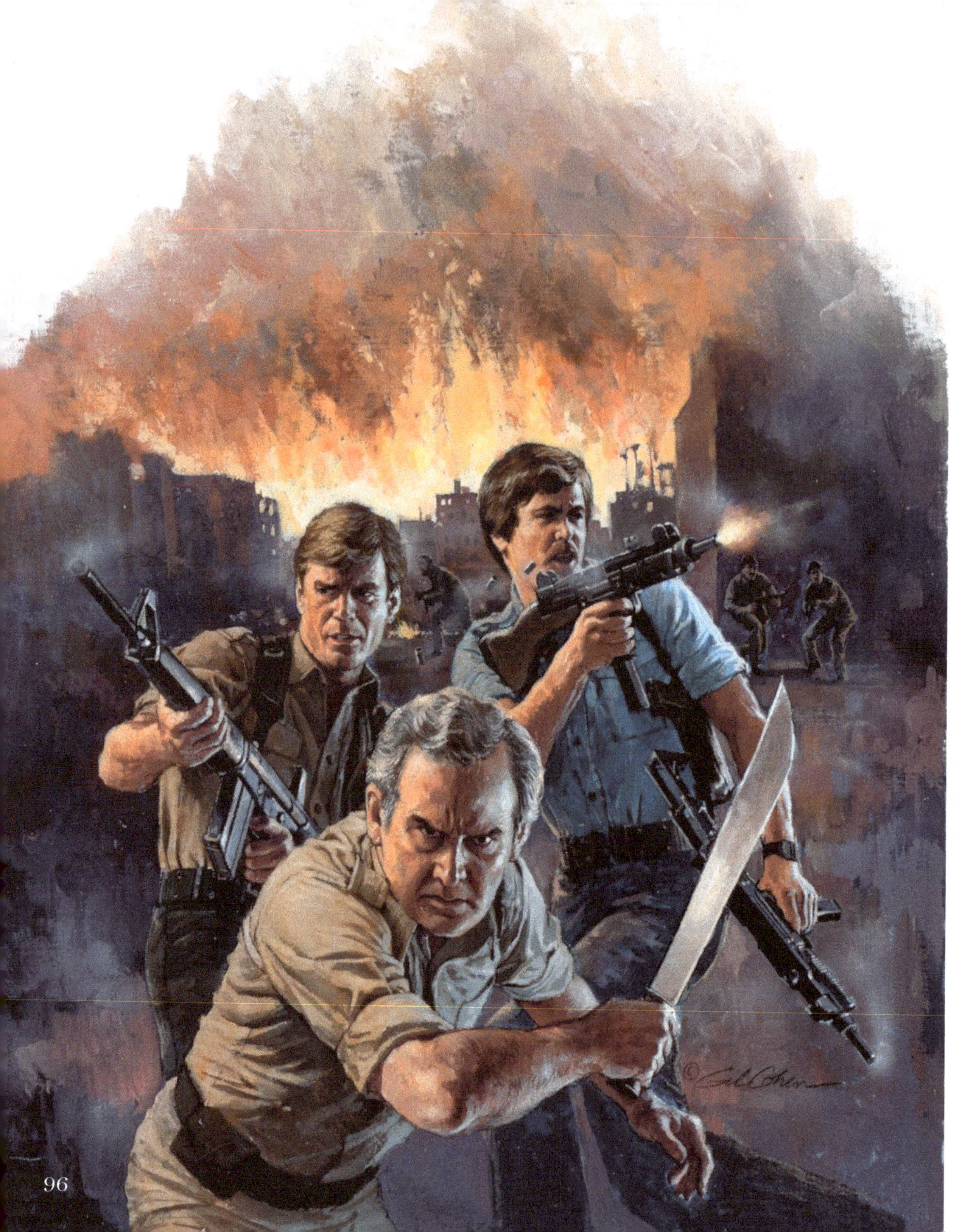

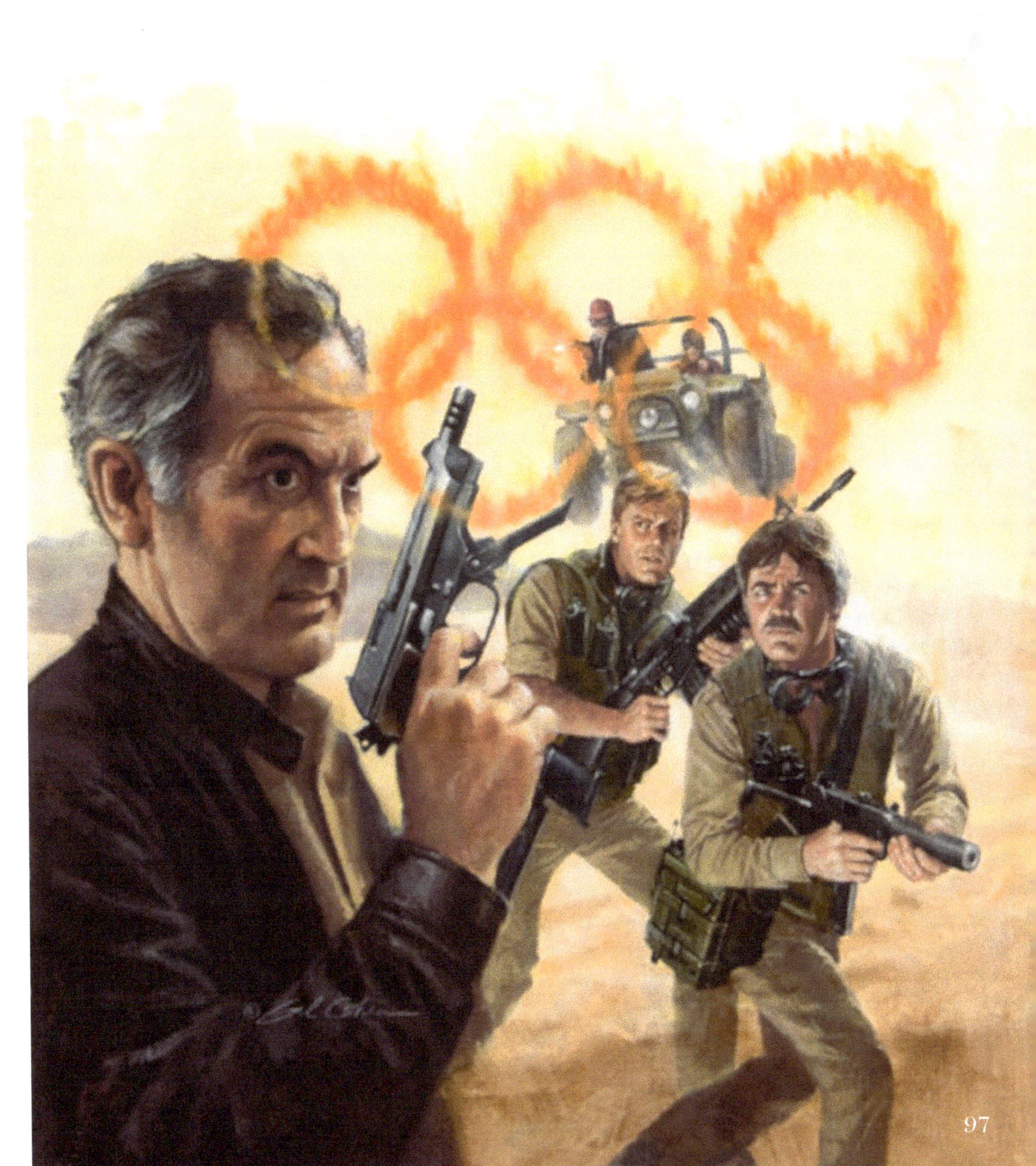

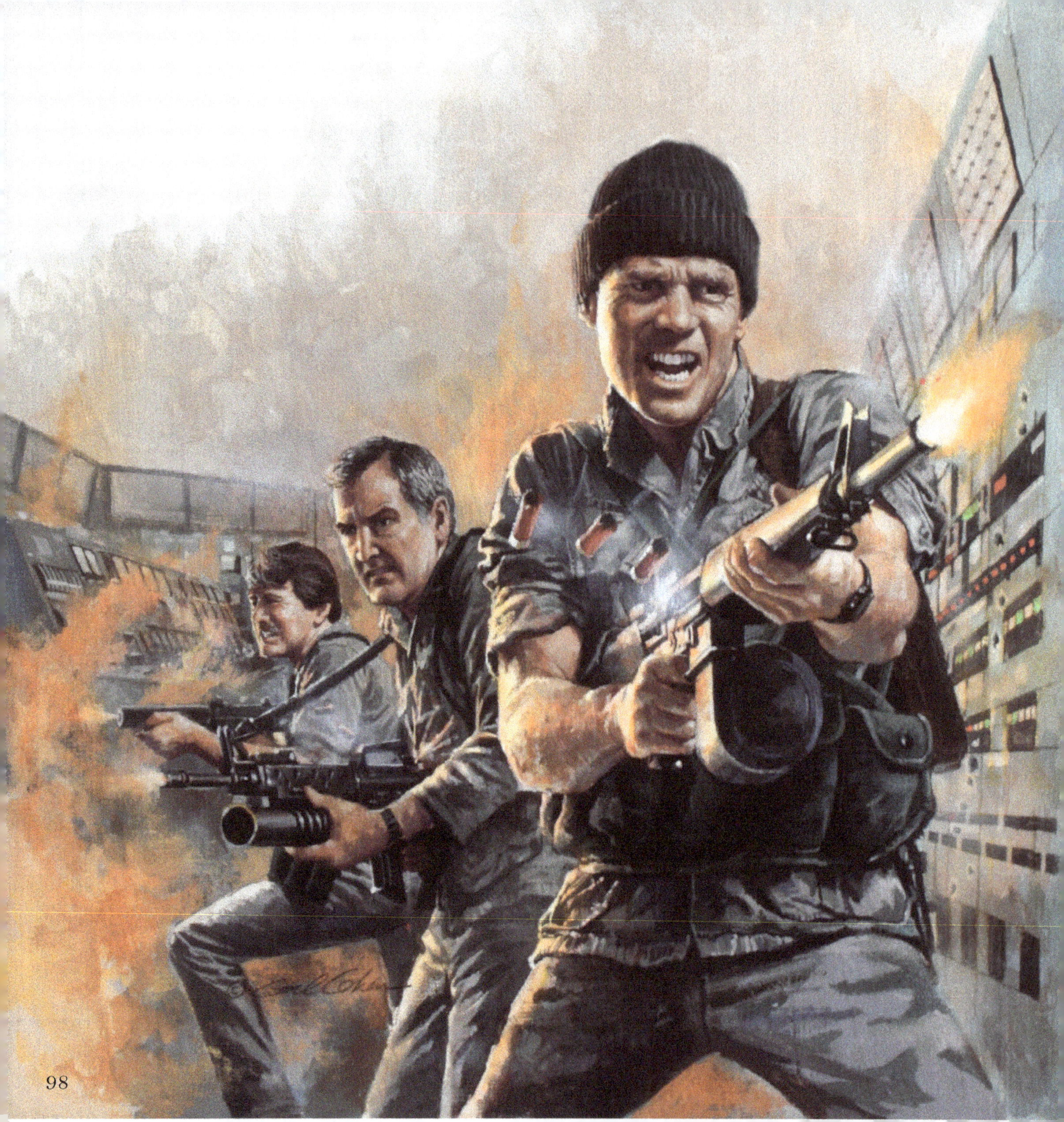

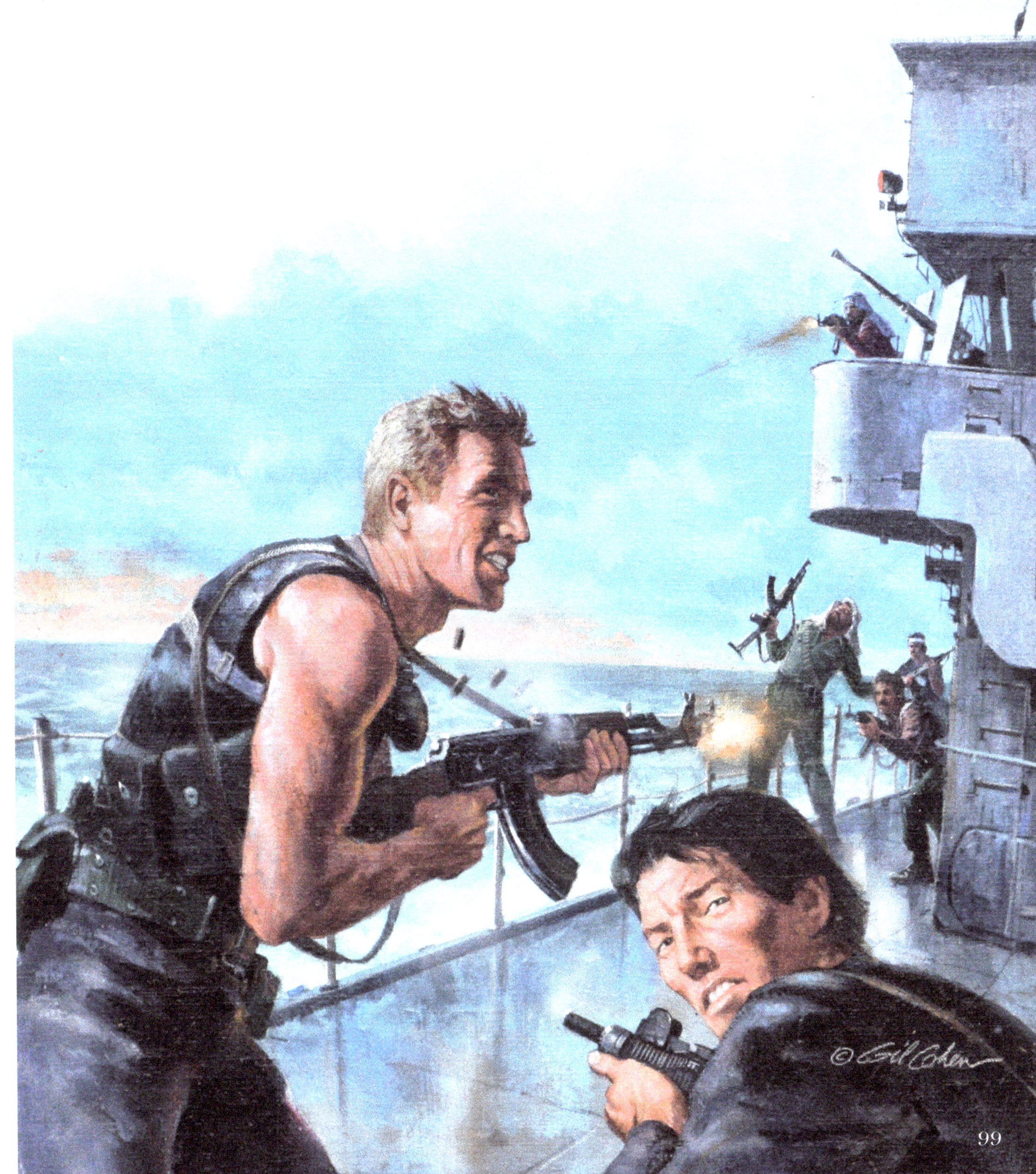

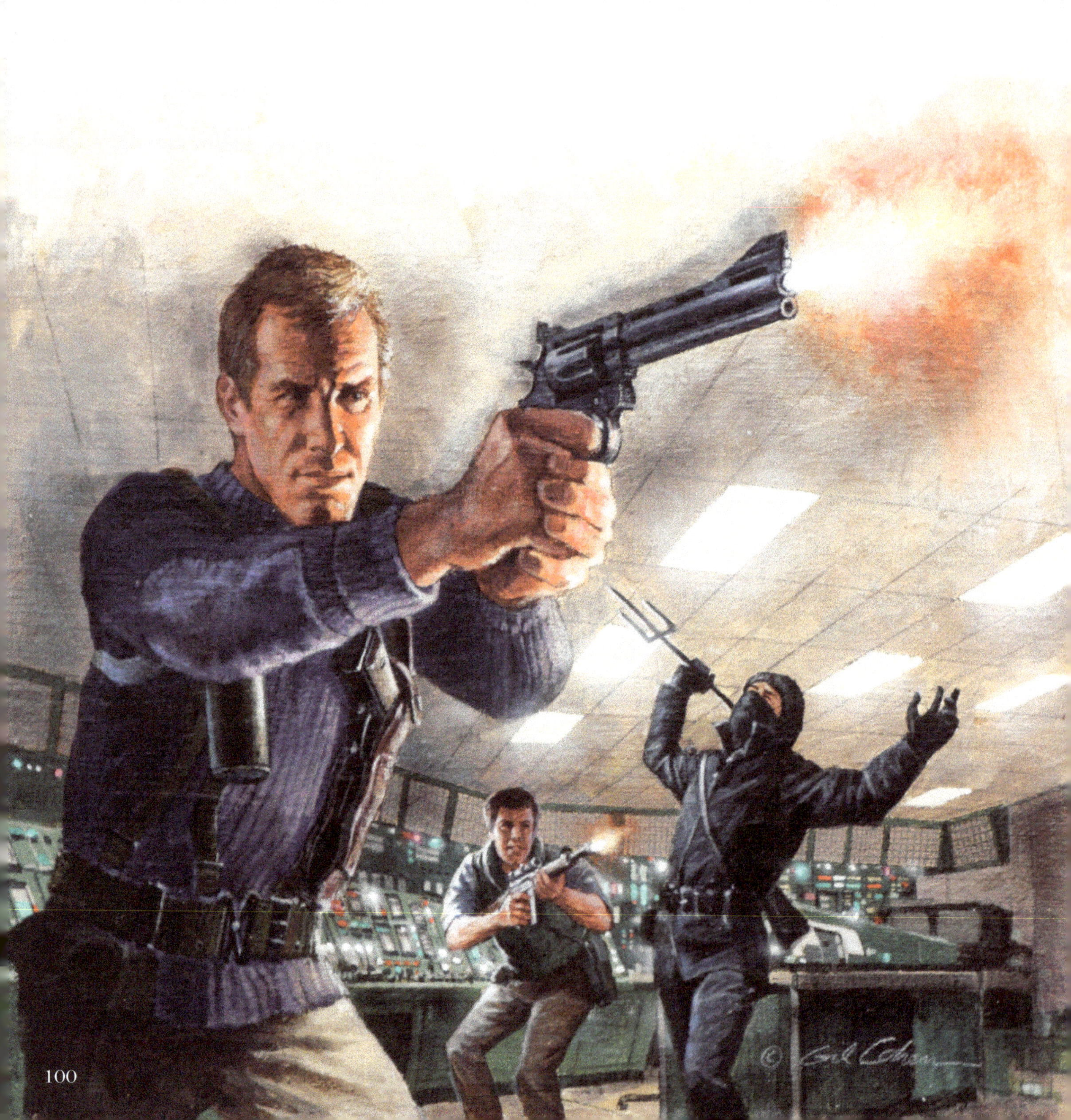

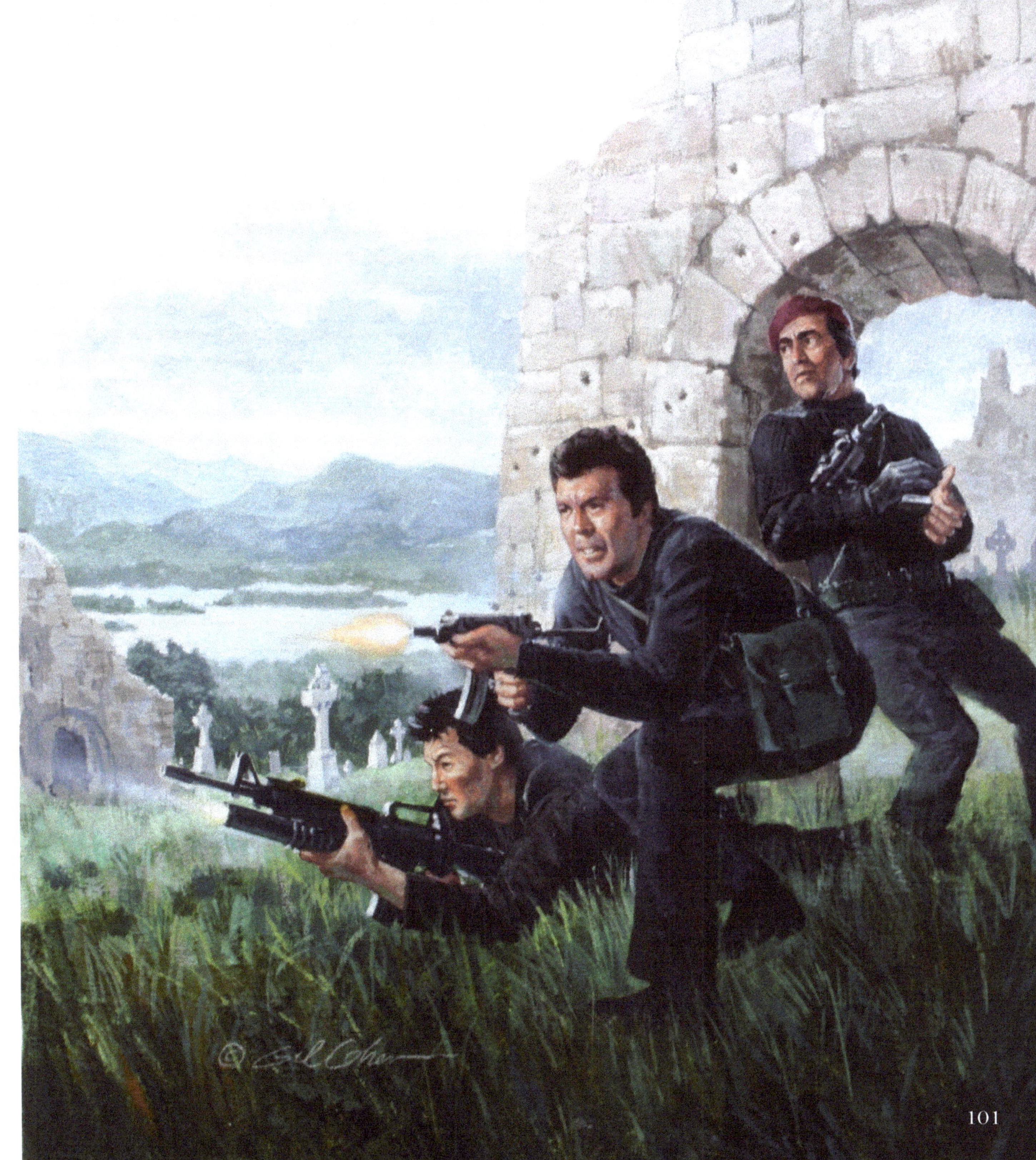

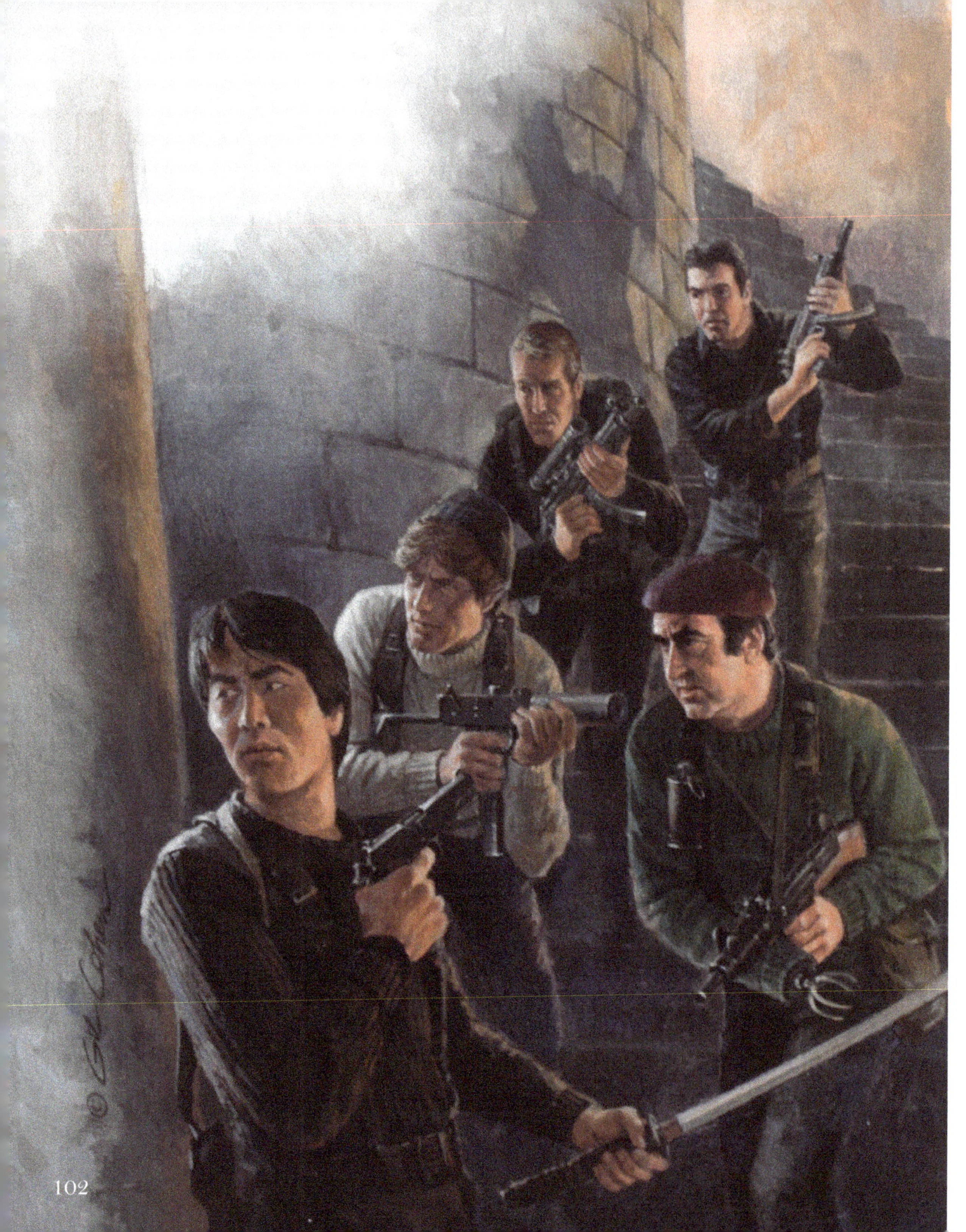

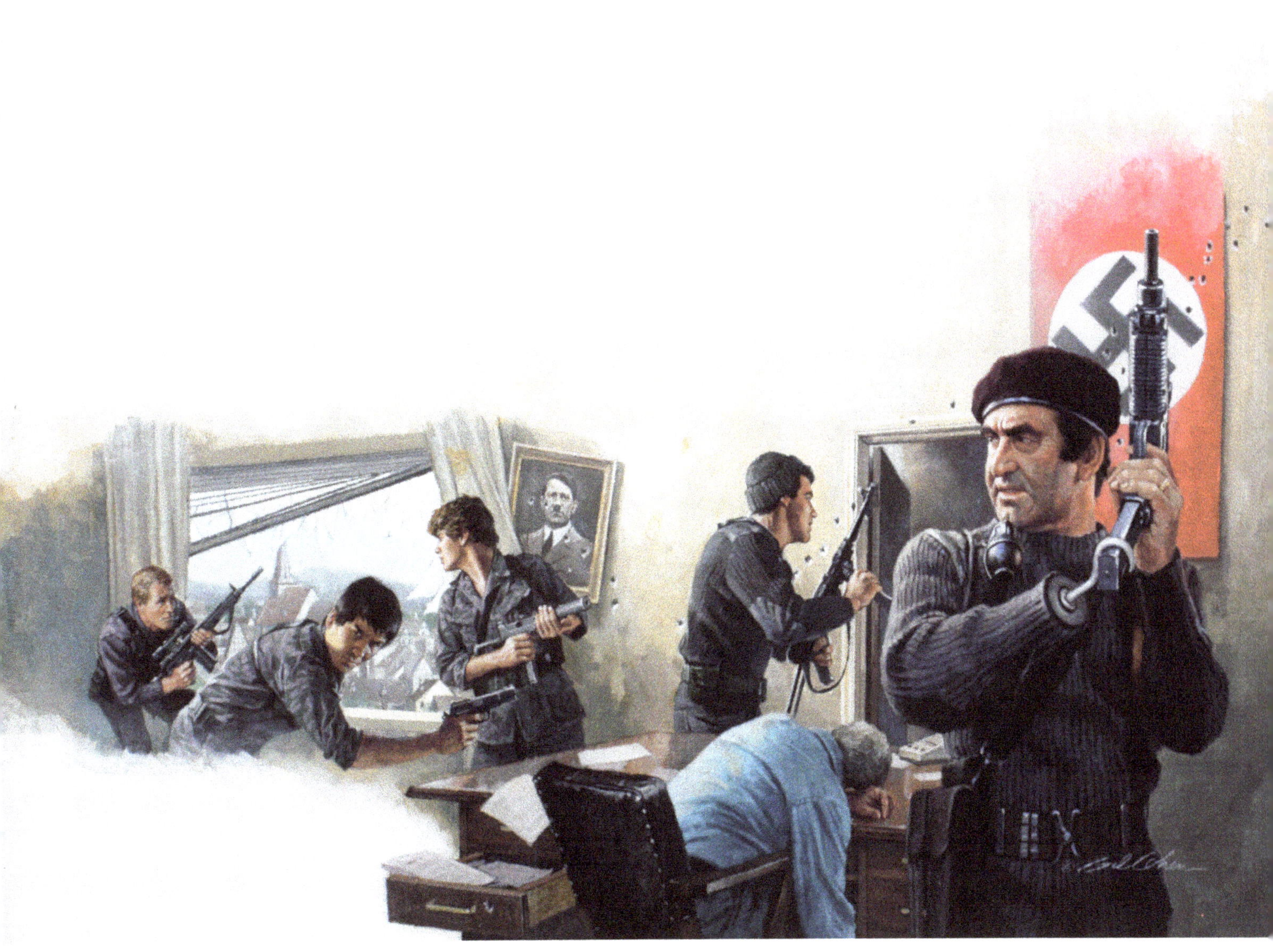

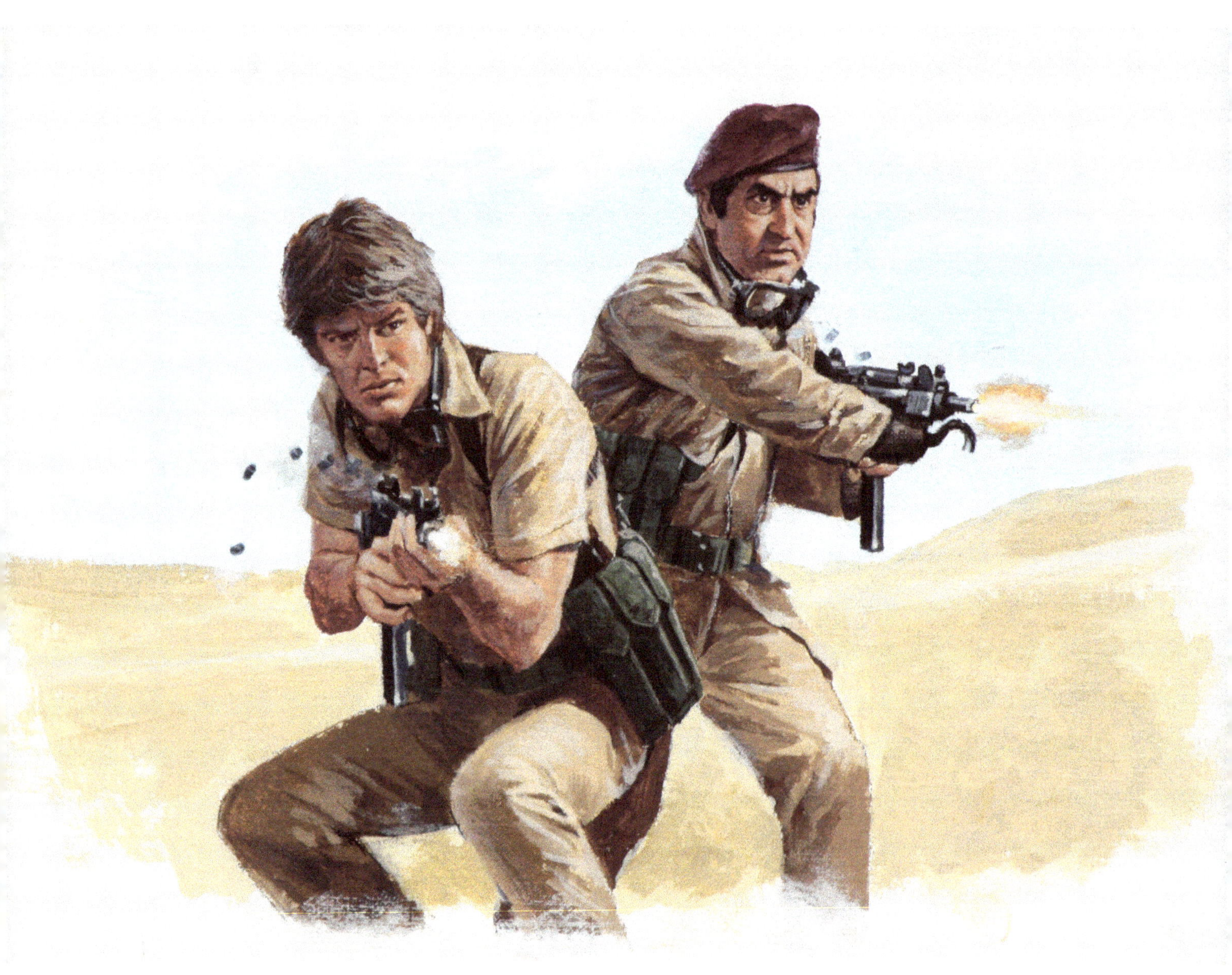

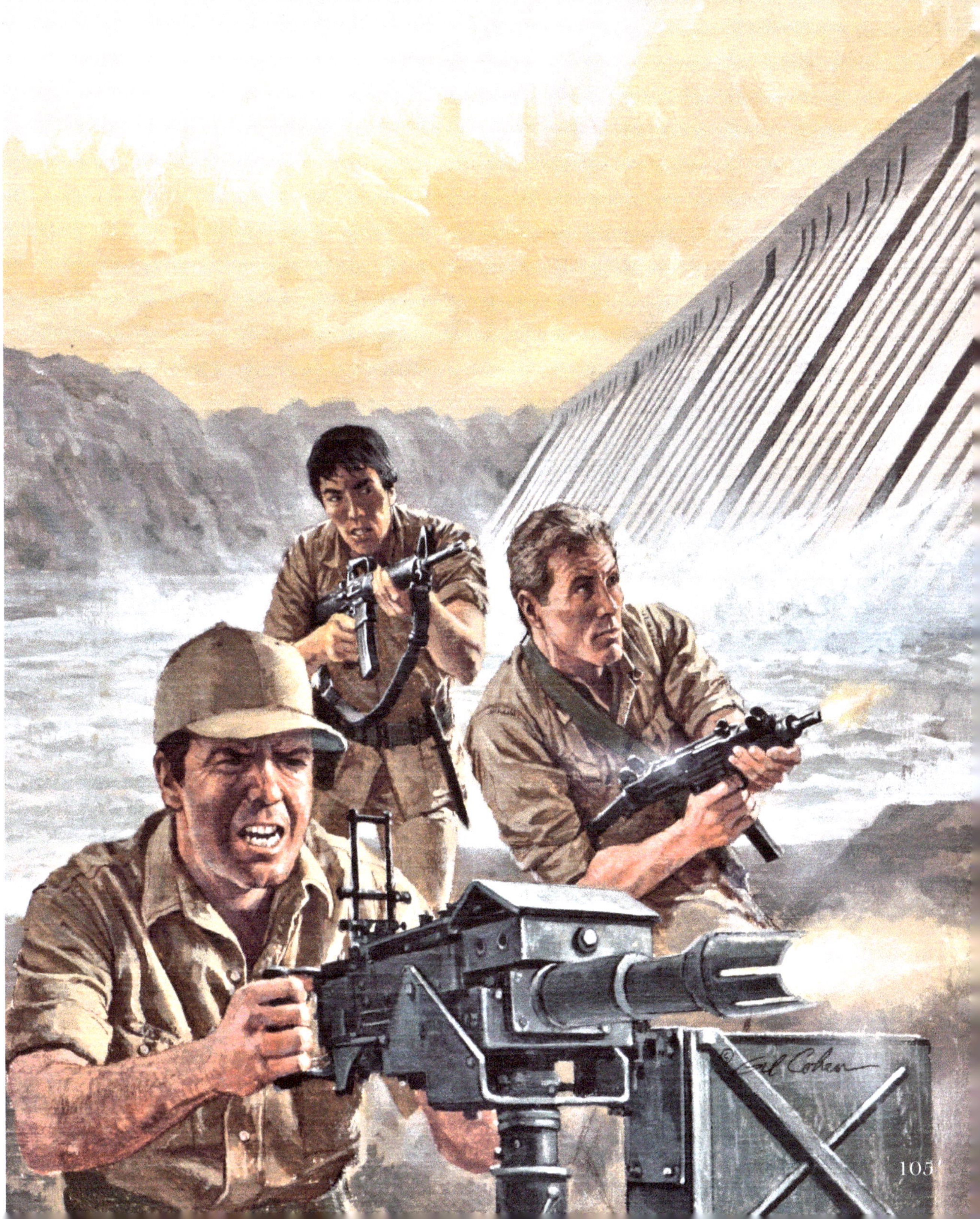

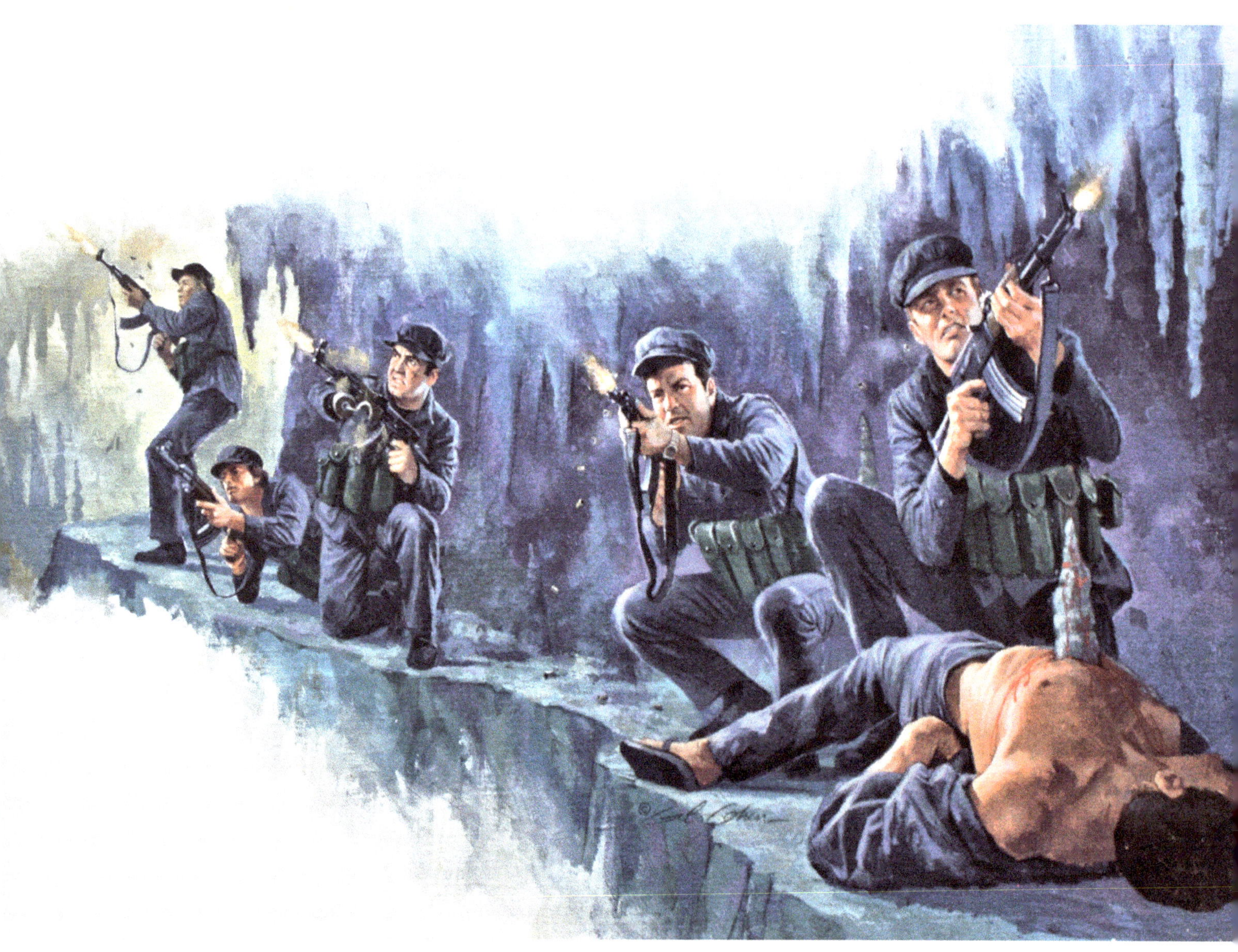

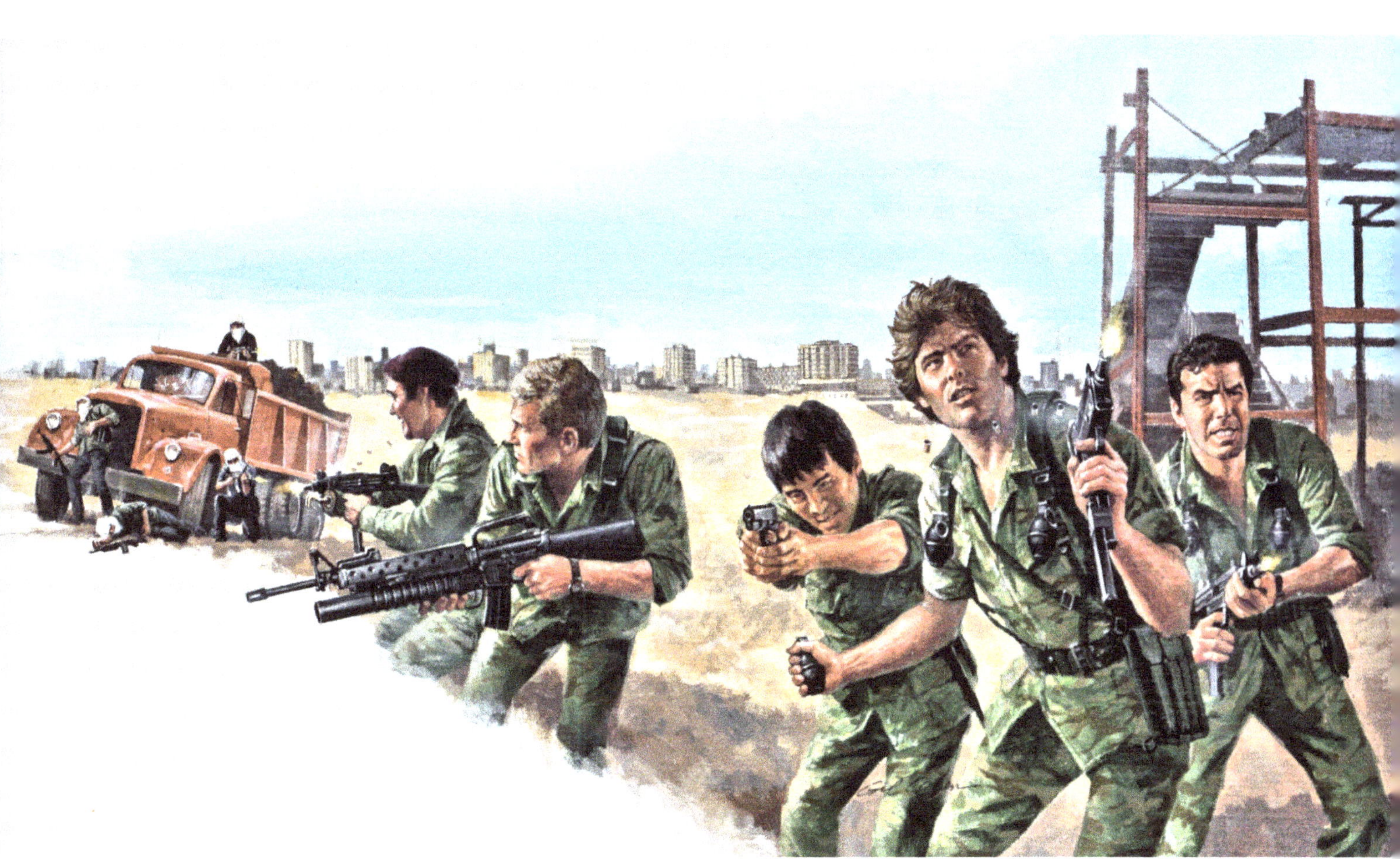

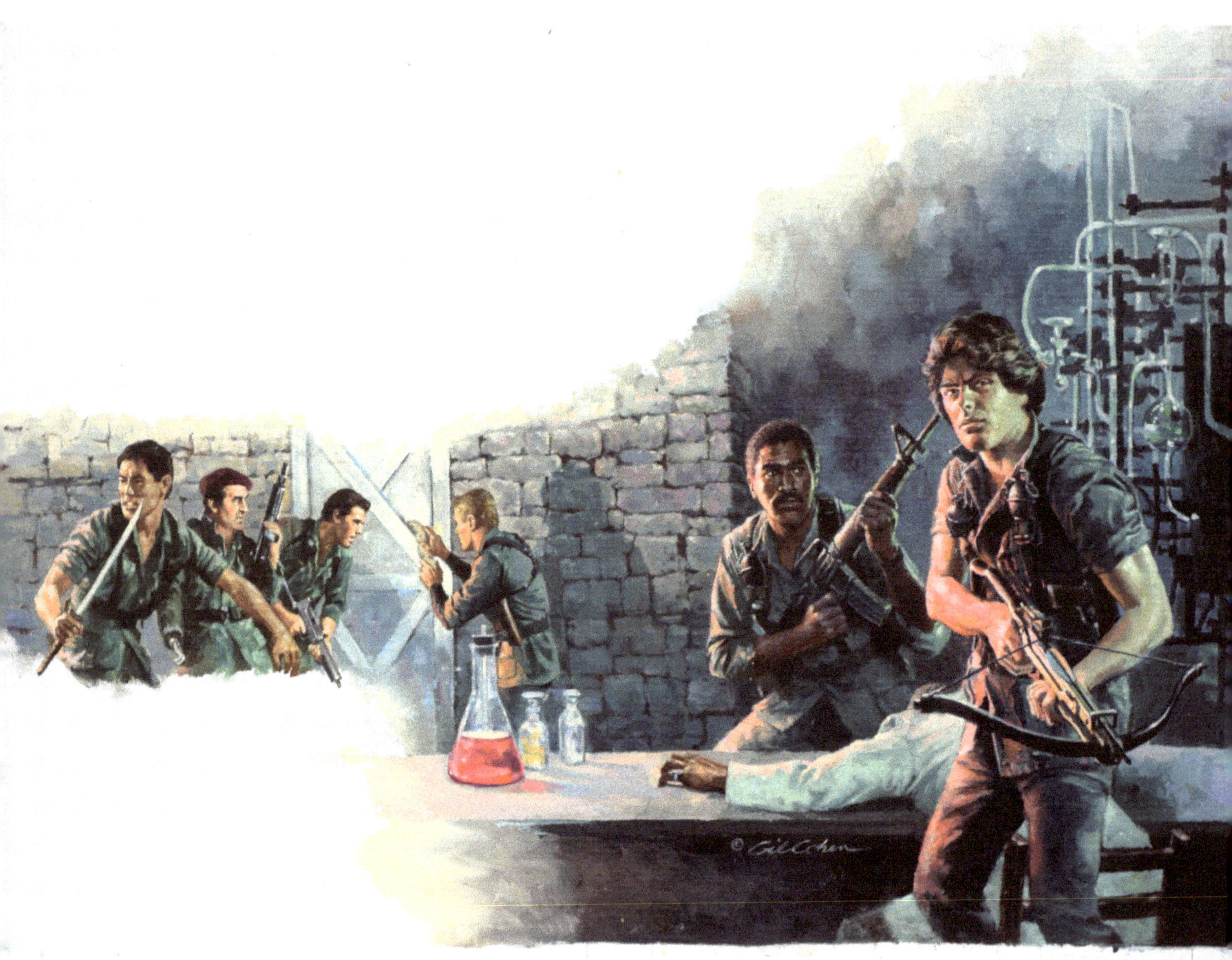

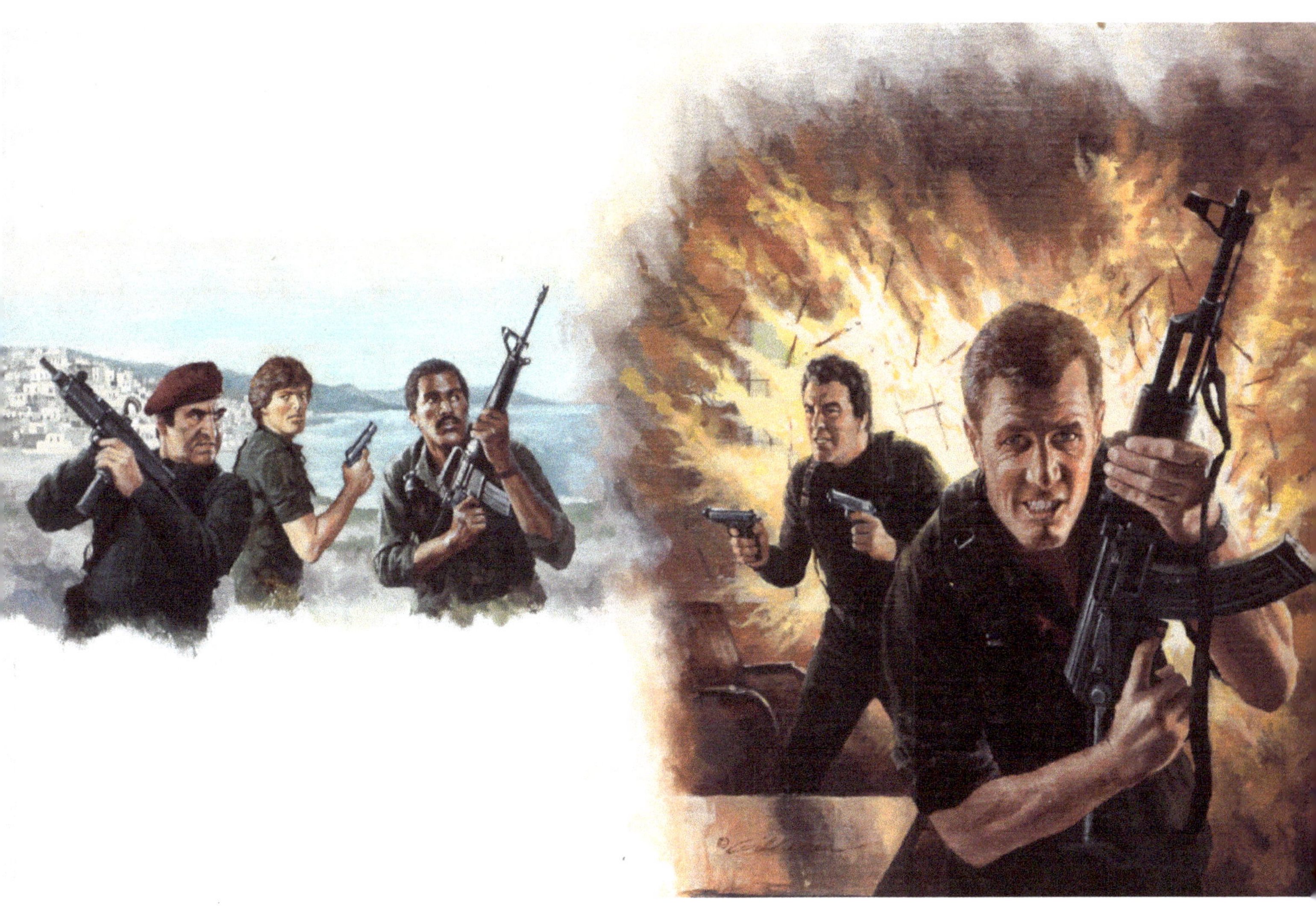

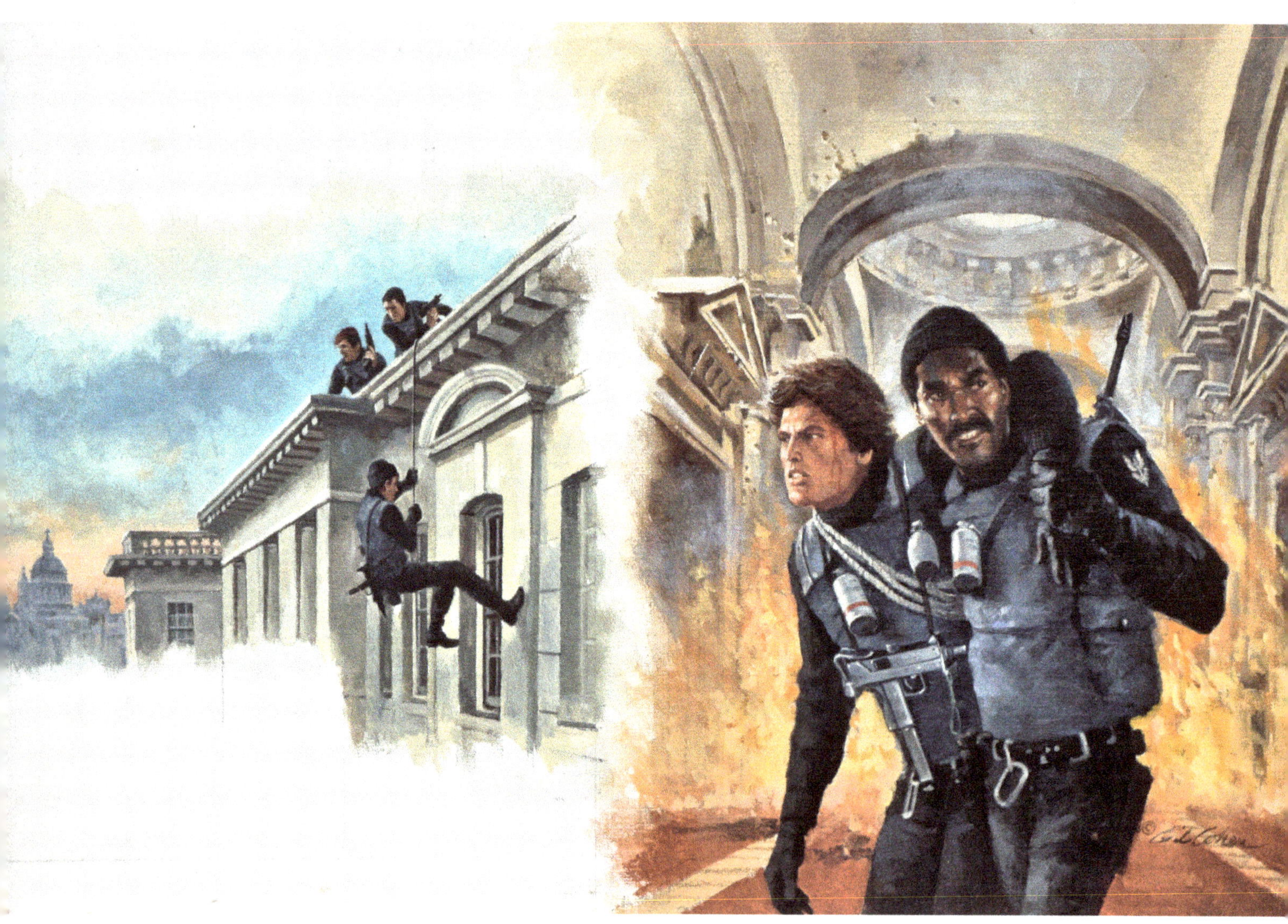

THE EXECUTIONER / MACK BOLAN

** Initial cover art replaced by GC in 1973*

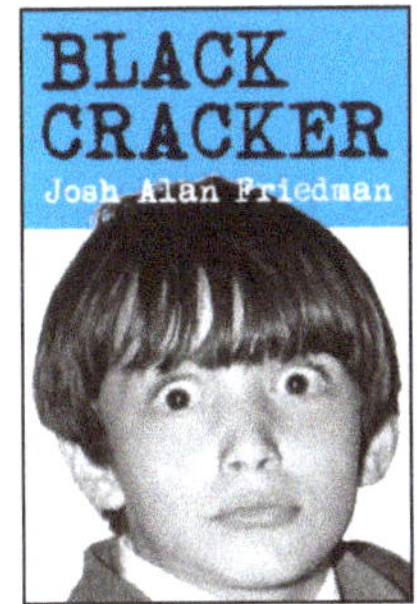

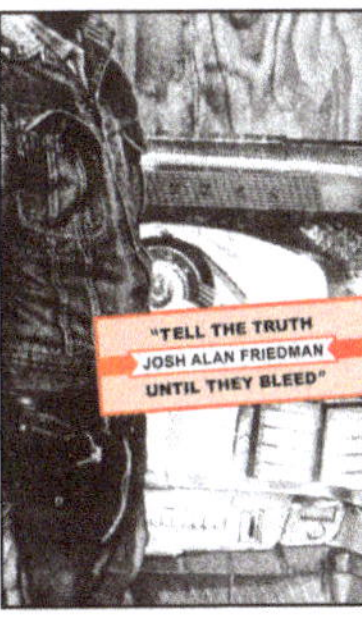

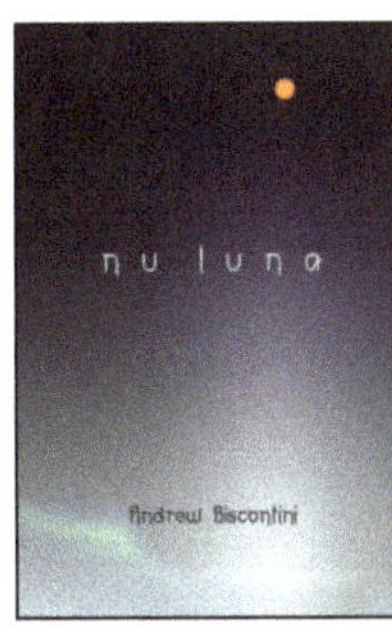

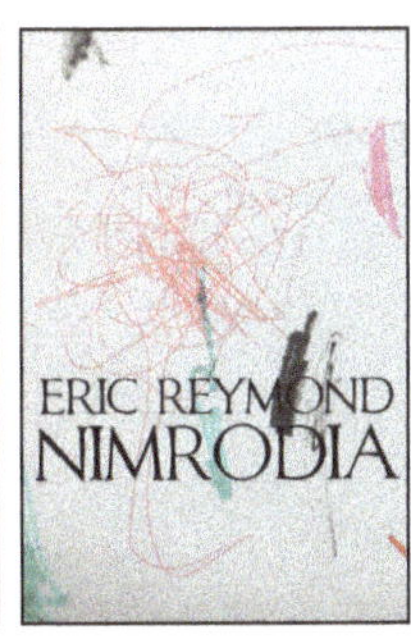

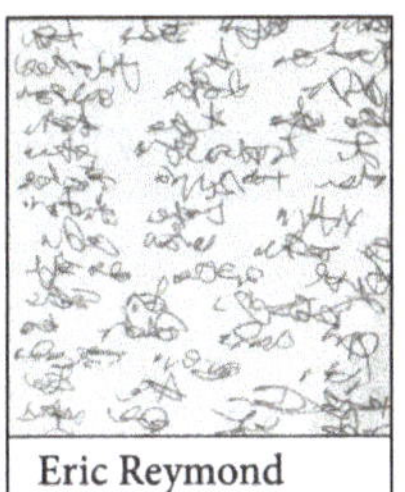

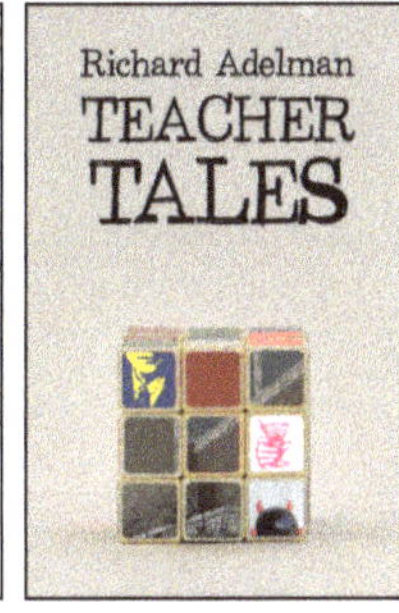

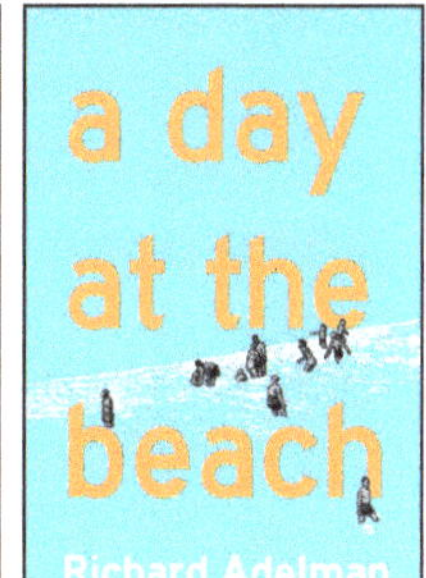

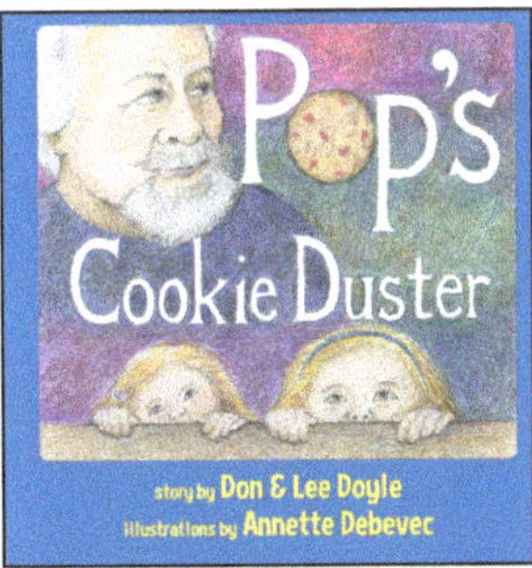

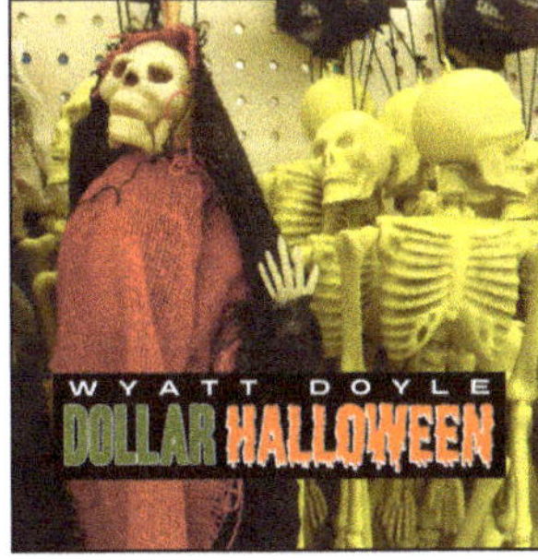

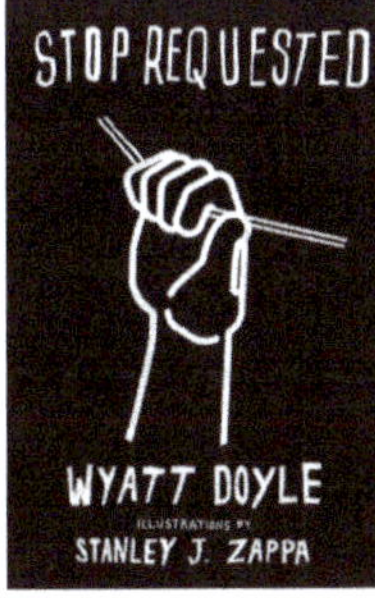

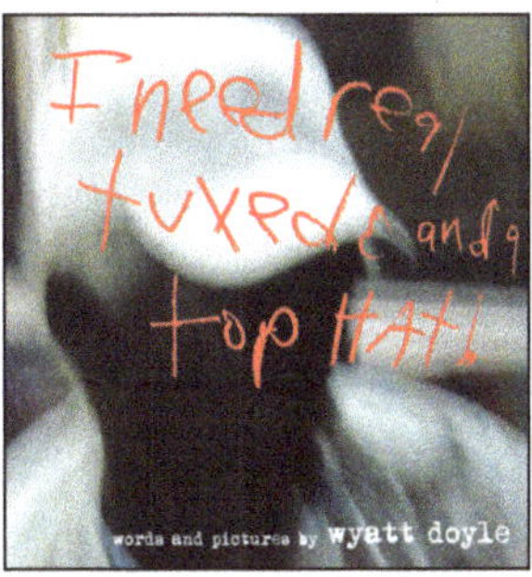

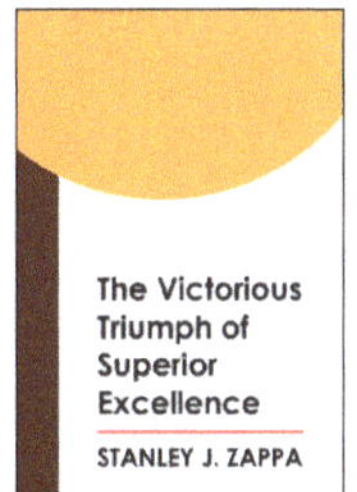

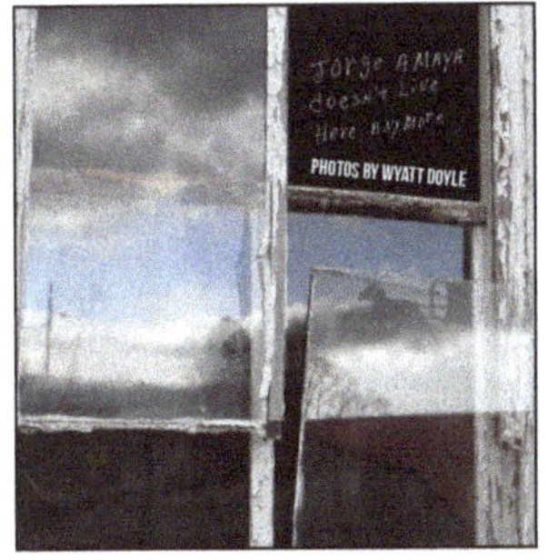

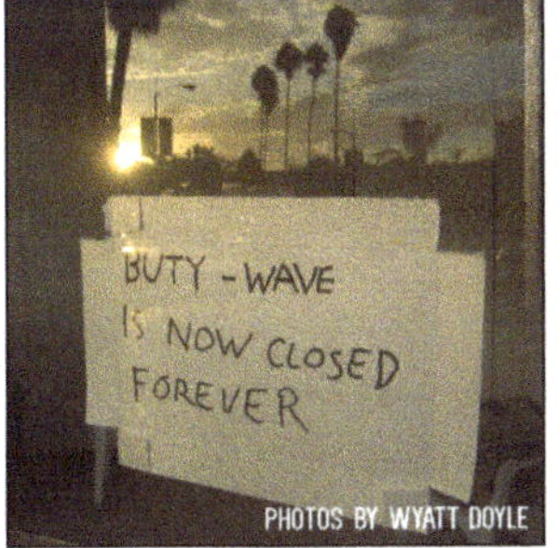

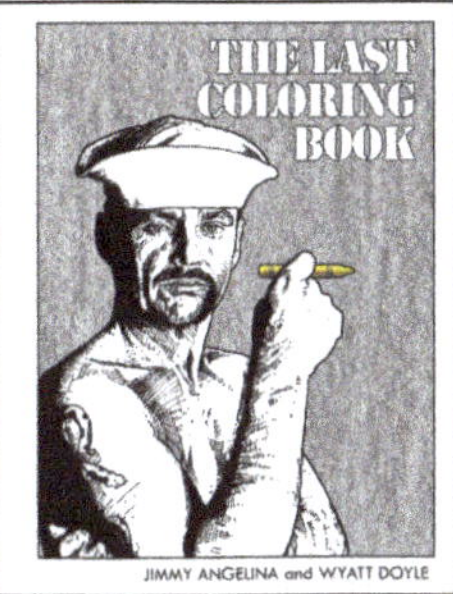

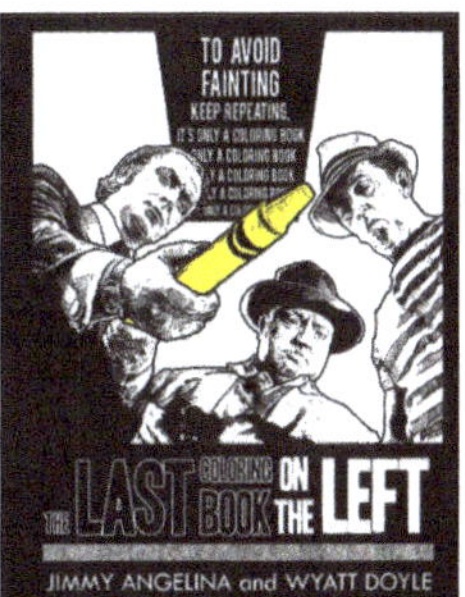

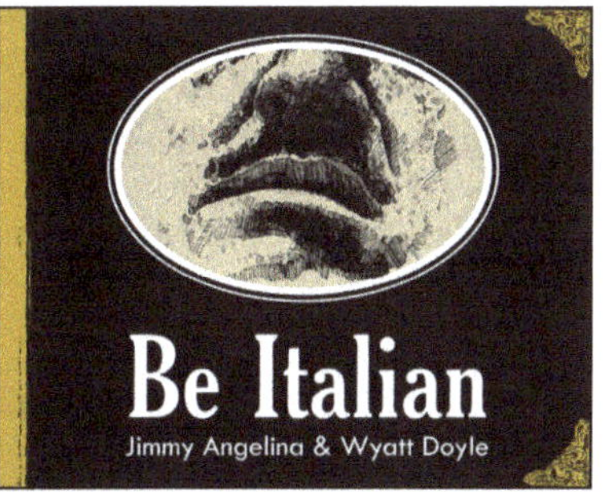

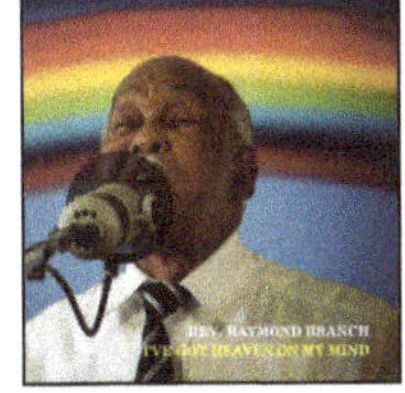

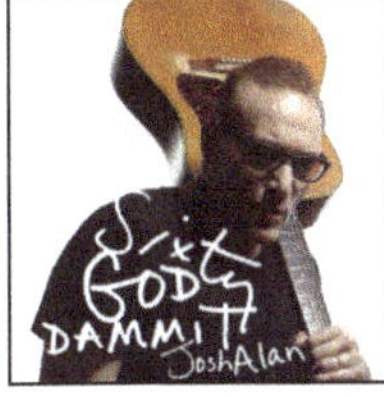

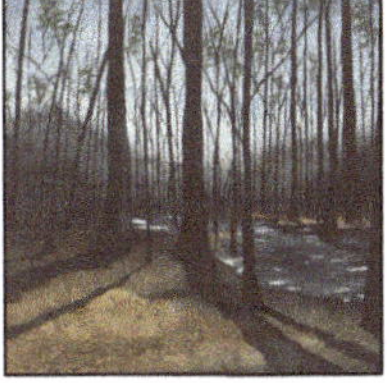

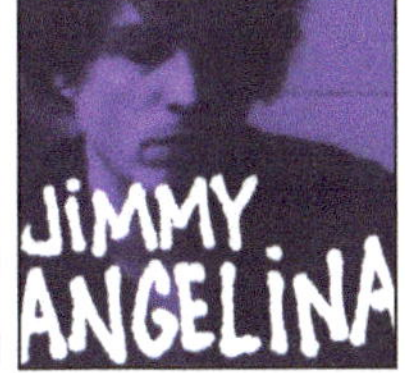

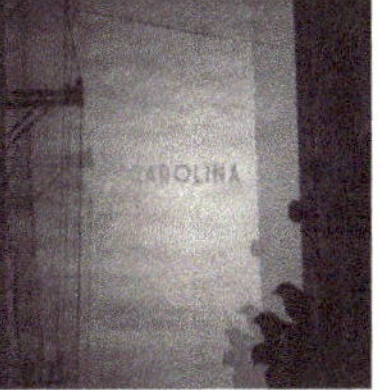

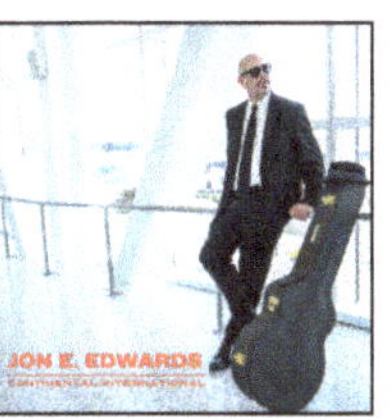

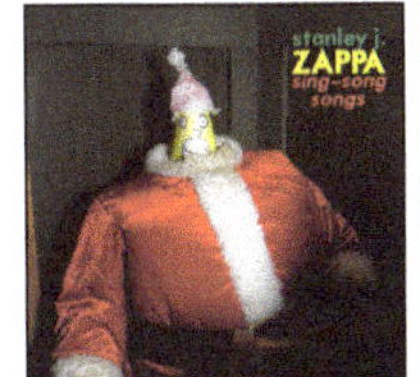

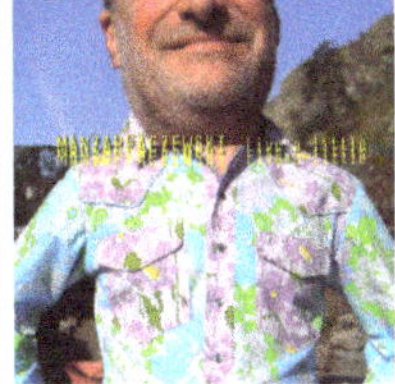

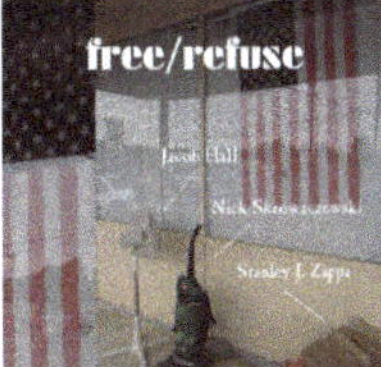

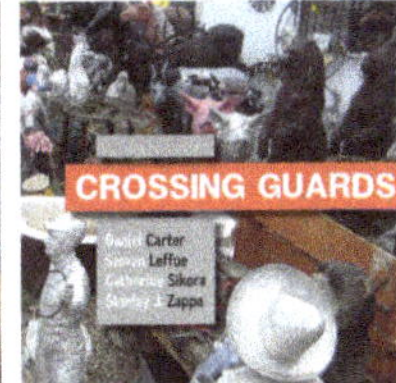

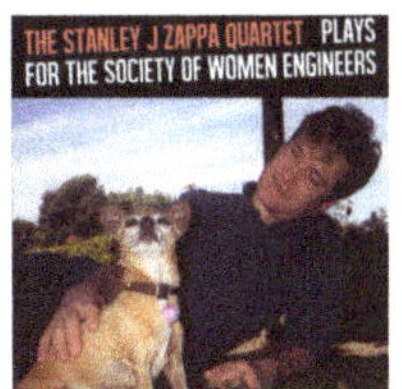

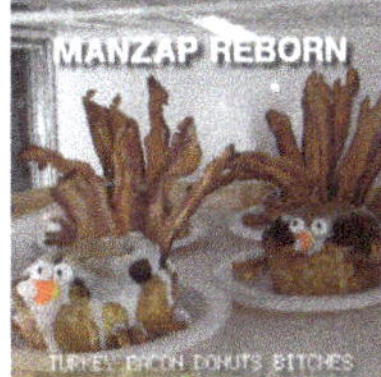

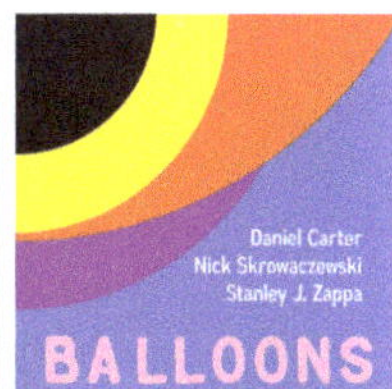

Words and Pictures and Music

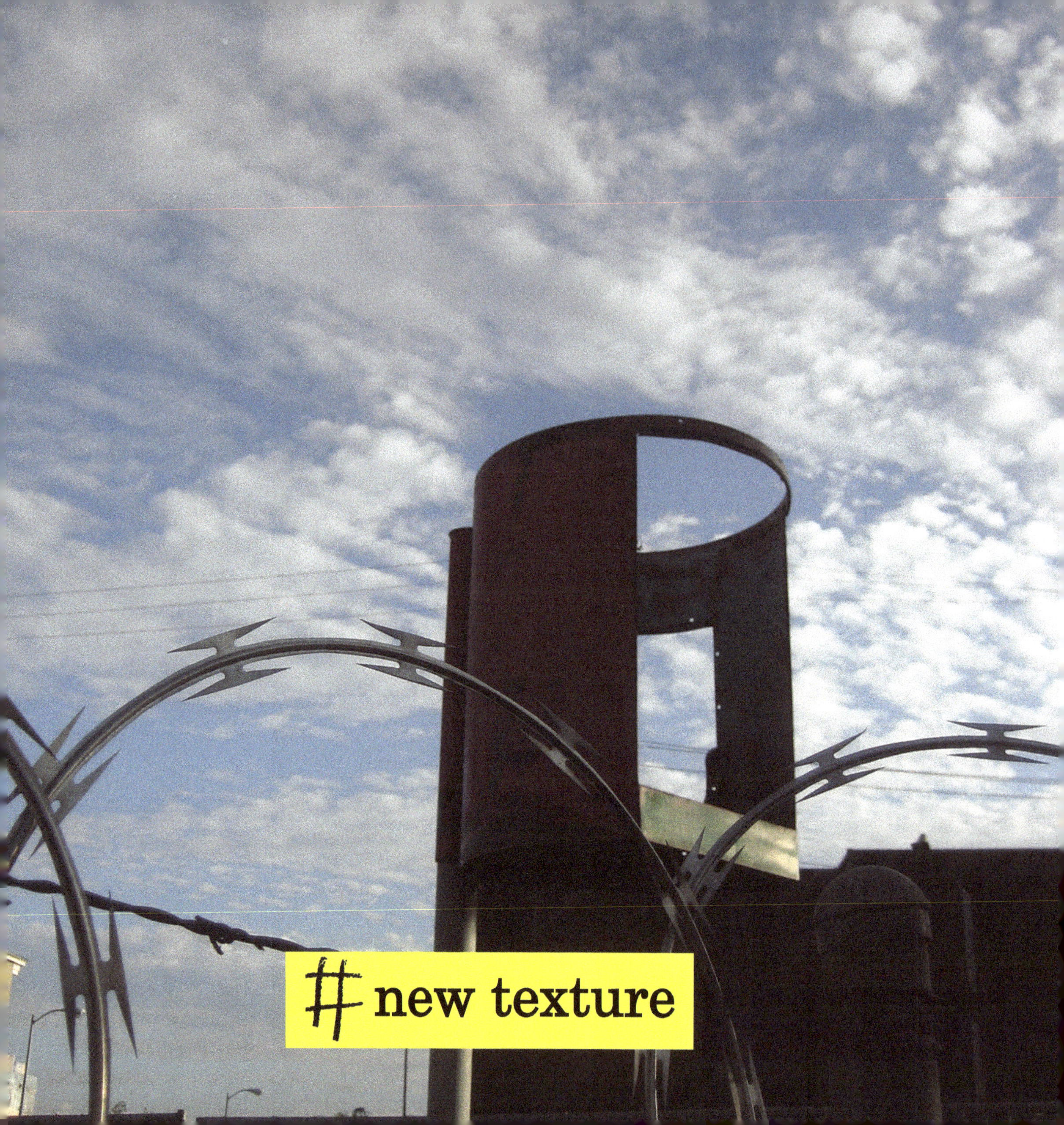

new texture

www.ingramcontent.com/pod-product-compliance
Lightning Source LLC
Chambersburg PA
CBHW042047030726
47599CB00019B/2399